MAN

AND ENVIRONMENT

NEW VIEWPOINTS | A DIVISION OF FRANKLIN WATTS, INC.
NEW YORK 1975

A NEW YORK TIMES BOOK

LINCOLN

MAN
AND ENVIRONMENT

EDITED WITH AN INTRODUCTION BY AMOS H. HAWLEY

301.31
HAW

Lincoln High School Library
Tacoma, Washington

54748

Library of Congress Cataloging in Publication Data
Hawley, Amos Henry, comp.
    MAN AND ENVIRONMENT.

    "A New York times book."
    Bibliography: p.
    Includes index.
    CONTENTS: The population explosion: Fremont-Smith, E. Malthus—
again. Davis, K. Too many people. Lilienthal, D. E. 300,000,000 Americans
would be wrong. Dempsey, D. The fertility goddess vs. the loop. [etc.]
    1. Human ecology—Addresses, essays, lectures. 2. Population—
Addresses. essays. lectures. 3. Pollution—Addresses, essays, lectures. 4. Natural resources—Addresses, essays, lectures. I. Title.
GF8.H38   301.31   74–32298
ISBN 0–531–05574–4

The publishers are grateful to the contributors herein for permission to
reprint their articles.

CONTENTS

INTRODUCTION
1

PART 1 │**THE POPULATION EXPLOSION**
Introduction
20
Malthus—Again │ ELIOT FREMONT-SMITH
21
Too Many People │ KINGSLEY DAVIS
26
300,000,000 Americans Would Be Wrong │ DAVID E. LILIENTHAL
36
The Fertility Goddess vs. the Loop │ DAVID DEMPSEY
46

PART 2 │**FOOD, RESOURCES, AND NATIONAL DEVELOPMENT**
Introduction
64
Symposium on World Food Resources
66
Waiting for the Monsoon │ KHUSHWANT SINGH
76
A Report from the Majority of the World │ JAMES P. STERBA
89
We Are All Developing Nations │ BARBARA WARD
102

The World Is Running Out of Raw Materials │ WALTER SULLIVAN
111
Technology to Be King │ ROBERT K. PLUMB
115

PART 3 │ENVIRONMENTAL POLLUTION
Introduction
122
That "Hellish and Dismal Cloud" │ GEORGE H. T. KIMBLE
124
Santa Barbarans Cite an Eleventh Commandment:
"Thou Shalt Not Abuse the Earth" │ ROSS MACDONALD and ROBERT EASTON
130
Our Arctic Will Never Be the Same:
That Unstoppable Pipeline │ THOMAS M. BROWN
146
We Are Killing the Sea Around Us │ MICHAEL HARWOOD
164
What to Do With Waste? │ LAMONT C. COLE
181
Symposium on Population and Pollution
189

PART 4 │ECOLOGY AND THE FUTURE
Introduction
198
Can the World Be Saved? │ LAMONT C. COLE
200
Continuous Growth or No Growth? │ BERTRAM G. MURRAY, JR.
213
Don't Knock the $2 Trillion Economy │ PETER PASSELL and LEONARD ROSS
223
Human Ecology and Ethics Are Inseparable │ ROGER REVELLE
233
The Link Between Faith and Ecology │ EDWARD B. FISKE
239

SUGGESTED READINGS
243
INDEX
245

MAN

AND ENVIRONMENT

INTRODUCTION

It is possible that the 1960's will be recorded in history as the decade in which the literate public, and not just the intelligentsia, became deeply concerned with the quality of life on earth, now and in the future. This ground swell of interest is unique not only for its massiveness, but also for its far-ranging character. It reaches beyond political and continental boundaries to take into its purview circumstances and events in the world at large. People everywhere seem to have awakened to the recognition that there can no longer be any independence; the effects of happenings on the opposite side of the globe are brought home with the speed of sound. Air travel at near sonic speeds, instantaneous communication via satellite, and the universal sharing of ideas and products are making a world citizen of the common man.

While the issue that first provoked the widespread interest in circumstances affecting the quality of life may be debatable, there is no questioning the fact that population and its increase occupy a central place in public discussions of the matter. Nor is that entirely surprising. For throughout history man has been actively concerned with population numbers and their relation to welfare. His preoccupation with population trends reached a new intensity in the past twenty-five years, however. Underlying this unusual focusing of interest on a single factor are such conditions as the persistence of international tensions in the world, the political and economic maturation of former colonial and other underdeveloped nations, the belated appreciation of the problems of underprivileged peoples at home as well as abroad, the acceleration of the rate of change, and above all an unprecedented upsurge in the growth of world population. Because this latter factor is so often put forth as an explanation of events in the twentieth century it is important that the nature of its influence be clarified. A brief review of the historic pattern of population growth will contribute to that end.

During most of the 2 million-odd years that man has occupied the earth his number has increased at an almost imperceptible rate. The evidence available indicates that although through most of that long period occasions of slow growth alternated with population declines, the net effect was a very gradual increase in numbers. From the beginning to the year 1650 the average growth rate was approximately two thousandths of a percent per year. The number of people on earth in 1650 was slightly above 500 million. That is not a very impressive achievement, for it is well within man's capacity to double his number in a generation.

Thus the events that followed the mid-seventeenth century are extraordinary. In the two hundred and fifty years preceding 1900 the average rate of increase rose to half of 1 percent per year. The rate leaped to 1 percent per year in the period 1900 to 1940. And it doubled again to 2 percent per year between 1940 and 1960. Stating the increase in absolute terms, to the 500 million people on earth in 1650 another billion people had been added by 1900. But only fifty years were required for the accumulation of the next billion people, making the total 2.5 billion in 1950. Yet another billion was added in the years since 1950. The total stands currently at more than 3.5 billion people.

It must be recognized, however, that population figures for early years are of uncertain dependability. They are based on various estimating procedures, some fairly systematic, others rather crude. The practice of census taking, in which everybody in a given area is counted at regular intervals, is a product of the nineteenth century for the most part. Although census taking is now virtually universal, fully half of the nations of the world have less than twenty-five years' experience in enumerating their citizens. They have much to learn about procedures and organization before their counts will approach accuracy. The state of knowledge is even less satisfactory in regard to the numbers of births and deaths that occur annually. It is probable that not more than 60 percent of these vital events are regularly reported at this late date. In analyzing population trends, therefore, one is on much safer ground if he confines his attention to the modern period. Historical reconstructions and small-scale field studies have helped fill many of the gaps that exist in official population statistics. It is with the modern period, of course, that we are mainly interested.

In close association with the technical revolutions that began around the middle of the eighteenth century in Western Europe there occurred a phenomenon commonly known as the "demographic transition." This was a process of population increase involving a shift from high levels of fertility and mortality, of the order of 40 or more per 1,000 population, to low levels of vital rates, of about 15 per 1,000 population. Two phases can be identified in that transition. Phase one began with a decline of the death rate which, over the next century or more, fell to approximately one-third of what it had been. In the meantime, and until late in the nineteenth century, fertility remained at its traditionally high level. The widening gap between fertility and mortality rates gave rise to an accelerating growth of population. Near the end of the nineteenth century phase two began. In the third quarter of that century fertility entered upon a long-term decline, approaching once more the level of the death rate. Population growth decelerated as fertility rates subsided. The transition period in Northwestern Europe between the downward turns of first the death rate and then the birth rate—the lapsed time between phase one and phase two—was very close to one hundred years.

The demographic transition has been repeated wherever modern industrial technology together with its organizational forms have taken possession of local economies. It followed the spread of Northwestern European peoples to North America and to Australia and New Zealand and subsequently it moved southeasterly across Europe. In the present century the transition has been repeated in

Japan, Taiwan, Hong Kong, Singapore, and in two or three other small populations. Noteworthy in these Asiatic instances is the reduction of the time lag in the appearance of phase two from the one hundred years in European history to roughly thirty years in modern times.

But in continental Asia, Africa, and Latin America, which together contain some three-quarters of the world's people, the demographic transition has not advanced beyond phase one. The entrance of the new nations in these areas upon this course of change has been spectacular, however. Owing to their progressive adoption of western technology in agriculture, industry, medicine, and public health, their death rates fell precipitously in the years after World War II. In less than twenty-five years death rates dropped from around 40 per 1,000 to 20 and less per 1,000 population. In but a few of these areas has the fertility rate given any indication of deviating from its traditional level of 40 to 45 per 1,000 population. In consequence growth rates in the so-called developing countries have leaped from around one-half percent per year to more than 2 percent and in some countries to more than 3 percent per year. Growth rates of these magnitudes, if uninterrupted, can double population size in twenty-four to thirty-five years, or in the span of a generation.

The pace of population growth in the developing countries contrasts sharply with that of European peoples during their modernization period. Economic and social change in the transformation of the West was a relatively slow, cumulative process that occupied a century and a half or more. Seldom did the rate of population growth rise above 1 percent per year. That modest growth rate was sustained partly by massive migrations to the New World areas. The opportunity to drain off the excess numbers of people created in the transformation from an agrarian to an industrial society is not available to the developing countries, for there are no unclaimed lands left in the world. Therefore, the developing country must resolve its population problems within its own boundaries.

The important question raised by these trends is: What are the social and economic implications of population increase? An answer that has long had wide appeal was supplied by Thomas

Malthus almost two centuries ago. His ideas can be set down in a few lines. According to Malthus, in any given state of the arts, resources, after having been brought to full use, can only be increased arithmetically, while population possesses the power of geometric increase. Hence, population increase tends invariably to outrun subsistence and would do so were it not for checks to growth resulting from war, famine, disease, and vice. The starvation and suffering into which the human being is dragged by his propensity to reproduce are subject to no more than temporary relief. Any increase in available subsistence is quickly taken up by another surge of population increase. The only gain is in the number of people who can live in misery. Its gloomy outlook for the future of mankind notwithstanding, the theory has survived many generations of criticism.

The vitality of the Malthusian theory must be due to its combination of many of the virtues of good theory. It is neat and parsimonious, it offers an explanation of the general phenomenon of change, and it is addressed to a salient problem of social policy. No doubt this is why most population thought begins or ends with the ideas put forth by Malthus. His influence, however, has reached well beyond the work of population students. It became the cornerstone of classical economics. Even more important, it supplied Charles Darwin with the key idea—the struggle for existence—in his theory of evolution. Modern biology is greatly indebted to Malthus. We shall see this when we turn to the nature of ecology.

This is not to say that Malthusianism is without faults. There are, in fact, two rather glaring defects in the argument. The first has to do with the assumption that human beings are driven to multiply to the maximum supporting capacity of available resources. It is doubtful that such an assumption is applicable to the reproductive behavior of many lower forms of animal life. Certainly every human group has various means of keeping its numbers within the manpower needs of the group. These range from contraception through delayed marriage, abstinence, abortion, and enforced migration to induced mortality as in infanticide and patricide. Malthus recognized this in the second and later editions of his essay. To the harsher checks to growth he added "moral restraint," a rather grudging concession to the influence of society on population. This belated acknowledgment that reproduction is not solely the function of a biological imperative should have alerted scholars to the need for a more searching examination of the theory.

The second defect becomes relevant at this point. It lies not so much in the theory as in the use made of it. The error consists in employing what is essentially an analytical model in the diagnoses of real-life situations. Specifically, the circumstance limiting the direct applicability of the theory is the assumed fixed "state of the arts." It is one thing to take such a position for the purpose of studying a relationship between two other factors; it is quite a different matter to proceed on the understanding that the "state of the arts" is in fact fixed. To do the latter is to convert a perfectly logical procedure in a reasoning process to a practical fallacy. Nevertheless, that is what has happened very generally and Malthus is responsible for setting the pattern. The uncritical thinker, having allowed his attention to be diverted from the determining importance of the organization of society, has been able to see only the finiteness of resources. Since population is the only factor that can vary, it seems to follow that changes in individual and collective welfare are a function entirely of population size. As one increases, the other must decline.

Historically, the "state of the arts" has been anything but constant. The fund of technical knowledge and of procedures for putting technical knowledge to use have proven not only highly changeable but cumulatively changeable. The cultural repertory has grown at an accelerating pace and continues to do so. With each major advance along that path, population has grown more numerous and in some areas of the world improvements in the level of living have raced far ahead of population increase. A hunting and gathering economy cannot support more than three or four persons per square mile, even though the soil and other resources may be rich. A pastoral economy in the same area can support twenty or twenty-five persons per square mile. The introduction of a simple agricultural use of the land raises the number of people who can live there by more than 100 percent. Agricultural improvements will raise density levels to two hundred or more persons per square mile. Much higher densities are possible when agriculture is mixed with trade and industry. In short, it is evident that the limiting factor is not resources as such; it is rather the opportunities that exist in the social, economic, and technical organization of society for providing access to resources to members of the population.

Consider, for example, the second phase of the demographic transition as it has been experienced in the developed nations. Birth rates have fallen to levels approximating those of the prevailing death rates and, accordingly, growth rates have subsided to a fraction of what they were. Yet there is no pressure in the West of population on resources, no curtailment of sustenance. Rather have rates of consumption soared to new heights. Economic growth and technological change appear to have gained a complete independence of population size.

I have lingered long over the Malthusian theory for the reason that it is the mold in which so much thought about population is cast. It is indeed seductive in its simplicity. It appeals to the tendency present in all of us to seek very simple explanations for highly complex phenomena, especially when knowledge of those phenomena lies outside our ranges of competence. Thus a veritable mythology of population has come into being. It is commonly believed that population growth is the cause of economic growth, of starvation in crowded countries, of pollution on land, at sea, and in the air, of psychic disturbances and pathological behavior in cities, of war, and of the acceptance of communist ideology. All such notions rest implicitly or explicitly on the assumption that all other things, that is, "the state of the arts," are constant. That is the assumption underlying most of the contraceptive programs currently being promoted in many of the developing countries.

The implication that population is the only factor that lends itself to change is in error on two counts. First, as already mentioned, "the state of the arts," or the social, economic, and technical organization, is changeable, and its capacity to affect the level of welfare in a society is decisive. Second, a reduction in the birth rate, should that be accomplished, offers no quick solution to problems commonly described as population problems. At any given moment all of the persons entering the labor force from within a particular country during the next twenty years have already been born. Hence, no early relief from unemployment or under-employment can be expected from birth-rate decline. Furthermore, even though rates of reproduction do decline, the large numbers of young people that have resulted from recent high birth rates will, as they age into the reproductive years, give rise to many babies. The population will continue to grow until the large cohorts of reproducers age out of the reproducing years. Important changes in age composition are at least twenty years in the making. Two decades is enough time for significant shifts to occur in the social and economic system and to begin to exert their effects.

Although population cannot be held to be the cause of stresses in society, it may be an important source of their aggravation. Where population growth exceeds the rates of technical and institutional changes, as may happen in the short run, the production and distribution of a food supply is apt to fall short of what is needed. As often as not the problem lies on the side of distribution rather than of production. A lagging development of efficient marketing facilities, a lack of agricultural credit, and a persistence of primitive means of transportation and storage maintain high costs of getting food from producer to consumer. The poor suffer most severely from distribution costs. Food prejudices may add further complications to an already difficult situation. It has been observed, for example, that pellagra, the principal disease of malnutrition in India, could be eliminated by stopping the polishing of rice and changing the method of preparing the grain for eating. Present practices remove all vitamin content from the grain.

In point of fact, the food supply has kept pace with population growth since World War II. Had it not done so, obviously enough, the growth of population would not have occurred. There is even some evidence to indicate that the average level of living in developing countries today is higher than it was among European peoples in the sixteenth and seventeenth centuries. Most of the increase in food production accomplished in developing countries up to 1966 or 1967, however, resulted from bringing marginal and waste lands into cultivation. Less than two-fifths of the increase can be attributed to improved agricultural methods. But while there are rather definite limits to the increase of area under cultivation, there are no known limits to the improvement of technology.

Since 1966 a new and dramatic agricultural revolution appears to have been in the making. I refer to the development of new strains of wheat and rice and their rapid adoption in many cereal-producing areas of Latin America and Asia. The new seeds yield crops 200 and more percent larger than the seeds they replace. In 1965–66 the new strain of wheat was introduced to 37,000 acres on a trial basis. Three years later, in 1968–69, 34 million acres were planted to the new seed. A similar reception was given the new rice seeds. Since 1969 the acreages have doubled again. The Food and Agricultural Organization of the United Nations reported that agricultural production increased by 4 percent in 1971 over 1970, an amount twice the rate of population growth. Countries that formerly were food importers have become exporters, notably Mexico and Pakistan, and to a lesser extent thus far the Philippines and South Vietnam.

But the "green revolution," as it is called, is not fully established as yet. There are numerous problems still unresolved. It is not known what new fungi and other pests will appear to attack the wheat and rice plants. There are also problems associated with the shortening of growing seasons and the drying and storing of grains while the wet seasons are still in progress. The most significant problems, however, are economic and social in character. A much heavier capital investment is required for the best utilization of the new seeds. Heavier applications of fertilizer, a more extensive use of irrigation, and a greater application of mechanical tools demand larger farms and a relatively smaller labor supply. The displacement of farm population may swell the migrant streams to cities and to the ranks of the urban unemployed. It is not unlikely, too, that a cheapening of food costs will bring another reduction in death rates and further increases in population. Implicit in the green revolution, in short, may be a major reorganization of the institutional structures of the societies concerned. It might, of course, only hasten what was inevitable anyway.

Nor is there any population pressure on nonagricultural resources currently being felt or likely to be felt in the early future. Substantial reserves of most of the materials used are known to exist, though in no part of the world has there been a full exploration of mineral resources. It must be acknowledged, however, that the growth of industrial civilization with its rising levels of living have led to accelerating rates of consumption of nonreplaceable resources. The very finite character of the earth would seem to set a definite limit to either or both population growth and level of living advances. Still, resources are relative to technology; the one changes with the other. The history of mechanical technology is a record, among other things, of resource substitutions. Coal replaced wood as a source of heat and power, to be later replaced by petroleum and hydroelectric energy, which may soon be replaced by nuclear energy. We are told now that solar energy is a mechanically, though not yet an economically, feasible substitute for nuclear energy. Resource substitutions have involved shifts from high grade to more economically usable lower grade deposits, from deposits near centers of consumption to remotely located resources, and from metals and solids of various kinds to chemical and electronic resources. More often than not a substitution occurs for reasons other than resource exhaustion.

That there will be further technological change is beyond question. Historically, the accumulation of technical knowledge has followed an exponential curve. A simple extrapolation extends that curve ever more steeply into the future. The expectation of further developments need not rest solely on a mathematical exercise. It has a sound basis in the enormous fund of information that has been gathered into our libraries, data repositories, and the minds of technical specialists. The unexploited potentialities that lie in that vast accumulation are immeasurable; they may be infinite. And the fund of knowledge continues to grow. This is not to say that the future will take care of itself. It argues rather that there is no support for an assumption that change has run its course.

Unfortunately, technology is a concept that is commonly used in much too narrow a sense. It includes a great deal more than tools and the engineering lore that enters into their manufacture and use. Every tool requires one or more organized groups for its production, its application, and the administration of the processes its use engenders. A work organization, such as a factory, had to be invented, perfected, and applied; it is as much a tool as is the hardware it employs. So also is the corporation, the government, and even the family. Moreover, many important industrial advances have required no additional tools; they have resulted from administrative or organizational innovations. The factory assembly line is a prime example. Technology, in short, should be thought of as a term for the instrumental aspects of culture. In view of the complexity of all that is or should be subsumed under the term it is entirely possible, and indeed it is often the case, that technology advances unevenly. Some components develop belatedly or retain imperfections long after others have been proven feasible. The automobile appeared years before appropriate traffic controls and administration were devised. Driver education is still more recent, and later still is the means of controlling the emission of atmospheric pollutants. The corporation existed centuries before it was adapted to the organization of business and industry. Without laboring the matter, the point to be made here is that many problems attributed to technology are due to irregularities and disjunctions in the process of change.

A second major issue linked to population growth has to do with environmental pollution. Discussions of this problem have become so clouded with rhetoric that fact and propaganda are not easy to separate. Pollution is a value-laden term and as such it has many meanings. The victim of hay fever looks upon the air loaded with pollens as polluted. Similarly a stream carrying minerals and silt has little appeal for the person who wishes to use the waters directly. Pollution does not gain acceptability by being of natural origins. Moreover, anyone who has visited an Asiatic or an African village or who has read the literature on the medieval city knows that there is nothing new about man's fouling his habitat. The difference between industrial and agrarian peoples or between the present and the past in respect to environmental misuse or neglect is one of scale and possibly also of aesthetic standards.

That environmental maintenance has become more difficult as populations have grown larger is scarcely debatable. But only the most uninformed reasoning would infer a cause-and-effect relationship from that association. Many other things have also increased with the environmental problem; literacy, for example, yet few people would argue that literacy is the cause of pollution. Misuse and deterioration of the environment result not from people as such; it is caused by people who are careless, inconsiderate, or unwilling to submit to the costs of maintenance.

There are three conditions that have contributed to the increased intensity of pollution and to its heightened visibility. Foremost among these is the great increase in the use of nonsoluble materials—chemicals, paper, metals, and plastics—in the manufacture and packaging of consumer goods. This trend has produced a waste disposal problem without precedent in kind or in magnitude. A second circumstance is the progressive urbanization of population. The effect has been to concentrate waste as well as people. Huge quantities of potential refuse and pollutants are funneled into areas of population density in the normal course of supplying ordinary consumer needs. Third, there has been a failure on the part of the public to accept responsibility for environmental maintenance, to recognize the costs of neglect, and to provide the means necessary for an adequate protection of the land, the air, and the streams. This might be construed as a lag in technological progress. However interpreted, the neglect has its roots in ancient beliefs and practices. A tradition of belief in free land and the abundance of nature has seemed to absolve everyone of responsibility.

Environmental problems are often treated as simple relations of an act to the thing acted upon, of a misdemeanor committed against nature. Barring the occasional litterer, polluting practices normally have their origins deep in the institutional structure of the society. They cannot be exorcised by punitive measures applied to an agent close at hand. The elimination of the motor vehicle cannot be contemplated unless we are also prepared to dismantle a great part of the economy and to restore the settlement pattern of the nation to what it was near the turn of the last century. Solid waste is a by-product of a high level of living. If we are prepared to give up that rate and kind of consumption, return to doing many things for ourselves, and restore the family and other institutions to where they were seventy years ago, we might eliminate the waste problem. But these possibilities are not real; the trends of change are irreversible. We must take up the pollution problems where we find them and plan to attack them with the technology at our command.

When the concerns over rapid population growth and the maintenance of environmental quality are joined the result is recognized as an ecological problem. For ecology is loosely defined as the study of the relation of organism to environment. The term is derived from the Greek words *oikos,* meaning household or living place, and *logos,* translated as knowledge, learning, or reason. Thus, strictly speaking, ecology denotes the study of the household or sustenance activities or organisms. It was in this sense that the word was first given currency by biologists near the end of the nineteenth century and it is within biology that the study has been most vigorously pursued down to the present. In principle ecology is a very inclusive subject; it embraces all of life. But there are differences among plants and animals and among lower forms of animal life and man. Hence there are plant, animal, and human ecologies. To understand what links these subdivisions of the field and what sets them apart, it is necessary to consider a few of the elementary notions of ecology.

The relation of organism to environment is necessarily an adaptive one. Environment, though always in a state of flux, is a passive factor in the drama of life. Responsibility for survival and growth lies exclusively with the organism. Every living creature seeks an accommodation with environment that maximizes its life changes. One of the great ecological observations is that adaptation is rarely, if ever, accomplished by the individual acting alone. It results instead from individuals establishing relations of mutual aid and division of labor and thereby gaining the capacity to act in concert. Adaptation is a collective rather than an individual phenomenon. This is manifest in both very general and in fairly specific levels of observation.

On the most general level, interdependencies among living things are seen to constitute a vast and intricately ramified system of relationships. Organic nature, to use Charles Darwin's metaphor, is a "web of life" in which every creature is connected directly or indirectly with every other creature. Accordingly, influences exerted at any one point in such a complex system produce repercussions at one or more other points. To draw again upon a Darwinian example, the size of the clover crop in the English countryside was shown to be dependent on the number of ground-nesting bees, which in their pursuit of honey pollinated the clover. But the greater the stores of honey the larger the number of field mice. Hence, a large population of mice meant few surviving bees in the following season and a reduced clover crop. That outcome was avoided, however, where there were many cats, for they preyed on the mice. The number of cats, in turn, rested upon the number of cat lovers residing in the rural villages. Keepers of cats, therefore, quite inadvertently helped regulate the size of each season's clover crop.

When the web of life is examined within a specific locality it takes on the aspect of a biotic community. That is, the assembled organisms are found to be engaged in a set of well-defined and hierarchically ordered roles, not unlike that which characterizes the human community. It possesses regulatory mechanisms that control the relative numbers in the several roles and lend a measure of stability to the organization as a whole. This community-like affair is the conclusion of an adaptive process.

Adaptation, it should be noted, involves the biotic community in systematic relations with environment to constitute an ecosystem. This concept refers to a unit of organization comprising a community and its physical and chemical environment between which there are cyclical flows of energy-producing matter. Applications of the ecosystem idea also vary from the specific to the general. In some instances it is employed to identify a highly localized unit of territory and its occupants. Where this is done the ecosystem bears a close resemblance to the Malthusian model described earlier. That is, there is the assumption that an association of species resolves its life problems within particular boundaries and that it fills the enclosed space to a maximum degree. For many purposes, however, this is regarded as an overly simple view of adaptation. Ecosystems, it is observed, are not discrete units; they overlap one another at many points. In fact, energy flows between biotic and physicochemical realms may reach far afield. Thus ecosystem is merely a term for the existence of systematic relations with environment.

Now a question of more than passing interest is: What has the idea of a biotic community to do with the society of mankind? There are two kinds of answers to the question. The first points to the fact that the human species is one of many species that make up biotic communities. Man's role has been a changing one, of course. He started many millennia ago in the humble position of an omnivore that was a food object as often as not. With the evolution of culture man rose through the ranks, as it were, to a position of dominance in the biotic community. In that capacity he determines which species shall live where and under what conditions they shall so live. As an agriculturalist, man is often instrumental in creating entirely new associations of species that could not survive without his continuous protection. Where he makes intensive use of space, as in cities, man dispossesses all species, barring only a few pets and a larger number of parasites. Through such changes in the landscape man often deprives himself of the assistance of useful species. On the more constructive side, knowledge of the interrelations among species has become an important tool in land, water, and resource conservation.

A second response to the question concerning the import of the biotic community concept for mankind has to do with its uses as a source of analogues for the study of the human community. The latter, for example, is also an adaptive mechanism, though its member parts are occupational specializations rather than species. Moreover, the environmental relationships, or more operationally, the procurement of sustenance, is a preoccupation that pervades and colors every feature of the human community. Again, the population that can be sustained in a locality is a function not of the environment directly, but of the way in which the community is organized. Even when no further useful analogues are obtainable there remains a way of formulating problems for investigation that has proven to be highly fruitful, that is, in terms of interactions and energy flows within civilizations.

An important difference between biotic and human communities lies in the extent to which the latter become interrelated. Improvements in transportation and communication technology have multiplied and extended relationships to every corner of the globe. Consequently, every human community has become a consumer of an almost unlimited diversity of physical and biotic resources. So varied are the flows of materials that it has become virtually impossible to render any measured account of the actual environment on which each modern human community is dependent. Environmental contact, moreover, is increasingly indirect, for it is mediated to each community through the productive efforts of many other communities. While this has created stability so far as the relation to the physical-chemical environment is concerned, it has brought a new source of instability, namely, variability, in intergroup relations. Technological changes, competitive shifts, market fluctuations, alterations of transportation rate schedules, industrial relocations, and political upheavals are separately and in combination almost continuous threats to the orderly processes of daily life in every community. As the new nations are brought more fully into the world scene they are made subject to the same kinds of social, economic, and political disturbances.

The expansion of man's resource environment has a local counterpart in an expansion of the daily living space. Improvements in short-distance transportation and communication facilities, such as the motor vehicle, the telephone, and the pipeline, have all but eliminated the importance of proximity in daily life. The destinations outside the home that are routinely visited have spread over a widening area as they have multiplied in number. Daily vehicular travel miles per household have tripled in the past three decades. By the same token, the urban resident chooses his friends and associates over a widening area at the expense of interactions within the neighborhood and surrounding vicinity. Whether the neighborhood has any viability as a social unit under the dispersion of activities taking place remains to be determined. One important qualification needs to be made, however. The range of daily circulations appears to vary with social-economic status. Thus, proximity may still have its traditional significance among the poor and underprivileged and may diminish as a limiting circumstance at each higher level in the social-economic scale.

One of the costs of the expansion of the scope of life is a decline of interest in the immediate locale. As the individual's affairs become more widely dispersed, the time available to him for attention to local conditions decreases. The neglect of the surrounding vicinity is further encouraged by the increasing dependence on vehicular travel in lieu of pedestrian movement. Environmental deterioration may have some of its basis in the widening sweep of interest that has come with expansion, but it is also true that the declining intensity of land use reflected in the broadening horizons has allowed many areas to revert to their natural state or to be made eligible for reconstruction. Large tracts of land formerly devoted to agriculture have been dropped from use. Similarly, increasing spaces in the cores of urban areas have lost their expected use value and are waiting adaptation to new, low-intensity uses. These reversals in the trend toward increasing intensity of environmental usage should at least lead one to reconsider his anxiety about the future.

Ecology knits together the many strands of life. The discipline demands a holistic view so far as it is practicable. It is thus incumbent on one who appeals to ecology for an analysis of society's problems to make sure that he has tried to encompass all of the relevant factors at work in a given situation and not just the few that intrigue him most. That is a difficult intellectual feat. It is especially difficult when man is involved, for human society is complex and in constant flux. That there is much still to be learned about how society operates in its relations with nature hardly needs to be emphasized. And much effort is being directed to that end. It is already abundantly clear that the major problems are problems of social structure and process. Problems of population numbers and of environmental pollution invariably resolve themselves into problems of societal organization, of failure to provide and enforce adequate measures to protect against misuse of the environment.

PART 1

THE POPULATION EXPLOSION

The papers in this first section deal with various aspects and problems of the population explosion. It is useful to return to Malthus, particularly for enlightenment on the social and political context in which his now classical theory was first put forth. Eliot Fremont-Smith offers a lucid account of the problems of the time and of the intellectual and political storm created by Malthus' ideas on the subject of population.

Kingsley Davis, one of the world's most distinguished demographers, examines world trends in population change in his article "Too Many People." He notes that the burden of growth is falling most heavily on the poorest nations. Poverty, aggravated by excess population, can produce serious political repercussions; the least fortunate nations might drift into the Communist camp and thereby alter the balance of power in the world. But it is just as probable that tensions between sparsely and densely occupied nations will arise over the issue of freedom to migrate and resettle. These and other possibilities argue strongly for aid from developed nations in the implementation of population-control programs in areas of rapid growth.

Population increase is not exclusively a problem of poor nations. As David E. Lilienthal shows, it also affects the United States. If trends continue as they have since World War II, our economy will be sorely strained, our cities will be severely congested, and our parks and open spaces will be stripped of their natural beauty by overintensive use. He urges fertility control and the improvement of contraceptive technology.

David Dempsey's article is a biographical study of Dr. Alan F. Guttmacher, the unquestioned leader over the past several decades of the birth-control movement. As the president of Planned Parenthood–World Population, a federation of national Planned Parenthood organizations, Dr. Guttmacher has been an indefatigable speaker, consultant, and advocate. His views and the policies of the federation have often been unpopular, for they have taken strong stands where others have been timid. If nothing else, however, they have stirred governments and foundations to vigorous action in programs of population control.

Malthus—Again
BY ELIOT FREMONT-SMITH

The word "Malthusian" has been taking on fresh significance of late. In New York, United Nations demographers have announced that the world's population passed the 3 billion mark in the middle of last year and is now rushing ahead at an average annual rate of increase of 1.8 percent—as much as 2.7 percent in Central America and some parts of Asia—a figure not far from the Malthusian projection of the population's doubling every twenty-five years. And China, whose population is fast approaching 700 million, has given signs of relaunching the intensive birth-control program it abandoned five years ago with the "Great Leap Forward." In doing so, it has opened itself to charges of what the Communists call the "Malthusian heresy."

"Malthusian" refers of course to the English economic philosopher Thomas Malthus, and to the theory of population growth he published in 1798 under the title "An Essay on the Principle of Population, as it Affects the Future Improvement of Society, With Remarks on the Speculations of Mr. Godwin, M. Condorcet, and Other Writers."

From *The New York Times Magazine,* September 23, 1962.
Copyright © 1962 by The New York Times Company.
Reprinted by permission.

"The power of population," Malthus wrote, "is indefinitely greater than the power in the earth to produce subsistence for men. . . . Population is always and everywhere, in some measure, pressing against the available food supply."

More specifically, Malthus' essay held that population, unchecked, increases geometrically, while the earth's food resources can increase only arithmetically: "In two centuries and a quarter, assuming a doubling every twenty-five years, [the population] would be to the means of subsistence as 512 to 10; in three centuries as 4,096 to 13 . . . ."

Although the theory was not entirely new—Plato, Aristotle, and Hume had previously addressed themselves to demographic problems, and Benjamin Franklin had first suggested the twenty-five-year doubling period—it was Malthus who brought the matter to public attention. Clearly, if one accepted his figures and assumptions, catastrophe was at hand.

Many did not, and for more than half a century—until Darwin engaged the theologians—"The Principle of Population" was the subject of heated debate. In the past decade, "Malthusian" has once again come into common usage.

Thomas Robert Malthus was born in 1766 in the town of Dorking, Surrey, where his father owned a small estate. He attended Cambridge University and, despite a pronounced shyness owing to a cleft palate and resulting speech impediment, took holy orders. In 1798, the same year he published his essay, he was appointed to a curacy. In 1804 he married and the following year was appointed to the East India College at Haileybury as professor of political economy, a post he held until his death in December 1834.

For two centuries the study of social philosophy had gyrated around the issue of man's "innate" moral quality. Jean-Jacques Rousseau was the principal spokesman for the positive or optimistic view (optimistic because, if man was good, Utopia was possible), and among Rousseau's English followers was his close friend and executor Daniel Malthus.

It can be argued that it was partly in revolt against his father that son Thomas aligned himself with the opposite view—that man was fundamentally evil and, left to his own devices (that is, without authoritarian guidance), would soon degenerate into a morass of "misery and vice." Yet "misery and vice" were also important factors in Malthus' theory of population control.

"The Principle of Population" was explicitly prompted by the writings of Rousseau's disciples, the Marquis de Condorcet and William Godwin. An extreme rationalist, Godwin had claimed, in his "Enquiry Concerning Political Justice" of 1793, that mind would triumph over matter in the coming perfect society to such a degree that death itself would be conquered. Further, "there will be neither disease, anguish, melancholy, nor resentment. Every man will seek, with ineffable ardor, the good of all."

To Malthus, this was not only ineffable poppycock, but dangerous as well, for disease, anguish, and the rest, which Malthus lumped under "misery and vice"—"all unwholesome occupations, severe labor and exposure to the seasons, extreme poverty, bad nursing of children, excesses of all kinds, the whole train of common diseases and epidemics, wars, plague and famine," plus celibacy, nonprocreative promiscuity, and "vicious practices" (by which he meant birth control)—these were the essential checks against overpopulation.

Malthus assumed that the bottom of the social pyramid was always at the bare minimum of subsistence; thus, in effect, the fate of the poorer classes determined the size of the total population. Disaster came either (1) when the food supply suddenly increased (through new agricultural resources or following a great plague), so that life for the poor became more comfortable, people married earlier, had more children, and died later—thereby quickly increasing the population which, multiplying geometrically, soon outran the food supply—or (2) when one or another of the natural checks was legislated out of existence. This second possibility Malthus saw as an immediate danger arising from the government's new poor-law bill.

For some time the old English workhouse had become increasingly limited to the old and infirm, poor relief being made in the form of direct payments whenever wages fell below a set minimum.

In 1796 Prime Minister William Pitt proposed to formalize this practice and, further (reading a lesson from the Napoleonic wars, which suggested population as an index of a country's might), actually to promote population growth by establishing relief rates in accordance with the number of children in any given family.

In Malthus' view, the proposed bill would not only negate the necessary checks of "misery and vice," but compound disaster. Direct relief, he reasoned, would kill incentive to work—to produce more food—for man is naturally "inert, sluggish, and averse from labor, unless compelled by necessity."

Thus, while population leaped, food supplies would actually decline; the poor would increase in suffering as they increased in number. (Despite his harsh theories, Malthus was not without humanitarian feeling. "The parish prosecution of men whose families are likely to become chargeable, and of poor women who are near lying-in," he added, "is a most disgraceful and disgusting tyranny.")

Largely because of "The Principle of Population," Pitt finally withdrew the proposed law, but Malthus became the center of a storm of criticism. Not only did Godwin attack him, but such luminaries as Coleridge as well, charging him with hypocrisy and worse. William Hazlitt accused him of having a "warm constitution and amorous complexion" and a tale sped the rounds that the "parson" had fathered no fewer than eleven daughters (which added nine fictional daughters to fact and curiously ignored Malthus' son).

Both Dickens and Disraeli later satirized Malthus in their novels, and Karl Marx denounced Malthusian theory as a vicious capitalistic plot to limit the proletariat and stifle revolution—a judgment that has caused considerable hand-wringing in the Communist world.

In 1804 Malthus published a greatly expanded and revised edition of "The Principle of Population." It contained an implicit but crucial shift of emphasis from "natural" forces to social forces—specifically, acknowledgment of the aspirations of the poor to middle-class status and to liberty.

Because this shift compromised some of his previous conclusions—and also because a man is more likely to be remembered for his extreme first assertions than for his gentler second thoughts—Malthus is known today for the essay of 1798, not the revision of 1804.

Since Malthus' time, the population of Great Britain has multiplied itself five times over, the population of America thirty-five times. The total number of people in the world, estimated at 907 million in 1800, has more than tripled—and half the additional number has arrived in only the last three decades.

The current Malthusian "crisis" was postponed during most of the nineteenth century because of technological progress (inadequately foreseen by Malthus) in agriculture and the processing and distribution of food.

But with the social and medical revolution of recent years, which has so mitigated "misery and vice"—especially infant mortality—in the underdeveloped areas, demographers, economists, politicians, and social scientists on both sides of the Iron and Bamboo curtains have been training worried attention to the potentially disastrous population spiral.

A variety of methods for increasing the food supply have been suggested, and it now appears technologically feasible to feed many times the earth's present estimated 3.1 billion inhabitants. Eventually, however, the Malthusian explosion will have to be contained; there is only so much standing room. Unless, of course, we colonize other planets, or as one writer recently suggested in a flash of inspiration, we find a way to reduce the size of the human animal.

Too Many People
BY KINGSLEY DAVIS

The amazing increase in the earth's population in recent years, justly described as an "explosion," is shown by the United Nations' latest projections to be merely a forerunner of a still greater burst of human multiplication to come. Only sixteen years from now, according to the U.N.'s medium estimates, the earth will contain a billion more people than now, and in forty-one years nearly 4 billion more. The rate of increase during the second half of the present century will be twice as fast as it has been during the first half.

The U.N.'s figures are set out on the following page.

Are these estimates accurate, or do they merely serve to scare us into "doing something about population"? The answer is that these are not "scare projections." They are the most systematic and responsible population forecasts on a global basis that we have.

Admittedly, nobody can predict future populations with certainty. The world's inhabitants in the year 2000 may exceed 6 billion

	1900	1925	1950
World population (in millions)	1,550	1,907	2,497
Percentage increase in 25 years		23%	31%
Years to double population at this rate		84	64

FUTURE

	1975	2000
Population (in millions)	3,830	6,280
Percentage increase in 25 years	53%	64%
Years to double population at this rate	41	35

or may number only a few thousand sufferers from nuclear radiation. Since future populations depend on what people do and decide, there is nothing automatic about them. The U.N. projections are based on statistical models that show what will happen if each nation's population follows the course implicit in its present stage of development. Only some world catastrophe or revolutionary innovation would cause the estimated world total by the close of the century to be far wrong.

If anything, the U.N. estimates are conservative. Not only do the experts who prepared them regard them as so, but it is a curious fact that nearly all modern forecasts of population have proved too low. In 1924, for example, two reputable experts, Pearl and Reed, forecast a world population of 1.8 billion in 1950, but the correct figure turned out to be 2.5 billion. Each new set of forecasts exceeds the old set. This being true, the picture the U.N. figures give is ominous. By 1975 the number of people being added to the human race each year will be 77 million, and by 2000, 126 million!

Why is this speed-up taking place? Reduced to the simplest terms, the reason for the coming rise in the already unprecedented rate of increase is this: Two-thirds of the world's people still live in underdeveloped countries where spectacular declines in death rates are occurring with little change in traditionally high birth rates. At the same time, the industrial countries have had a postwar recovery in births which, along with a continued steady drop in mortality, has brought their population growth back to pre-Depression rates. Since the underdeveloped countries can lower their death rates still further, and since the other nations seem disinclined to return to the low fertility level of the Depression, the net result is an anticipated scale of human growth scarcely dreamed of a few years ago.

It follows that the countries expected to have the greatest ballooning of population—the poorer ones—are precisely the wrong ones to have it. If the medium U.N. projections hold true, the currently underdeveloped areas will grow twice as fast as the industrial countries. Their share of the earth's people will rise from 65.5 percent in 1950 to 76.3 percent in 2000. This means that the poorer regions, to make any headway against the more advanced nations, must buck a very strong current. So far they are losing the fight, because the gap in wealth between them and the developed nations is widening.

One mitigating circumstance is that among both the industrial and the nonindustrial countries it is the "new" ones that are showing the fastest population growth. In the industrial group, for example, those in the New World are expected to increase nearly three times as fast as the older industrial countries of Central and Northern Europe, and in the nonindustrial group, tropical Latin America is scheduled to multiply roughly twice as rapidly as nonindustrial Asia. This tendency will prevent the world's most densely settled areas as a whole from showing the highest rates of population growth.

It is not true, as some fear, that the Communist countries will necessarily outmultiply the free world. According to the U.N. projections, these nations will have roughly the same proportion of the world's people in 1975 and in 2000 as they have now—about 35 percent.

The reason for this is that both the Communist and the free blocs include industrial and nonindustrial peoples in nearly the same proportion. The Communist bloc contains neither the world's fastest-growing region (tropical Latin America) nor the slowest-growing region (Northwestern Europe). If, therefore, communism does not spread by conquest, the world will probably remain two-thirds non-Communist. The "if," however, is a big one.

From a numerical standpoint, Red China is the world's most important nation. With 650 million people, she now encompasses nearly one-fourth of the human race, and her population is apparently increasing above the average world rate, with an absolute increment each year of approximately 15 million (almost equal to the entire population of Canada). By 1975, according to U.N. medium estimates, her population will reach 894 million, more than four times ours at that time. By the end of the century China may well have more than 1.5 billion.

Although Russia is expected to expand its population more slowly than China, it still will gain slightly over the United States. The figures for the world's four most populous nations, today and in 1975, are:

TODAY

	Population (*millions*)	Ratio (*U.S. = 1*)
U.S.A.	175	1.0
U.S.S.R.	208	1.2
India	406	2.3
China	650	3.7
1975		
U.S.A.	217	1.0
U.S.S.R.	275	1.3
India	563	2.6
China	894	4.1

Although we think our population is growing rapidly—and so it is, at just about the current world average—the gains south of our border make ours seem small. Mexico's birth rate, for instance, is 47 per 1,000 as against 25 for us, and her death rate 12.9 as against our 9.6.

The resulting rate of natural increase (the difference between the birth and death rates) is more than twice ours. Indeed, the population growth in Mexico, as in some other parts of Latin America, is close to 3.5 percent a year—a rate which, if continued, will double the population in twenty years and increase it tenfold in sixty-seven years!

What are likely to be the chief consequences of this immense increase in world population? Some of the dangers may be clearly foreseen.

The central fact is that population growth will tend to be greatest where people are poorest. In this desperate situation the less developed nations will hardly be squeamish about the means they adopt to further their national goals. Caught in the predicament of having an ever larger share of the world's people and an ever smaller share of the world's resources, they will be driven to adopt revolutionary policies.

Obvious possibilities along this line are the reduction of population growth by speeding birth control and/or the transformation of the economy by totalitarian methods.

Not only is the glut of people in the poorer areas itself conducive to communism, but in the past communism has made its gains by conquest rather than by population growth. In 1920 it held less than one-tenth of the world's people under its fist; today it holds more than one-third. The lack of unity in the rest of the world against communism suggests that Red expansion may continue. If this happens, and if the conquests are made in the poorer countries, superior population growth will join territorial expansion in increasing communism's share of the world.

One of the questions of the future centers on China, whose sheer size poses a major political problem for the world—including Russia. The Communist bloc has achieved greater cohesion among its member nations than has the free world, but, as Yugoslavia and Hungary have shown, nationalism can plague the Communist group too. This may be a negligible factor so long as it concerns only the lesser satellites, but it can become acute when the "satellite" has three times the population of Russia.

At the moment China is not quite in a position to challenge Russia or America. She has more manpower than anything else; indeed, she has too many people and too fast a rate of increase to realize her economic or military potential. But she is apparently bent on converting her weakness into strength by radical economic methods. To the surprise of the Russians, China is out-communizing Russia. By the tightest of controls she is directing her masses into the most productive channels and trying to avoid the dissipation of scarce capital that would result if these masses were allowed more than a subsistence consumption.

In addition, the Chinese state is directly transforming excess people into capital by using underpaid surplus labor on vast schemes of public construction. At the same time, appalled by the annual population increase, the government has fostered a program of diffusing birth-control methods, and it has made a huge effort to settle sparsely inhabited areas in the north and west.

These measures cannot all be laid to communism. The policies, and to some extent Chinese communism itself, are the result of the desperate situation in which China finds herself in view of her low economic development and her runaway population growth. In any case the picture of a Communist elite organizing and driving an ocean of humanity evidently frightens the Russians themselves.

If the venture succeeds, China, with a projected 1975 population almost double the expected figures for the United States and Russia combined, would be the strongest contender for world leadership. Such a mass, equipped with modern arms and disciplined by a dictatorship, if bent on conquest, could be stopped only by a united world outside.

In the Western Hemisphere our own superiority of numbers, which has long bolstered our leadership of the area, is destined to diminish quickly. Whereas in 1920 we had more inhabitants than the rest of the hemisphere put together, in 1975 we will probably have only two-thirds as many as the other nations, and in the year 2000 less than half. Brazil, the hemisphere's second most populous nation, in 1920 had only a fourth as many people as we did: It will probably have half as many in 1975.

One question raised in connection with population trends is that of color. If color prejudice were the strongest force in the world, and if all so-called "non-whites" were united, they would certainly dominate the whites. The areas controlled or soon to be controlled by non-whites embrace about 64 percent of the human population; and this preponderance is likely to increase to about 72 percent by the year 2000.

But race has never been the main basis of conflict, and if it were it would not crudely pit all "whites" against all "non-whites." Far more important are differences of religion, culture, and nationality. The conflict of Moslems and Hindus in the Indian subcontinent has nothing to do with race, nor does the antagonism between Arabs and Jews in the Middle East, between Chinese and Malays in Malaya, or between South and North Koreans.

One potent source of conflict, however, is international migration, which creates alien minorities or majorities within nations. Further growth will probably increase migratory pressures and, as a result, bring stiffened barriers to such movement. Human migration, when unrestricted, generally flows from areas of low income to areas of high income. Since the fastest future population growth will be in underdeveloped areas, and since their relative poverty is growing greater rather than less, the demand there for admission to industrial lands will become enormous.

In 1950 almost 56 percent of the world's people lived in the already crowded and impoverished agrarian regions of Asia, North Africa, Middle America, and the Caribbean. According to the U.N. projections, the same regions will contain 59 percent by 1975 and 65 percent in 2000.

To keep their proportion simply at the 1950 level, they would have to send out, by 1975, 140 million emigrants and, from 1975 to 2000, about 571 million. In view of the troubles attending a few thousands of Caribbean and West African immigrants in Britain, the slaughter accompanying the movement of only 12 million migrants between India and Pakistan, the present plight of Arab refugees, and the history of alien fifth columns in many lands, human movement on such a fantastic scale seems inconceivable except by conquest.

The dangers implicit in the present and future uncontrolled population trends raise the question, what can we do about it?

The late Pope Pius thought, hopefully, that interplanetary travel might alleviate the earth's population pressures. But merely moving people on the earth itself is costly. For example, adding one thousand migrants to Canada's population is estimated to entail capital outlays of $12 to $13 million. Assuming that an individual could be moved to another planet at the ridiculously low cost of $1 million, it would take $45,000 billion to get rid of the earth's current increase for one year—a sum exceeding the earth's total income.

The curious thing about such drastic suggestions is that they assume man to be permanently and blindly driven by his own reproduction. They say, in effect, that the only way for human beings to avoid starvation is to emigrate into space, produce food out of algae and wood, or give up every enjoyment for sheer, grinding subsistence. If the assumption were true that the limit to population is a shortage of food, man's numbers would be increasing fastest in areas where food is most abundant, but this is not the case. No human population lives merely to eat.

Actually, the main cause of high death rates in the past has been not scarcity of food but the prevalence of disease. The unprecedented population growth of recent decades has been due chiefly to the control of infectious diseases. It is unrealistic to calculate the "carrying capacity" of the earth as a way of finding an "ultimate limit" to population growth.

All such ideas focus too exclusively on the death rate. They assume that growth will be limited, if it is limited at all, by some death-dealing agency such as starvation, disease, or war. But human beings, unlike other animals, can voluntarily control their population growth by limiting their reproduction. They have already demonstrated this capacity in industrial societies.

We are thus living in the key period of a new demographic revolution. The first step in this change was the drastic decline of death rates all over the world, especially in nonindustrial areas brought on by twentieth-century science. The decline, still going on, has not come automatically but has been achieved by a vast and costly international effort. As a consequence of the decline, the high birth rates once needed to offset the death rates are no longer necessary. Yet in nonindustrial and some industrial areas high birth rates continue.

They continue in part because it takes time for parents to realize the new hardships resulting from excessive family size, but in the main because no effort remotely comparable to the public health effort has been made to help parents reduce their reproduction. Our tax dollars go generously to help control malaria, Bilharzia, yaws, dietary deficiency, and a hundred other ills throughout the world, but virtually none go to protect the people of underdeveloped areas from the appalling effect of this beneficent work—overpopulation.

A vital issue of our time is the next step in the new demographic revolution. Will world leadership make an attempt to control births as well as deaths? Will the frantic multiplication of people be reduced by planned effort rather than by possible catastrophe?

So far, official thinking in the West about this matter has been dominated by obscurantist attitudes dating from the Middle Ages, when death rates were high. Most of the so-called "theories of population" unconsciously distract attention from the main problem because they assume that reproduction must go blindly on.

We therefore find some of the advanced nations, where birth control is practiced—for instance, Belgium, the United States, and the Soviet Union—officially uncooperative on this subject in their dealings with the underdeveloped nations. The latter, however, are beginning to show themselves to be less superstitious. Some of them (Japan, China, India, Mauritius, Puerto Rico) are going ahead on their own with birth-limitation programs.

With the U.N. projections showing starkly what lies ahead unless action is taken, a policy of intransigence in this matter seems hard to justify. It is inhumane to have impoverished populations growing so fast that their economic development is hindered. It is shortsighted, in a world increasingly dependent on science, to have the bulk of the next generation reared in regions that cannot afford even an elementary education. It encourages parasitism to give economic aid and migratory opportunities to peoples who are irresponsible about such an important matter as reproduction.

It remains to be said that excessive population growth seems to intensify the struggle for scarce raw materials, to build up explosive migration pressures, and to encourage *Lebensraum* wars, and that communism is making its greatest conquests precisely in the impoverished and crowded countries. Thus, the leading nations of the

West might well consider giving every encouragement, including money, to foreign countries in their efforts to control fertility, simultaneously setting an example by officially encouraging birth control at home.

300,000,000 Americans Would Be Wrong
BY DAVID E. LILIENTHAL

By the year 2000, just one generation away, the population of the United States will probably be about 300 million, 100 million higher than it is now and 200 million higher than it was in 1920. Yet in comparison with many underdeveloped nations, population growth would not seem to be a serious problem in America.

Certainly this vastly increased population will not lack for food. While population growth in Latin America, for example, has brought per capita food production below pre-World War II levels, we in the United States worry about overweight, spend huge sums to restrict farm production, and give away enough food to prevent famine in poor nations throughout the world. In contrast to less developed nations, we have enough space, too. Just fly over this country and see the huge sparsely populated areas that could easily accommodate additional tens of millions.

Great differences in resources, technology, and education help explain why Americans regard overpopulation as a menace only to other peoples. It can't happen here, they think. I used to think so, too. I don't anymore.

During the past ten years, much of it spent overseas, I came to the easy conclusion that if we succeeded in tripling or quadrupling food production in hungry nations—and in some areas in which I worked we did just that—the problem of overpopulation could be solved. But gradually I learned I was mistaken to believe that increased food production was the complete answer to the crisis of population abroad. Gradually, I also learned that America's overflowing cornucopia has obscured a deeper crisis developing here, a population of at least 300 million by 2000 will, I now believe, threaten the very quality of life of individual Americans.

An additional 100 million people will undermine our most cherished traditions, erode our public services, and impose a rate of taxation that will make current taxes seem tame. The new masses, concentrated (as they will be) in the already strangling urban centers, cannot avoid creating conditions that will make city life almost unbearable. San Francisco, to take a still tolerable example, once was one of my favorite cities—cosmopolitan, comfortable, lovely. Now the high-rise buildings have sprouted like weeds and suburban blight is advancing on the Golden Gate. The value of real estate has increased, while people's enjoyment of life declines.

Historically the United States owes much of its vigor and power to population growth. (Only 50 million people rattled around in America in 1880.) Large markets, skilled manpower, huge factories, a country able to spend billions on war, space, and social welfare—all this, plus 75 million passenger cars—is surely a consequence of rising population. But no economy and no physical environment can sustain infinite population growth. There comes a point at which a change in quantity becomes a change in quality—when we can no longer speak of "more of the same." And another 100 million people will, I fear, make just that change in the joy of life in America.

It is probably true that as the population will grow, so will the dollar value of our output. U.S. wealth, measured by the gross national product, is now $670 billion; barring a major economic setback, total output will be doubled in about two decades. With GNP climbing at the rate of $40 billion a year, the United States probably can afford to build the schools, housing projects, roads, and other necessities of life for 300 million Americans.

But if our resources are mainly spent merely to survive, to cope with life in a congested America, then where is the enjoyment of living? Our teeming cities are not pleasant places today; imagine them by the middle of the next century when the areas of some might be one hundred times larger than they are now. This is the real possibility envisioned by Roger Revelle, director of the newly established Center for Population Studies at the Harvard School of Public Health. And it will be to the cities that tomorrow's millions will flock. Or consider the picture, drawn with characteristic wit, by economist John Kenneth Galbraith: "It is hard to suppose that penultimate Western man, stalled in the ultimate traffic jam and slowly succumbing to carbon monoxide, will be especially enchanted to hear from the last survivor that in the preceding year the gross national product went up by a record amount."

Nor does the nightmare consist only of traffic jams and a bumper-to-bumper way of life. As we have seen in the history of the last twenty-five years, public services that only the federal government can provide will continue to expand. Moreover, state governments, until now unable (or unwilling) to pay their share of the bills, show signs of awakening to their responsibilities. But bigger government efforts do not produce better results for human beings: They are simply a way of getting a job done when no more feasible methods exist.

Even today, most of the nation's most serious problems are caused largely by the pressures of a too rapidly rising population. In the next generation the problems may become unmanageable. Take four basic needs: education, water, air, and power.

The quality of education is closely related to the problem of numbers. Within the next five years, we are told, the number of high school students will rise to 15 million (a 50 percent increase over 1960), forcing hundreds of communities to consider imposing stiff new taxes. Many taxpayers will refuse to accept the added burden and their children will attend even more crowded classes. Farsighted citizens will approve new-school bond issues, but the increased financial drain probably will not result in an improved education.

Our standard of democracy entitles everyone to free schooling through high school. But our educational standards are rising. Two-year junior colleges, many of them supported by cities and states, loom as the next step in our system of free universal education. Along with the surge in enrollment at traditional four-year colleges and universities, higher education is expected to attract about 12 million students in 1980 (triple the 1960 figure).

Merely building the physical facilities for such huge increases is a formidable prospect. Creating a sympathetic atmosphere for education and filling the need for qualified teachers is a much more staggering problem. Of course, we may argue for the radical reform of U.S. education. We may plead for overhauling the existing system of teacher training, as James B. Conant has eloquently done. But I see few signs that we are about to undertake such vast changes in the machinery of U.S. education; nor does it seem possible, even if the mood for drastic reform was overwhelming, simply to order new procedures, new goals, and new solutions and then put them into practice. Good teachers cannot be turned out by fiat. We do not live in a planner's paradise. Ask Robert Moses.

With increased urbanization and industrialization, demands on the water supply will be much greater than most Americans have remotely imagined. The drought in the Northeast United States last summer was an indication of even greater shortages to come. And though engineers and scientists can, and will, tap new sources of water and devise ways to purify polluted rivers like the Hudson, the cost will be fantastic—hundreds of billions of dollars. Add to the current strain the pressure of a 50 percent increase in population and the result may well be a chronic water shortage that can hardly be solved at any tolerable price.

Imaginative but impractical water schemes have been proposed, such as one to bring to the United States the almost limitless supply of far northern water, carrying it a thousand miles and more to our own boundaries. Assuming that Canada would agree to the politically prickly diversion of her waters, the cost is estimated in the neighborhood of $100 billion. But it has taken more than a generation of hot dispute and interminable litigation to decide priorities of water among our own sister states of the West. How much greater the difficulties of diverting Canada's water to care for U.S. needs.

As for nuclear-powered desalination plants, quite apart from the cost of constructing the huge installations we would need and the pipelines to carry the water inland, there is the additional problem of safety in disposing of radioactive waste. Technicians may solve the problems, but at what social cost? The conversion of precious open spaces into atomic garbage dumps?

Just as easily accessible water supplies dwindle, air pollution will increase. Air pollution is the result of congestion, industrialization, and the multiplication of automobiles—factors in direct relation to population density in urban areas. Los Angeles is not an industrial city, yet at times its air is hardly fit to breathe. And with the spread of industry in the sprawling cities of the nation, more and more places will be Los Angelized.

We have long assumed that at least the air we breathe is free. It won't be for much longer as we expand our efforts to purify the atmosphere. In California, for example, an aroused public finally insisted that automobile manufacturers install exhaust filters to trap toxic chemicals. Keeping automobile fumes and industrial poisons out of the air we breathe is going to be an increasingly costly business. By the year 2000 the high cost of breathing will be a real issue, not just a phrase.

Packing too many people into an urban area increases the cost of providing still another essential of everyday living: electric power. Even more serious, such concentrations of people may make absolutely reliable electric service more and more difficult to maintain. I doubt if it was a mere coincidence, for example, that New York City needed ten hours to restore electricity after the recent Northeast power failure, while smaller communities were able to turn on their lights in a much shorter time. Growth is desirable up to a point; then the advantage of size diminishes and the multiplication of complexity multiplies the headaches. And by 1980 we can expect at least a 300 percent increase in the nation's electrical energy needs. Most of this will flow into urban areas. The present difficulties of maintaining absolutely reliable service to such concentrations of people and industry, and holding down costs, will thus be magnified.

As chairman of TVA and the Atomic Energy Commission, and in my present work in Asia and Latin America, I have become familiar with the problems of producing and distributing electricity on a large scale. Indeed, it was TVA a generation ago that pioneered the concept that the greater the use of electricity the lower the cost per kilowatt hour. This is still generally true. But for great cities the exact contrary is coming to pass. To distribute electricity in a large, densely populated areas such as New York is more costly than in smaller urban markets. Huge generating power plants produce ever lower generating costs; but to bring this power to the consumer in massive concentrations of population grows more and more expensive. Consequently, the price of this essential of modern life probably will go up in the great cities as population growth continues.

Without realizing it, we are fast approaching what may be called the population barrier beyond which lie unpredictability and, I fear, problems of unmanageable size. Consider, for example, the relationship between population growth and the poor.

The Federal Aid to Dependent Children program has doubled to more than 4 million cases during the last decade, while the costs have soared from about $600 million to more than $18 billion. Even more depressing than the numbers of families who cannot survive without welfare assistance is the phenomenon known as the "cycle of dependency."

More than 40 percent of the parents whose children receive ADC funds themselves had parents who received relief checks. This cycle is sad but not surprising. Poor people tend to have more children than they want or can afford, and the children have less chance to receive the education and training they need to break the pattern. Thus, even the third generation appears on relief rolls in the United States, the most socially mobile nation in the world. In America, reports the National Academy of Sciences in a recent study, "The Growth of U.S. Population," "the burden of unwanted children among impoverished and uneducated mothers . . . is much like that experienced by mothers in underdeveloped countries."

Since the poor cannot contribute their share of the mounting costs of education, medical care, public housing, and similar necessary government enterprises, the money must be supplied by the rest of the population through taxation. But the most painful loss is not measured in dollars but in human resources. And one measure of the potential loss is the fact that one-fourth of America's children are the offspring of poor parents.

Belatedly, we are helping poor couples who need and want financial and medical help in family planning. The White House Conference on Health in November gave high priority to birth control as part of federal efforts to halt the cycle of dependency and poverty. Tax-supported activities in forty states, combined with such large-scale private efforts as Harvard's Center for Population Studies and the $145 million grant by the Ford Foundation for basic research by the Columbia-Presbyterian Medical Center and the Population Council, herald new progress in a long-neglected field.

We tend to patronize the poor by preaching to them about birth control: Though poverty-stricken parents with four, five, or six children are the most publicized aspect of population growth, they are by no means the most important numerical aspect of the problem. As a matter of simple arithmetic, the four-fifths of the nation's families who earn more than the poverty-line income of $3,000 a year, and who can afford two, three, or four children, produce a greater total of children than the one poor couple out of five who may have six youngsters.

In fact, the latest census information reveals that though poor families may have more children than do better-off families, the difference is much smaller than many people believe. According to the National Academy of Sciences analysis, in 1960 married women forty to forty-four years old in families with incomes below $4,000 and above $4,000 differed in the average number of children by less than one. The postwar baby boom, for example, was more pronounced among middle- and upper-income families than among the poor.

Thus, these relatively well-off families are the ones mainly responsible for our rapidly rising population curve. They and their children are the ones who will account for most of the 100 million additional Americans by the end of the century.

How many children a couple should have is a decision only they should make; a government inducement or deterrent—a tax, for example—is morally repugnant and politically impossible. We cannot penalize the poor in order to limit the size of their families while we allow more prosperous parents to have as many children as they want. The large majority of middle- and upper-class parents need no birth-control help from government, nor will they welcome outside advice on so personal a matter. Yet it is this group of families who will want to have three, four, or more children for the very natural reason that they like children and can afford to support them. The question is, can the country support them?

Any notion that the pill or some other scientific device is the sole and complete answer is very dubious. At a symposium on birth control not long ago, Dr. Stephen J. Plank, a professor at the Harvard School of Public Health, cautioned against "the facile assumption . . . that we may be able to contracept our way to the Great Society." Birth control, he said, is a question of motivation rather than technology alone.

The neglected arithmetic of the population problem facing us is depressing. Look at this table showing the birth and death rates over the past quarter century in the United States.

Year	Births	Rate (per 1,000 pop.)	Deaths	Rate (per 1,000 pop.)
1940	2,360,399	17.9	1,417,269	10.8
1945	2,735,456	19.5	1,401,719	10.6
1950	3,554,149	23.6	1,452,454	9.6
1955	4,047,295	24.6	1,528,717	9.3
1960	4,257,850	23.7	1,711,982	9.5
1964	4,027,490	21.0	1,798,051	9.4

Although the birth rate has been declining since the mid-fifties, while the death rate has remained relatively stable, the drop in the birth rate is too little and too late to prevent an oversized population. The surge in the number of births over deaths continues (2.3 million were added to the population in 1964).

Or examine these low and high population projections prepared by the Census Bureau:

	Low	High
1970	206,000,000	210,000,000
1985	248,000,000	276,000,000
2010	322,000,000	438,000,000

The high figure would be reached if birth rates returned to the levels of the early 1950's. The low estimate—enormous as it is—is based on the possibility that the rates may decline by 1985 to the comparatively low levels of the early World War II years.

One theoretical way out of the dilemma would be to say that since America can no longer sustain complete "family freedom," some form of compulsory birth control is, regrettably, necessary. It would not be the first time in our history that government intervened to restrain individual impulse in the name of collective welfare. Yet, where children and parents are concerned, I do not believe we can yet advocate the sacrifice of one freedom for the sake of preserving another. Such a "solution" would make no sense at all, theoretically, practically, or ethically.

Government policies and private programs must make plain the kind of life we all face if economically comfortable families reproduce at rates they personally can afford. With equal urgency we must make plain the dangers if poor families have children in numbers they cannot afford.

Obviously, a stationary population—one in which the birth rate matches the death rate—is out of the question for many years to come. It is probably not feasible, nor even desirable. All we can hope to achieve is a slower rise in the size of our population rather than the present steep increase. What is needed is a far more drastic cut in the birth rate—a voluntary curtailment of the right to breed. It is needed, but I have no great conviction that it will happen.

For though scientific ingenuity may be able to solve many of the technological problems, we are only beginning to understand that people always change more slowly than technology. It is easier after all, to design a new industrial process than to redesign a cultural tradition. Yet that is the order of change we face if we are to preserve life's dignity and quality. Confronted by the crisis of population growth, we must, at present, appeal to private conscience for the sake of the general good.

The Fertility Goddess vs. the Loop
BY DAVID DEMPSEY

At a conference on the population crisis a few years ago in London, Dr. Alan F. Guttmacher, the tall, bouncy seventy-year-old president of Planned Parenthood–World Population, was listening to a speaker decry the soaring birth rate in developing countries. "Mind you, every half second while I stand here a woman is giving birth to a baby," the man declared solemnly.

After a pause, during which the audience attempted to project this frightening statistic into a yearly figure (it works out to 63,072,000), a voice from the rear of the hall boomed: "Sir, we must find and stop that woman at once."

"Alan all but leaped out of his chair," a colleague remarked later. "It was as though he wanted to start looking right away. After all, he's the most influential birth-control advocate in the world."

Guttmacher terms this description of his powers exaggerated, yet it is doubtful that anyone in our time has done more to propagate the idea of less propagation. The author of several books on family planning, an indefatigable lecturer on the subject and a traveling ambassador in behalf of birth control for the international arm of Planned Parenthood, he has become a symbol of hope for millions of women who served their time with Dr. Spock and want out. "I give the movement an image," he says.

To many, the Guttmacher image is that of an airborne missionary whose dedication to the cause has propelled him three times around the world—into sixty-five countries on three continents—bearing contraceptives for African natives, money for clinical outposts in Pakistan, and pungent remarks for banquet audiences in the United States. ("When you give the kids the keys to your car," he once told a Los Angeles group, "be sure to give them contraceptives, too.")

There are others, however, who contend that Guttmacher simply likes to travel and to listen to the sound of his own voice. "Alan is the third most egotistical man I have ever met," says a colleague in the birth-control movement, "but I don't mean this disparagingly. He just enjoys being Alan Guttmacher—and he's good at it."

The real Guttmacher seems to lie somewhere between these two characterizations. An associate who has worked closely with him for the last six years calls him "incandescent—a man with flavor, sensitivity, and conviction." In a sense, his awesome professional standing—he was at one time professor of obstetrics at Johns Hopkins University and later chief of the department at Mount Sinai School of Medicine in New York—explains his value to a traditionally humanitarian movement that has lately been infiltrated by hard-line demographers advocating coercive methods to halt population growth.

Guttmacher stands firmly on the side of voluntary planning and thus speaks with the "dove" element in a controversy that swirls about him with increasing velocity. His critics point out that even if such "crisis" countries as India and Pakistan should achieve their goals in reducing the birth rate the problem would not be solved; for every nation that has an effective program there is at least one that doesn't. World population is now doubling every thirty-five years, and time is running out. If mass famine is not to solve the problem, then governments must; what might be regarded as harsh solutions are, by comparison, humanitarian.

"Alan came into the movement when it was a medical concern focused on the individual and family," says Dr. Christopher Tietze of the Population Council, a research group that supports birth-control programs abroad. "But the emphasis is shifting to a demographic concern for survival, and he is just now catching up." Guttmacher is aware of this but believes that the new contraceptive technology and changing social attitudes toward family size promise to reduce the birth rate quickly enough to make the problem manageable. In any case, he says, compulsory birth control is not only morally wrong but probably impractical. "Just who is going to round up 200 million Latin American men and sterilize them?" he asks. The situation is most serious in countries where voluntary programs have not been tried, and Guttmacher thinks that this is the place to begin.

The controversy has been heightened by disagreement within Planned Parenthood on what constitutes an ideal family size. The organization, which has never come out with an official position on the subject, is under increasing pressure to recommend a birth rate that would "average" 2.3 children per family. This would stabilize the population, but, as Guttmacher points out, it would eventually give us a median age of sixty-five. "I find this depressing," he says. At present, the federation remains committed to the principle that a woman should be encouraged to have as many children as she wants, but not more than she can provide for. If "Freedom to Choose," Planned Parenthood's theme for 1969, has left some supporters of the movement unhappy, it nevertheless expresses Alan Guttmacher's faith in people. Given the facts and an opportunity to act, he believes, they will choose wisely.

To an outsider, Guttmacher is an accessible and friendly man whose natural vigor belies his age. Visitors are soon on a hearty first-name basis with him and are made privy to his boyish enthusiasm for anything athletic that comes out of Baltimore, where he was born and grew up. During the baseball season, he sneaks out of meetings to catch an inning or two of the Orioles on a transistor radio. The success or failure of the Colts he regards as his personal responsibility; when the Colts were unexpectedly beaten by the New York Jets in the Super Bowl game early this year, Guttmacher did penance by spending the remainder of the Sunday working on a medical paper.

Erect and agile, he still plays tennis and walks to and from work each day—a total of almost seven miles. He wastes little time on the trappings of executive success; guests who are invited to lunch with him may be surprised, and perhaps dismayed, to find themselves eating a delicatessen sandwich and drinking coffee at the president's oiled walnut desk. Guttmacher lunches on a cup of bouillon and a bowl of cottage cheese.

The office in which this takes place resembles the trophy room of a man whose sporting blood has been crossed with a social conscience. ("Guttmacher," he reminds visitors, "means maker of Good.") Above his desk a bearded, rabbinical great-grandfather of Hassidic mien peers down on the photographs of enough Guttmachers to suggest that the family was not always in favor of birth control. On a window sill stands the ceramic figure of an Indonesian fertility goddess with nine babies clinging to it, back and front. It is so ugly that Guttmacher's secretary frequently pulls the drape to hide it when she takes dictation. He promptly undrapes it when she leaves. On the front wall are pictures of the professors who influenced him most at Johns Hopkins, where he took his medical degree in 1923. Near these is one of Guttmacher's rarest trophies, a framed letter from Richard Cardinal Cushing culminating a correspondence on birth control. "Don't worry about my attitude toward the cause in which you are interested," the cardinal wrote. "In due time I will make a statement that is in harmony with the teachings of the faith which I profess." Indeed, the cardinal's statement, when it came, was so liberal that it became the prime lever in the repeal of Massachusetts's restrictive birth-control laws.

Guttmacher's desk holds mementos and amulets that do not lend themselves to framing. He keeps paper clips in an English pewter pap cup (once used for giving milk to babies) and has a baseball autographed by the Cuban minister of health for a paperweight.

In the six years since Alan Guttmacher became head of Planned Parenthood–World Population, its staff and budget have tripled and it has grown from a struggling, WASP-supported advisory service for the middle class into a slum-oriented mother church that supplies 472 Planned Parenthood clinics in the United States with medical scripture, proselytizing tracts, and an impressive armamentarium of contraceptive devices. "I have the largest pill practice in the country," Guttmacher boasts, referring to the hundreds of thousands of women who receive birth-control pills regularly in the federation's clinics.

At a testimonial dinner given him a year and a half ago by seven hundred admirers in Baltimore, the traditional gift of appreciation was a pair of gold cuff links. Guttmacher wears them proudly. On each is embossed a replica of the Lippes Loop, an intrauterine device developed by Dr. Jack Lippes of the University of Buffalo's College of Medicine in 1961 and now used as a contraceptive by an estimated 8 million women the world over. "The thing you've got to realize," says Dr. Tietze, "is that the loop was discredited in the 1930's, when it was called the Graefenberg Ring. But it was obvious that the pill was getting nowhere in the poor countries—you have to know how to count to use it and the majority of village women in the Far East can't do this; something else had to be tried, and Alan decided that the IUD's ought to have another chance."

In 1964 Guttmacher persuaded the Population Council to set up a conference on the use of the new IUD's. Six hundred medical men and government officials from forty countries attended. "Alan fired them up like a tent-meeting evangelist," Dr. Tietze recalls. "It was a dangerous precedent—like endorsing Krebiozen, the sort of thing a quack might be accused of. But it proved to be a real breakthrough. The IUD's have their limitations, but they may give the world breathing space until a more foolproof technique is developed."

"Guttmacher is impatient," declares Dr. Louis Hellman, a former student of his at Johns Hopkins and now chief of obstetrics and gynecology at the Downstate Medical College. "He wants to get things done. The medical profession in this country was slow to adopt the pill when it first came out—too little was known about possible side effects and long-term risks. It's been even slower to prescribe the loop. Alan believes in telling the public both advantages *and* risks and letting the patient make the decision. He is not a cautious man."

Guttmacher believes this is no time for caution. Like nuclear war, he says, the population explosion is so terrifying that most people don't want to think about it. He adds: "My job is not only to make people think about the problem, but to do something about it."

This has not been easy. Most physicians, he declares, are guilty of "intellectual cowardice" in the interest of good business: "It's safer to do nothing than to risk getting involved with social problems." He believes, for instance, that women should be able to have abortions on demand. "The patent hypocrisy and holier-than-thou attitude of the medical profession in regard to this problem are revolting,", he charges.

On the average, Guttmacher travels about half the time, almost always in the company of his wife, an independent-minded woman who shops for her husband's razor blades, socks, and other necessities and shares with him the ceremonial rigors of state dining in such places as Topeka, Kansas, and the Fiji Islands.

On overseas journeys, the doctor carries a supply of IUD's and a film showing how to insert them. He visits tribal hospitals, lectures to medical councils, and solicits audiences with heads of state. A stop at Hong Kong, where he observed a physician inserting IUD's at a clinic, inspired the sports reporter in Guttmacher. "It was as exciting as watching a great shortstop field a ball hit far to his left," he wrote in the monthly President's Letter, which is mailed to thousands of the federation's supporters throughout the country.

When he's in the United States, Guttmacher makes as many as fifteen one-night stands each month before university groups, Rotary Clubs, medical societies, economic forums, nurses, YMCA's, and private schools. To senior citizens he talks about overpopulation ("they're no longer interested in sex as such"). Physicians and nurses receive a professional discourse on the medical aspects of birth control and maternal health and sometimes a mild tongue-lashing for their backwardness. Groups of young marrieds are treated to a question-and-answer session that, in effect, instructs them on how to make the most of marital sex without overloading the baby carriage.

The Guttmacher charm is also effective on an individual basis. A few years ago word was received that an eccentric, eighty-seven-year-old heiress to the McCormick reaper fortune had announced that she would bequeath $500,000 to Planned Parenthood. Guttmacher hurried off to thank her, spent an hour explaining the good works to which the money would be put, then considerately listened as she played the piano. When the woman died a short time later, the $500,000 bequest had grown to $5 million. "I'd like to think I had something to do with it," the doctor concedes.

"There's a bit of the ham in Alan," says Dr. Hellman. "He talks well, makes a good appearance, and enjoys shocking people. He particularly likes to talk about sex in girls' schools."

Guttmacher's prep-school circuit includes a number of coeducational institutions whose students look forward keenly to his annual visit, knowing that they will not receive the customary lecture on reproductive physiology, but an unblushing, down-to-earth talk on *sex* and what to do about it.

Guttmacher's dignified manner and appearance, his white hair, and his correct dress reassure headmasters that this is like a visit from the family doctor, someone who is about to make an ordinarily risky subject harmless. The persona, however, is deceiving. The family doctor unsheaths a large display board on which is mounted, like a collection of exotic butterflies, every contraceptive device in use. At the unveiling, eyes pop and there is a nervous cough from teacher. But Guttmacher disarms his listeners at once. "The surest way to prevent pregnancy," he announces, "is to practice chastity. That is what I recommend to you."

Since the student will not always remain a student—or chaste, for that matter—Guttmacher spends the next twenty minutes explaining the workings of the contraceptives in order of their reliability, beginning with the pill ("If a woman forgets for three days, she can't take three pills on the fourth and make up for it. God doesn't give her any credit for that. He may even punish her by making her pregnant") and including the loop, diaphragm, condom, vaginal foam, jelly, cream and suppository. For Catholic students there is a discussion of the rhythm method. A blackboard is used to diagram fertility periods and to show the mysteries of conception. These chalk talks are often enlivened with metaphors from the world of sports. "The male sperm is like an Olympic swimmer," he declares, "as it races to seek out and fertilize the ovum. It is out to *win*. . . ."

The talk ends with a little lecture on premarital intercourse. Guttmacher advises against the practice, but suggests that if a girl indulges in it she should protect herself against possible pregnancy. "I do not advocate sexual freedom for adolescents," he insists. "I do believe in sexual responsibility." But, he adds, "Better contraception before intercourse than an illegal abortion after."

The net result of a Guttmacher visit to a boarding school is difficult to appraise. Some of the older girls are clearly frightened by the doctor's unusual frankness, whereas the boys show gratitude for the forthright, avuncular advice. (Father would never tell us all this.) Some of the information, however, seems to sail right over the heads of very young students. At the end of one lecture, a thirteen-year-old boy, sitting in the rear of the room, raised his hand and asked: "Dr. Guttmacher, would you tell us more about the Olympic swimmers?"

Despite the popularity that mentioning the unmentionable evokes among the young, adults who attribute our decline in sexual morality to the sort of precautionary advice that Guttmacher hands out frequently take a stern view of his talks. The doctor not only stands his ground in the face of such criticism, but sometimes confounds his more personal detractors with the statement, "Madam, I am a monozygotic monster," which simply and irrelevantly means that he was born an identical twin.

This unusual birth—it occurs only once in 279 cases among whites—took place on May 19, 1898, in Baltimore, where Guttmacher père was rabbi to a Reform congregation. Alan, his twin brother, Manfred, and an older sister, Dorothy, attended Baltimore schools. When the boys were seventeen, their father died, and for a time it looked as though they might have to go to work. A family friend offered to set them up in the ladies' ready-to-wear business, but school officials intervened; loans and after-school jobs were secured and Alan and Manfred entered Johns Hopkins. After medical school and a year on the staff of the University of Rochester, Alan married a New York girl, Leonore Faith Giddings, and went back to Hopkins for his residency in obstetrics. He remained there to teach.

Manfred, meanwhile, had become a psychiatrist. Until graduation, the twins had lived at home, occupying the same room for twenty-five years and often wearing each other's clothes. "When Manfred died in 1967," a close friend declared, "he took part of Alan with him. They were not only indistinguishable, but inseparable."

"Even their wives got them mixed up," an ex-Baltimorean remembers. "There were times when they simply answered to each other's names." Talk about the Guttmacher twins, legendary in Baltimore, frequently concern patients who got into the wrong office by mistake. One woman, worried at the undue hypertrophy of her breasts following the birth of a child, bared them to Manfred; he commented that while it would please him no end to examine them, he doubted that she would be helped much by the opinion of a psychiatrist.

Of Alan Guttmacher, Dr. Alex Schaffer, a former student and now a professor at Hopkins, said at the testimonial dinner: "On the wards, in the delivery room and operating room and classrooms, he taught with vigor and fire, a perpetual stimulus, almost a goad. Some jealous competitors thought that he interlarded his presentations with a few too many Anglo-Saxon expletives, but in my opinion they added a dash of accent to the casserole."

In the early 1930's the two Guttmachers became active in the city's only birth-control clinic. Alan's views on the subject were becoming more pronounced as he became more outspoken. Commonplace today, these views were strong meat in Baltimore thirty-five years ago, when the Guttmacher creed—that it is a basic human right for every woman to choose whether she wants children—was developed. Abortion, he argued, should be a question for physicians to decide, not law enforcers. The poor should have the same access to contraception as the well-to-do. (Private maternity cases were sent home fitted with diaphragms if they wanted them, Guttmacher recalls. Ward patients were simply sent home.)

Alan's growing reputation for free speech, both secular and profane, appealed to the Baltimore sage Henry L. Mencken, who invited both brothers to join him in an occasional evening of beer drinking and *Gemütlichkeit* at Shellhase's Restaurant on Howard Street. "This was not the famous Saturday Night Club, where Mencken played the piano and the other members tooted away on horns," Alan says. "We discussed the issues of the day and told stories." With Mencken's older brother, August, and Louis Hellman joining, the group met on Mondays. Manfred had written a psychiatric study of King George III that tickled Mencken's anti-British prejudices, and Alan was preaching birth control, legal abortion, the democratization of medical care, and in general acting the *enfant terrible* of Baltimore medicine. A local publication deplored the fact that Mrs. Guttmacher had not used birth control at the time of the twins' conception.

After ten years of weekly sessions, the group disbanded with the onset of World War II. "As time went on," Alan reminisces, "Henry became increasingly pro-German. Unfortunately, he also did most of the talking." Nevertheless, Guttmacher values their relationship as a lesson in the limits of iconoclasm. As Mencken came to believe in less and less, the Guttmachers found themselves standing for more and more. Alan was chairman of the medical committee for the Maryland Chapter of Planned Parenthood, and Manfred had been appointed court psychiatrist for the city. (Two of his books, *The Role of Psychiatry in Law* and *Sex and the Offender,* are recognized today as pioneering works on the mental determinants of crime. Manfred's career ended on a note of distinction when he was retained by the defense to testify for Jack Ruby in 1964.)

In the early forties, Alan was appointed chief of obstetrics at Baltimore's Sinai Hospital. He had also built a fashionable private practice, his reputation as a radical notwithstanding. Rose Burgunder (now Mrs. William Styron), a Guttmacher baby whose family lived next door, remembers him as "a warm, amusing, gentle" man who, when he wasn't delivering babies or shocking Catholics, liked to play bridge. Mrs. Styron sought him out to deliver her own babies after Guttmacher had moved to New York.

Guttmacher had achieved some notoriety with his first book, *Life in the Making,* written in 1933, in which he predicted, with science-fiction panache, that within "a few thousand years" the whole matter of human birth would be taken care of in the test tube. "I am quite confident," he wrote, ". . . that creation by means of the sexual act, or by any other sort of fusion of egg and sperm, will be considered antiquated. Conception will be an impersonal process involving ions and atoms and flasks and fluids." (When this passage was read to him recently, he said: "Did I write that? We— I must have been rather immature.")

To the average infertile woman, theories on ions and atoms were of slight comfort. She was in no position to wait, and in any case she did not believe that sex was antiquated. Guttmacher, recognizing the need for practical therapy, began experimenting with artificial insemination—so successfully, in fact, that grateful parents sometimes named children after him.

In 1952 the Mount Sinai School of Medicine in New York lured him from Hopkins and Guttmacher moved with his wife and three daughters to a large, comfortable apartment on upper Fifth Avenue, just a few blocks from the Mount Sinai complex. Here, for the next ten years, he ran the department of obstetrics and gynecology, wrote a number of books, lectured, read papers to medical conventions, and carried on an extensive private practice. When Planned Parenthood sought a successor to the late William Vogt, who retired as president in 1962, Guttmacher took the job, changing a five-block walk north to Mount Sinai into a forty-block walk south.

With long strides, Guttmacher makes his daily trek to work in thirty-eight minutes—less time, he says, than the bus ride requires. At his Madison Avenue office, he assumes a three-part role: (1) directing the educational, membership, and publications work of the 160 Planned Parenthood staff members; (2) goading the 103-man board of directors into a more radical stance on birth control; and (3) "image building." Administrative donkey-work, for which he admits to being temperamentally unsuited, is carried out by a triumvirate of associates—Paul Todd, Jr., a former congressman from Michigan and now chief executive officer of the federation; Winfield Best, an energetic veteran of fifteen years in the movement who handles liaison with the 154 affiliates, and Fred Jaffe, a program developer who works with public agencies. A Negro, Mrs. Naomi Gray, is vice president in charge of field services.

On policy questions, the federation and its president occasionally find themselves at odds. In at least one instance the organization came around to Guttmacher's point of view when, a few months ago, it endorsed the principle of therapeutic abortion after years of opposition and after Governor Rockefeller picked Guttmacher to serve on a citizens' commission to recommend a liberalized abortion law for New York State. Defeated by the legislature last year in what Guttmacher calls "an exercise in futility," the bill has been reintroduced—with enhanced prospects of success—this year.

Boiling up in nearly all of Planned Parenthood's board meetings these days is the touchy question of whether contraception in itself, without a strict policy on maximum family size, can be effective in reducing population growth. Donald R. Strauss, chairman of the federation's executive committee, advances the argument that the whole problem is shifting from "unwanted" to "wanted" children. He is supported by a 1965 survey showing that four-fifths of the births that year were "wanted" children, not the result of accidental pregnancies. Says George N. Lindsay, brother of the mayor and Planned Parenthood's board chairman in 1968: "It is mainly the more fortunate Americans, confirmed contraceptive users, who are causing U.S. population growth by producing 'wanted' babies so abundantly."

Since contraception is largely a practice of the better-educated, facing this issue means a shift of emphasis in the birth-control campaign from the ghetto to the white middle-class neighborhood. And for a sizable number of the federation's board members—themselves preponderantly white and well-to-do—this means restricting the "freedom to choose." They argue that the elimination of the 20 percent of pregnancies that are "unwanted" would stabilize the birth rate.

"What it all comes down to," declares one dissenting board member, "is that we want the poor to stop breeding while we retain our freedom to have large families. It's strictly a class point of view." Guttmacher is caught in the middle of the argument, and in a sense he is impaled on his own ideals, which are sympathetic to the poor. "Even the unwed mother, if she wants the child, should have it," he says. "We're not trying to take away anyone's freedom. What we are trying to do is show ghetto families how to space their children and avoid having children they don't want."

Whatever the merits of the argument, the ghetto approach is now the federation's chief thrust, and it is also the policy of the federal government, which since 1966 has undergone a dramatic reversal, moving from almost no action on birth control to a proposed expenditure in 1969 of $31 million. Last month the Department of Health, Education and Welfare recommended the adoption of Planned Parenthood's "blueprint" for supplying free birth-control advice to some 5 million American women below the poverty line.

Among other things, this policy has brought the Planned Parenthood Federation under attack from black militants, who see "family planning" as a euphemism for race genocide. Crash programs, as in Lincoln Parish, Louisiana (where the birth rate was reduced 32 percent during 1966–67), Washington, D.C. (a 24 percent drop in the last three years), and Baltimore (down 36 percent since 1965), confirm the suspicion that black people are taking the brunt of the "planning." At least one clinic has been burned, others have come under verbal attack, and Guttmacher from time to time is picketed. He points out, however, that it is the men, not the women, who object: Because the level of maternal and infant deaths among Negroes is twice that of whites, birth control actually improves survival rates.

The controversy is far from dead. "Admit it or not," an official of the Population Council says, "the genocide faction has a lot of evidence on its side." He points to laws in many southern states that compel mothers on relief to seek birth-control advice. Guttmacher, who is more popular in the South than he would like to be, has fought these laws as an infringement on human freedom. Guttmacher's position is not popular with some of his own board members, but on balance, the country's black leadership supports the federation's approach to planning. A Negro, Dr. Jerome H. Holland, president of Hampton Institute, was elected chairman of Planned Parenthood's board for 1969, and about 10 percent of the board is black.

The hard-liners are a more formidable group. Justin Blackwelder of the Population Crisis Committee, a Washington-based organization, has said: "Family planning means, among other things, that if we are going to multiply like rabbits, we should do it on purpose." Others have pointed out that it is the freedom of the Indians and Latin Americans to choose that is insuring them a famine-ridden future. Dr. John Rock, a prominent Catholic advocate of birth control, predicts that a massive famine in many parts of the world is "inevitable" by the mid-seventies, and, he says, "There is nothing we can do to stop it."

Rock is a board member of the Population Policy Panel, a New York group, which urges a more aggressive government effort to lower the birth rate. In a series of full-page newspaper advertisements, the panel has equated the increase in crime with a rising population ("When Was the Last Time You Were Mugged? This is the Crime Explosion—and the Population Explosion is the Underlying Factor"). Guttmacher argues that no evidence exists to prove that a rising population *in itself* is the leading factor in the rise in crime. In any case, he says, a good deal of public concern for the problem is a smoke screen for something else—a vested interest in maintaining the status quo, in white supremacy, in keeping the poor from multiplying, or in containing communism.

Pressure for a harder line has also come from theoreticians in the movement, many of them respected academics. Sociologist Kingsley Davis of the University of California at Berkeley shook up Planned Parenthood a year ago with an article in the magazine *Science,* which challenged the concept of family planning as an effective approach to slowing down the birth rate. "There is no reason to expect that the millions of decisions about family size made by couples in their own interest will automatically control population for the benefit of society," he wrote. Reliance on such "planning," in Davis's view, may only create "a basis for dangerous postponement of effective steps."

Writing in the *Harvard Alumni Bulletin* in 1967, Professor Roy O. Greep carried this argument further by pointing out that reducing the birth rate is not the same as stabilizing it at a manageable level: "While we have some evidence that such control may be effective under the most favorable circumstances, the fact still remains that it has not yet had the slightest decelerating effect on the rates of worldwide population growth." What "involuntary" control might consist of is outlined by biologist Paul Ehrlich of Stanford University, who proposes that American tax laws be changed to discourage reproduction (by the imposition of luxury taxes on diapers and baby food and the elimination of tax deductions for children) and that birth-control instruction be made mandatory in public schools. Ehrlich would also refuse aid to countries with increasing populations that do not make the maximum effort to limit growth.

Guttmacher is against such a Draconian solution, and he refuses to admit that voluntary planning is ineffective. "Where it has been tried," he says, "it works. The United States now has one of the lowest birth rates in its history. Fifteen years ago, the average family size was 3.2 children. It is now about 2.7, and there is no reason why it cannot be stabilized at 2.3. Personally, I would prefer to see a slight population increase to give us a more dynamic, youthful society." He contends that it is population imbalance—not raw growth—that is creating the problems of megalopolis; during the 1950's, half of the counties in the United States lost population.

The growth rate in Europe, he adds, is flattening out, even in such largely Catholic countries as France and Italy. As for the developing countries—the "crisis" areas—he thinks the very seriousness of the problem will work toward imposing a solution: "Korea is halfway to its 1971 goal of a 2 percent birth rate. Taiwan is making significant strides. Even Latin America is beginning to wake up. It's senseless to argue that because a total solution hasn't been achieved there is no hope."

But can "significant strides" catch up with the exploding population before it is too late? One hopeful sign is a radically new contraceptive substance, progestin, which prevents ovulation. Its developers hope to be able to plant a "ribbon" of progestin under the skin and time it to last ten or twenty years—or a lifetime. The substance would be recoverable if the woman should change her mind. Unlike the pill, it would not have to be taken daily, and it would avoid the chief problems with the loop, which may fall out accidentally and can easily be removed by the wearer. Progestin's backers hope that, through "mass inoculation," it can do for overpopulation what the Salk vaccine did for polio.

Admittedly, Guttmacher is buying time. He thinks the voluntary movement should set a deadline of 1980. If world population growth has not dropped below 1.5 percent by then, he says, "we'll have to get tough." But toughness, in Guttmacher's vocabulary, does not mean coercion, which he believes would be impossible to impose without creating such distrust and hostility that governments would be thrown into chaos. "The coercive school simply hasn't faced the social consequences of its position," he says.

"Many countries with high birth rates are unstable. Compulsory birth control would be an invitation to revolt."

Guttmacher's "toughness" is positive: Pay men and women substantial bonuses to undergo sterilization after the second or third child ("A thousand-rupee bonus would easily solve India's problem in a few years"), concentrate on research in contraceptive technology, and revise the tax laws to favor smaller families. Even if such methods don't work, Alan Guttmacher will be remembered as the fighting symbol of a good cause. He is gambling now that in the precious world of human birth planning and freedom are not incompatible.

PART 2

FOOD, RESOURCES, AND NATIONAL DEVELOPMENT

The "Symposium on World Food Resources," with which this section begins, presents a representative sample of the many views on the capacity of the world to feed its growing population. The deep pessimism of Sir Charles Darwin is countered by the restrained optimism of Fred Hoyle, who feels that controls on population growth will bring numbers into an appropriate relation to food resources. Robert McNamara makes an even stronger case for the need for population control as an approach to a solution of the expected food shortage. A contrary argument is advanced by Dr. James Bonner. It is his contention that there need be no prospect of a food shortage if the best technology is brought to bear on the matter and if the waste of food substances is curtailed. None of these writers was aware, at the time they were writing, of the "green revolution," in which Dr. Norman E. Borlaug has had such an important role. As a result of Dr. Borlaug's brilliant work on the development of improved wheat strains in Mexico and of the work of the scientists at the Rice Institute in the Philippines, food problems are, seemingly, at the threshold of solution.

But the optimism engendered by the miracle seeds may have obscured one highly significant contingency, namely, the vagaries of weather. Three successive years of monsoon failure wiped out almost a decade of agricultural progress in India and brought many of its people to the edge of famine. "Waiting for the Monsoon," by Khushwant Singh, goes beyond the harsh facts of survival to reveal how the life and culture of an entire people are intertwined with the monsoon phenomenon. The depth of his understanding of man's relationship with nature in India could only be acquired by one who has shared the experience since childhood.

James P. Sterba's "Report from the Majority of the World" is a perceptive account of life in the rural sector of a poor country. In Indonesia the people appear to be living so close to the minimum level of subsistence that even relatively small reductions in the harvests of a year could result in large-scale disaster. The green revolution has already made progress in Indonesia. Whether it will bring down the price of food so that the landless will benefit remains to be seen.

The difficult and interrelated problems of development are expertly discussed by Barbara Ward. Despite years of foreign aid, the gap between rich and poor nations in productivity and economic well-being has widened. There are also informational, psychological, and political gaps, and these too seem to have grown larger and deeper. To reduce these discrepancies in understanding, trust, and development, requires a much closer partnership between rich and poor nations than has been attained thus far. Each, in fact, needs the other, for all are involved in a single technological and cultural revolution; in that sense all are developing nations.

Part II closes with two short papers on the state of raw material resources in the world. Walter Sullivan lets Dr. Charles F. Park, Jr., a professional geologist, speak on the probable exhaustion of the supplies of nonreplaceable materials. A survey of the raw material resources and of the possible substitutions that might be made inspires only pessimism in Dr. Park. A much more optimistic outlook, which emerged from a conference of distinguished scientists, is reported by Robert K. Plumb. Their confidence in the future rests not on estimates of raw material abundance, but on the effects of a continuously advancing technology. More to the point, "brain power" is the answer to the dwindling supplies of conventional resources. Trained manpower is the one great replaceable resource possessed by society. Every society should extend itself to the utmost, therefore, to preserve and enlarge its supply of scientists and skilled technicians.

Symposium on World Food Resources

Will the World Population One Day Starve or Simply Cease to Increase? | We have heard it said over and over again that man faces a gloomy future because his birth rate is rapidly outstripping his means of producing food. Millions are therefore doomed to death by starvation in a future not too remote.

Sir Charles Darwin is the latest of these prophets of doom. He published his dire forecast in *Engineering and Science,* a periodical issued by the California Institute of Technology. Along comes Fred Hoyle, a cosmologist who believes that the process of creation is continuous in the universe and who picks the Darwinian argument apart in the same periodical and rejects it in part.

There is no doubt that an increase in food supply is accompanied by an increase in our animal population. Reduce the food supply for a particular species of animal and that species decreases in number. Starvation is the controlling factor as Sir Charles points out, following the familiar argument.

Example of the Birds

Hoyle accepts this argument with reservation. To him, starvation is not the only way in which populations adjust themselves to food supplies. Certain species of songbirds automatically limit their number without starvation by a division of good and poor territory from the standpoint of food supply. Territory is divided not into a number of units equal to the number of contending birds but into the number that can provide enough food for a brood of chicks. If the number of contenders exceeds the number of good territorial units, there is fighting. Fighting means not death but the separation of the contending birds into two groups. One group appropriates the available rich territory and breeds; the other group contents itself with poor territory and does not breed. Thus the birth rate is determined automatically by the amount of food that is available. The unsuccessful birds do not starve to death. They find just enough food for subsistence.

Sir Charles also makes the point that we cannot rely on the advance of scientific knowledge to provide enough food for the needs of a rapidly increasing population. To him, man is no different from other animals. Give him more food and his numbers increase; give him less and his numbers decrease.

Hoyle agrees with Sir Charles on this point. Neither of the two believes that improvements in technique can keep pace with the increase in population. If the human species continues to multiply at the prevailing rapid rate and if that rate is maintained, "the amount of standing room on the earth will be reduced in about 1,100 years to a ratio of one square yard per person." In 5,000 years the mass of humanity will exceed the mass of the earth itself; in 11,000 years it will exceed the mass of the whole universe visible with the 200-inch Palomar telescope. To Sir Charles it follows that the rate of increase in the human population must decline.

But Not Starvation

What will bring about this decline? Starvation is the answer, a natural process to Sir Charles. He doubts if voluntary birth control will work because it will not be accepted by the whole of humanity. Those who accept it will limit their numbers; those who do not will multiply. Hence there will be no check on the increase in population. Those who will not accept the voluntary limitation of births will engulf those who will.

Hoyle concedes that this conclusion may be correct, but that it "is not logically compelling." He also concedes that there must be a feedback between food supplies and population but denies that this feedback calls for starvation. What happens if the population gets too large? Is death by starvation inevitable? In the case of the songbirds previously referred to no deaths are caused by starvation. There is simply no more breeding among the poorly fed. This is likely to happen in a human population. The excess will not necessarily die of starvation, it will cease to be born.

Is there any human example on a large scale of this operation of feedback? Hoyle finds it in the stability of the British birth rate in the last thirty years. Starvation did not stabilize the birth rate, but the lowered standard of living did, a very subtle form of feedback.

In the Nation: Population, Hunger, and Oblivion | Rather like a voice from the past, the earnest words of Robert S. McNamara at Notre Dame this week served with startling suddenness to restore some long-range perspective to the affairs of the world. While men still creep cautiously in reluctant pursuit of what seems an ever-receding peace in Vietnam, while politicians in this country bicker over ABM and a few millions for the hungry, while commissars in the Soviet Union fuss over Czechoslovakian dissent, while young people everywhere rail at the vast conspiracy of oppression and manipulation they seem to see overhanging all—while all this is taking the place of useful social and economic action, the human race proceeds apace toward breeding and starving itself into oblivion.

McNamara, returning to a theme he has sounded before, echoed some of the recent words of Lord Snow in Britain and Andrei D. Sakharov in the Soviet Union in insisting on a "humane but massive" population reduction.

So fast is the rate of population growth in most of the underdeveloped world, McNamara explained—from his vantage point as president of the World Bank—that even the most energetic and resourceful governments can do no more than stand still, maintaining an uneasy *status quo* in their totally inadequate standards of living. Most are actually slipping backward.

With his curiously American insistence that man's ingenuity and dedication can make things come right—seen before in his Montreal speech of a few years ago—McNamara suggested that agricultural technology was being advanced swiftly and dramatically enough to "buy two decades of time—admittedly the barest minimum of time"—during which man might reduce the population explosion to manageable proportions.

A Wiser Generation

This corresponds to Lord Snow's "Model B" for the future—the proposition that one of three possible outcomes of the population crisis would be just enough reduction of hunger to gain time for a wiser generation to come into power and confront the population problems in earnest.

In his Westminster College speech, Snow made it clear he considered Model B unrealistic and had even less hope for Model C—the idea that *this* generation might steel itself to the task and that the wealthy nations might make the enormous sacrifices needed to avert disaster. Hence, the British author and scientist thought Model A most likely—that the wealthy nations in their preoccupation with nuclear weapons and themselves would do little or nothing, so that in perhaps no more than thirty years millions upon millions of people would be starving, with some of the hungry, of course, turning upon the fat.

Here are some of the facts of the situation. Worldwide births and deaths are now in the ratio of 2 to 1, with a net gain in world population of about 70 million a year. Nearly 58 million of this increase—according to the authoritative *Population Bulletin*—occurs in the poor nations.

"To bring births into balance with low and still declining death rates," the *Bulletin* states, "would necessitate a cutback of some 50 million births a year." For this enormous and complex and delicate task, contorted by incredible problems of religion and ignorance and custom, there is no "framework remotely adequate to put the necessary billions of dollars and the essential brains and skills to work either to slow down human reproduction or to speed up agricultural productivity."

All Would Go Hungry

And Dr. Georg Borgstrom has pointed out that if all of the food in today's world were distributed evenly among its 3.5 billion human inhabitants, every one of them would go hungry.

Sakharov, putting the "expected date of tragedy" even nearer than did McNamara or Snow—at 1975 to 1980—believes the task of coping with the danger is so Gargantuan that the developed nations could only do it by quantum changes in their foreign policies, permitting them the closest cooperation; and even then, in his opinion, these nations would have to impose on themselves a "fifteen-year tax equal to 20 percent of the national income."

That, he quite correctly points out, would in itself ensure a significant reduction in expenditures for weapons.

McNamara, whose warning was more restrained but no less pointed, states his belief in a "rational, responsible, moral solution to the population problem"—a solution that he said all shared in the responsibility of finding.

Well, everyone shared the responsibility, all right, but not much else. The *Population Bulletin* states that the total outlay devoted annually to the population crisis outside the United States is about $80 million. Yet, all the world's nations spend $154.3 billion annually for military purposes (or did in 1966; the bill probably has gone up). That means that the world spends $2,000 for military purposes for every $1 it spends to control population.

Naturally, the Soviet Union and the United States, the only two nations that could do much about population or hunger, contribute more than two-thirds of the world military budget. That is madness, suggesting nothing like a "rational, responsible, moral" solution. And that kind of madness, if we keep on the way we have in this country and this world, is what we will continue to have right down to the last bitter dying gasp.

Farms Today Set Population Limit | If the brain power is available, there is no important limitation on the amount of food that the world can produce.

This is the conclusion of a study on "The World's Food: Need and Potential." It was made by Dr. James F. Bonner, professor of biology at the California Institute of Technology, as part of a glimpse at the world a century from now made by the institute for leading American corporations.

There is no technological reason why shortage of food should limit the population growth of the earth, Dr. Bonner reported. This is true, he said, despite the fact that more than one-half of the present world population receives barely enough food to maintain life at a minimum level. Another one-fourth of the population is undernourished, he said.

Human food comes directly or indirectly from plants, he said. Plants used as food and the plants fed to animals that produce meat, milk, and eggs take sunlight and combine carbon dioxide from the atmosphere with water to make fibrous tissues.

Each year plants on land and in water produce enough food for five hundred times the current world population.

Usable Food Not Used

But most people eat only cultivated plants, and these comprise only one-fourth of what is available. Also, these other factors reduce the amount of usable food from the plants grown today:

"About half" the cultivated food is fed to animals. The animal eats only part of the plant. What he does eat is returned to us as animal food with a caloric yield of only about 10 percent.

Man consumes only about 20 percent of the cultivated plant. He eats the wheat seed but does not eat the stems or leaves.

Insects, fungi, rabbits, rats, etc., consume one-third of the food grown in the world today.

The amount of land on which to grow food varies throughout the world from .2 of a cultivated acre per capita in Japan to .6 of an acre in Asia, .9 acre in Europe, 2 acres in the Soviet Union, and 2.4 acres in the United States.

The number of calories of food produced each day on a cultivated acre varies from a low of 2,300 in Russia to a high of 14,000 in Japan. The figure for the United States is 4,000 calories. Calories measure the energy-producing value of food. There are 100 calories in a tablespoon of honey, for example.

Half the world exists on a low calorie intake. This part of the population lives in most of Asia, Egypt, all of Central America, and parts of South America. Individuals there average less than 2,250 calories each day. Another 20 percent of the population, living in most of southern Europe and parts of South America and Africa, eat between 2,250 and 2,750 calories; 20 percent, including all of North America, much of Europe, Oceania, Argentina, and the Soviet Union, eat more than 2,750 calories.

One billion acres of new cultivated land could become available to agriculture if the warm and cold wet areas now neglected were farmed, Dr. Bonner estimated. This land can be farmed by planing new crops and by irrigating with distilled seawater and by other improvements that are feasible now.

Population to Rise

If this were done, Dr. Bonner said, and the productivity of all the world's cultivated lands were raised to the level prevalent in Europe, 3,700,000,000 people could be fed a diet "healthful, adequate, but not exciting." This population is expected for the world in twenty-five to fifty years, he said. There are now 2,600,000,000 people in the world.

Improvements in food supply will come, Dr. Bonner asserts, in these "nonconventional" steps:

Animals will be used less as food. Diets of plant proteins will supplement animal products. In the United States alone, he estimated, if the population increases to 200,000,000 in fifteen years the nation will have only two-thirds of its present animal food ration.

Grain crops will be replaced by crops in which more of the plant is eaten. Entirely new edible crops are a possibility. A meat beet or a fat plant might be produced.

Woody stalks and leaves might be utilized. They can be converted to edible sugars by methods now known.

Steppes and deserts now cover twice as much of the earth as cultivated lands.

Nine-tenths of the photosynthesis that occurs on the earth's surface is in the oceans, but little use is made of this. Cultivation of algae might raise food production.

Chemical synthesis of vitamins and of essential meat proteins is possible now.

Dr. Borlaug and the "Green Revolution" | The Nobel Peace Prize for 1970 was awarded last week to a fifty-six-year-old agronomist from Iowa who knows more about the seeds of wheat than the seeds of war.

Dr. Norman E. Borlaug was awarded his prize, valued at $78,000, for leadership of the "Green Revolution"—the development through "genetic engineering" of new cereal varieties whose introduction into developing countries has enormously increased crop yields and helped exorcise threats of famine.

Now visible across a great sweep of farm horizons, the revolution began obscurely in 1944 when the Rockefeller Foundation sent Dr. Borlaug to Mexico to develop new wheat strains that would enable Mexico to become independent of wheat imports.

There are thousands of wheat strains (all plants of a strain are genetically identical), and each has advantages and disadvantages in size, disease resistance, growing period, and the like. The point of creating new strains is to eliminate undesirable qualities and combine desirable ones. Dr. Borlaug's basic materials were Japanese Norin dwarf wheat—which has short, stiff straw and uses fertilizer efficiently in producing grain rather than excess straw—and Gaines winter wheat and its relatives, which have produced up to 216 bushels an acre in the Pacific Northwest.

How It's Done

Wheat is self-pollinated—its sex organs combine male and female elements within one structure—and Dr. Borlaug developed new strains by delicate cross-pollination. He opened one floret (sex organ) after another—the individual wheat head usually has more than fifty florets—and with a tweezer removed the anther (male element). When he had collected perhaps a hundred of these tiny, yellow, pollen-baring elements, he inserted each into an emasculated floret of another wheat strain.

From this forcible coupling of two strains, a child of new genetic makeup was born. Seeds from this new strain were then planted, and the planting process was repeated unto the sixth generation of the strain. This sixth, genetically pure for desired characteristics, was then accepted—or rejected as having failed to live up to Dr. Borlaug's hopes.

To speed the development process, Dr. Borlaug worked winters at plots in Mexico's subtropical Sonora state and summers in the cooler 10,000-foot-high valley of Toluca. Taking materials from one to the other, he got two generations of experimental strains each year.

Ten years after his arrival, Mexico stopped importing wheat; ten years after that, yields averaged thirty-nine bushels an acre of wheat (instead of eleven) with good milling and baking qualities and higher proteins. In 1966 Dr. Borlaug began helping India's farmers, and his 8,156th strain (the Indians called it Kalyon Sona, or Golden Savior) took hold marvelously and allowed double- and triple-cropping each year.

But if all wheat were of one strain, disease could be catastrophic. So India and Pakistan planted other Borlaug strains as well. And scientists stressed the "complete package"—which meant controlled irrigation, sophisticated use of pesticides and insecticides, optimal fertilization, mechanization, and improvements in marketing, storage, and credit facilities.

Some Problems

The revolution has not yet produced Utopia. It is upsetting traditional tenant-landlord relationships and threatens to increase unemployment in countries where unemployment is already massive. But it is producing greatly increased food supplies—and the revolution has extended to rice, corn, sorghums, and millets. It also threatens to dull the edge of arguments in favor of birth control. But Dr. Borlaug warns that this revolution will afford only a reprieve, not a permanent solution to the population problem.

He is now director of the wheat program at the International Maize and Wheat Improvement Center, an independent organization supported by the Rockefeller and Ford foundations and the Agency for International Development, with help also from the U.N. Development Program and the Inter-American Development Bank.

Dr. Borlaug still spends most of each day in the fields with young scientists (the "Borlaug apostles"), rising early, quitting late, working on new wheat strains and on triticale—a man-made species which results from a cross of wheat and rye. He also travels widely to work in foreign fields; Dr. Borlaug is that rarest of revolutionaries who finds a welcome at every border.

Waiting for the Monsoon
BY KHUSHWANT SINGH

Aurangabad, India. It was the hottest day of the year, 112 degrees in the shade and like the hellfires of Gehenna in the sun. I stood on a mound taking in the scene. Behind me was a range of hills, brown, barren, boulder-strewn. In front was a melancholy expanse of dun-colored fields divided by cactus and camel thorn. The flamboyant gulmohar was in flower, the fiery orange of its blossoms almost burning the eyes. Here and there was a laburnum drooping under the weight of its clusters of yellow petals. A hot wind picked up dust, churned it into a whirling dervish which spiraled its way across the wasteland and died out on the rocky hillside.

From the distance came the notes of a bugle. Men and women scurried over the parched fields, crouched on the ground, and pressed their hands over their ears. After a moment of petrified silence, there was a muffled roar. The earth shook, rocks flew into the air, a column of black smoke rose toward the gray sky. The bugle sounded again. The men and women ran back to the spot

From *The New York Times Magazine,* August 26, 1973.
Copyright © 1973 by The New York Times Company.
Reprinted by permission.

from which they had come. They made an awful racket, clanging tin cans and yelling.

I walked down to see what was going on. In a low hollow between the fields was a newly dug well, looking like a thirty-foot-long cylinder of gray slate bored into the earth. A hole blown out in the rocky floor shimmered like quicksilver. The water was muddy, probably brackish, but they clustered around it like wasps on a crystal of sugar. They scooped it up in their palms, put them reverently against their lips as if it were nectar, and splashed some on their faces.

Nakshatra Wadi, where I saw the blasting on a visit in the spring, is a small village four miles from the ancient city of Aurangabad, known to tourists who visit the Ajanta and Ellora caves. Aurangabad had been in the news again as the district worst hit by the drought. Last year's winter crop was lost. As the spring wore on, wells began to dry up. By April, the situation had become desperate. Many villages had to be supplied with drinking water by a fleet of tankers.

Nakshatra Wadi was luckier than its neighbors; two of its dozen wells had enough to slake the thirst of its 675 inhabitants. And they had struck another subterranean seam. Nevertheless, no one except the family of the headman, Vijay Dutt Deo Dutt Trivedi, who owned seventy-five acres of land and had his own well, had had a bath for many weeks. Most peasants had sold their cattle to butchers at less than half their price. They worked on relief projects, breaking stones to pave roads, digging tanks and wells. "How long can a man live without water?" Trivedi had asked me as we walked back to his house followed by a procession of villagers. "Two days? Three days? Here in Aurangabad District we have lived without it for three years. Our crops are destroyed; 90 paisas (out of 100) in the rupee were scorched by the sun."

Seventy percent of India's rainfall, which lasts roughly from mid-June to September, comes with the monsoon season. It is not enough to read about the monsoon in books, or see it on the cinema screen, or hear someone talk about it to understand what it means to India. Nothing short of living through it can fully convey all it means to people for whom it is not only the source of life, but also their most exciting impact with nature. What the four seasons of the year mean to the European, the one season of monsoon means to the Indian.

For three years the monsoon had failed. Even in the best of years the rain may be excessive in some places, like Cherrapunji in Assam, which gets 428 inches in the year, while parts of Rajasthan, Gujarat, and Maharashtra may not get a drop. But rainfall in 1970, 1971, and 1972 was far below normal in most areas of the country, and buffer stocks of wheat built from surplus raised in the northern states of Punjab and Haryana, along with imports from the U.S., began to dwindle. Last year, the harvest from the green-revolution belt in the north also fell below expectations. Soon the buffer stock was almost exhausted, but the government was loath to take around the begging bowl to affluent nations, particularly to the United States, which had supported Pakistan against India in the Bangladesh affair. Once again this spring, the dream of India's becoming self-sufficient in food seemed to be turning to nightmare; drought and famine stalked the land and the old lament was heard: India's prosperity is a gamble with the rains. In many hundreds of villages like Nakshatra Wadi, people were pinning their hopes on a good monsoon.

We entered the headman's house in Nakshatra Wadi with the peasants trooping behind us. The Trivedis were evidently prosperous. It was a large room with an electric fan and fluorescent light. The walls were plastered with garish prints of Hindu gods and goddesses and of political leaders—Gandhi, Nehru, Bose. The Trivedis owned a tractor, two motorcycles, and a transistor radio. Tea and biscuits were ordered.

"What will you do if the rains fail again?" I asked the peasants, who had squatted on the ground. For a while no one answered. Then Nelson Ingles, the revenue collector for the *tahsil* (a subdivision of the district), a Christian, who was accompanying me, spoke. "Don't even talk about it," he said to me in English to avoid the villagers' understanding him, and then, loudly in Marathi: "The rains will come in a few days, they must."

"Oh, yes, there will be plenty of rain this year," assured Trivedi, handing me a cup of tea. "There are signs it will be here soon."

"What signs?"

Sita Ram, an old *brinjarry,* one of a tribe of nomadic gypsies now settled on the land, was asked to explain. He stood up, scratched the stubble of his chin for a while before he deigned to speak. "The more intense the heat, the stronger is the monsoon that follows," he said, quoting a Marathi proverb. "I have never known it hotter in my seventy years. And I can smell rain in the morning breeze."

The villagers hung on his words as if he were a prophet. Saroo Bai, the woman member of the village council, stood up and said, "Tell him about the leaves!"

"Oh yes!" exclaimed Sita Ram. "The *karwand* and *heevar* [Marathi names for species of thorny bushes] are in new leaf." He quoted another proverb to the effect that if these bushes leaf in May, the rains must follow in early June.

"And the birds," prodded Trivedi, "tell him about the birds!" Sita Ram ran his hands over his face and, after a pause, said, "The *papeeha* [hawk cuckoo] has been calling, *'Paos ala, paos ala,'* which means, 'The rains are coming.' "

"That's only in Marathi," I corrected him. "In Hindi they describe its call as *'Pee kahan'*—'Where is my beloved?' "

"That's the same," he replied. "Rain is the time for beloveds." The men laughed; the women covered their faces with their hands and giggled. Sita Ram looked very pleased with himself.

"And the English interpret the bird's call as 'Brain fever'; they call it the brain-fever bird."

"Oh, the English!" exclaimed Sita Ram contemptuously. "What did they know of such things? That's why they are no more in India." His audience was more impressed. He continued: "I also heard the monsoon bird [pied-crested cuckoo] two days ago. That's a sure sign that it will rain in a few days."

"I heard the monsoon bird last year and there was very little rain," I told him.

Sita Ram looked unhappy. Trivedi came to his rescue. "It can't go on forever! If there is a God," he said, pointing to the ceiling, "He must send us rain—or send for us."

We left Nakshatra Wadi, drove through Aurangabad city and ten miles along the road toward the Ajanta caves. We stopped at the village of Chowka. Here, the conditions were worse. Not one well had water in it. Outside the village council office was an orderly line of women and children sitting on their haunches under the scorching heat of the midday sun with their brass pitchers, buckets, and empty gasoline cans, patiently awaiting the water tanker. "What will you do if the rains fail you again this year?" I asked the headman, Bhao Rao Jai Rao Wagh.

"What will we do if the rains fail us?" he replied. "What can we do except pray to Hanumanji [monkey god, the most popular deity in the villages around Aurangabad]?" Once more Nelson Ingles reprimanded me: "You must not break their morale. If it had not been for the employment we gave them, they would have taken to looting, robbery . . . anything." Ingles identified himself with the government. "We give them 3 rupees (39 cents) per head, per day at our relief works, which is more than what they earned from their land; we send them drinking water; we give them *sukhadi* [a mash made of ground wheat, molasses, and vitamins]. We are now ploughing their lands and giving them seed. All this has cost us hundreds of millions of rupees." He turned to headman Wagh and reassured him in Marathi, "I'm sure your prayers will be answered. Hanumanji is a very powerful god."

None of the peasants I had seen at Nakshatra Wadi or Chowka looked famished. I asked Nelson Ingles if any cases of death from starvation had been reported. No, he replied emphatically, thousands have gone hungry but no one starved. They have been able to buy enough rations from fair-price shops to keep alive. The state of affairs in these villages of Maharashtra was typical of what obtained in drought-stricken areas in Gujarat and Rajasthan in May. Trains and trucks bringing wheat from the north kept up stocks in ration depots. Even a slight dislocation in the transport schedule could have spelled disaster.

Later in the evening, Ramesh Chandra Sinha, thirty-one, the strapping revenue collector of Aurangabad, dropped in to see me at the government rest house where I was staying. With him was Joyce Abraham, twenty-four, the only Jewish member of the elite Indian Administration Service, who was training under Sinha. The two came in with armfuls of charts, which they proceeded to unroll and explain. "In this district there are 300 villages without a drop of drinking water. I have 115 tankers on the move all the time, but my biggest headache is this city," said Sinha. "It has a population of over 160,000. Its normal supply of water, which was meager enough, has had to be cut by half. Our taps run for exactly 40 minutes in 24 hours. We've dug hundreds of wells—some 380 feet without striking water. We've drilled holes in the dry beds of rivers and squeezed whatever we could out of the sand."

"How long can you hold out?"

"Till the monsoon breaks," he assured me, "and break it will. Although 1972 was the worst year in recorded history, there was some rain. We've dug tanks and raised dams in our rivers to trap whatever comes down. The expense has been enormous. In this district alone, I employ 457,000 men and women on relief projects and spend about $160,000 every day to save people from dying from thirst."

"Why did you not dig tanks, wells, and irrigation channels earlier?" I asked Sinha.

"I can't answer that question." he replied. "There never have been adequate water storage facilities in our state. But we have paid the price for it and we are now better prepared. I am sure if we have a good monsoon this year, I will be able to store enough water to see us through at least two bad years. I believe this is true of other drought-stricken areas of India as well. One lives and learns."

I turned to Miss Abraham and asked her what she knew of the problem. "Not very much except that the water that comes out of my tap looks like that," she said pointing to my bottle of Scotch. "It is absolutely undrinkable."

"But this is most drinkable," I assured her.

More than a dozen peasant leaders joined us for dinner. Among them was Manek Rao Palodkar, a swarthy, powerfully built man in his early fifties. He farmed fifty-five acres of land in the village of Palod, from which he derived his surname, and was the sitting member of Parliament from Aurangabad. All the men were sunburned, strong, stocky, and dressed in white handspun cloth and Gandhi caps. The talk at dinner was of the heat, dust, clouds, and the rain. "The monsoon first hits Sri Lanka, then the West Coast. We get it a week after it breaks over Bombay," said Palodkar with the assurance of a successful politician.

"Before the regular monsoon, there are pre-monsoon showers," said one of Palodkar's cronies.

"But the pre-monsoon showers are not important," Palodkar corrected him. "We divide the four months of the rains into eight periods of fifteen days each, depending on the signs of the zodiac. The pre-monsoon is the Rohini. Never trust the Rohini; it comes with dust-raising winds, locusts, and hailstones. Then comes the Mriga [Orion]. That is the real monsoon, a regular downpour, which cools the heart; it usually starts between June 7 and June 10."

His crony refused to be squashed. "What we need is prolonged rainfall." He quoted a Marathi proverb to the effect that the test of the real monsoon was when the gunny sacks that peasants drape over their heads and shoulders remain damp long enough to breed insects in them. "That is in mid-July or August," he said.

The dinner had ended with everyone convinced that the monsoon was around the corner. We came out into the garden. It was hot and still. A long, shallow pool, which last winter grew water lilies and goldfish, was almost dry. Over the corners, where some slimy ooze remained, flashed a couple of fireflies. "When the monsoon comes, the place will be full of them," said one of the party.

"Monsoon" comes from the Arabic word for season, *mausim.* The Arabs gave the name to the seasonal winds of the Arabian Sea, which blow for approximately six months from the northeast and six months from the southwest. In India, the word refers both to the winds and to a season of rains, and while there is also a winter monsoon, when Indians speak of the mausim they generally mean the drenching rains that come with the moisture-bearing southwest winds of summer.

The winter monsoon is simply rain in winter. It is like a cold shower on a frosty morning. It leaves one chilled and shivering. Although it is good for the crops, people pray for it to end. Fortunately, it does not last very long.

The summer monsoon is quite another affair. It is preceded by several months of working up a thirst. From the end of February, the sun starts getting hotter and spring gives way to summer. Flowers wither. Flowering trees take their place. Then the trees also lose their flowers. Their leaves fall. Their bare branches stretch up to the sky begging for water. The sun comes up earlier than before and licks up the drops of dew before the fevered earth can moisten its lips. It blazes away all day long in a cloudless sky, drying up wells, streams, and lakes. It sears the grass and thorny scrub till they catch fire. The fires spread, and dry jungles burn like matchwood.

The sun goes on, day after day, from east to west, scorching relentlessly. The earth cracks and deep fissures open their gaping mouths asking for water; but there is no water—only the shimmering haze at noon making mirage lakes of quicksilver. Poor villagers take their thirsty cattle out to drink and the animals are struck dead. The rich wear sunglasses and hide behind curtains of grass fiber on which their servants pour water.

The sun makes an ally of the breeze, heating the air till it becomes the *loo,* the hot wind that blows between April and June and precedes the monsoon. Even in the intense heat, the loo's warm caresses are sensuous and pleasant. It produces a numbness that makes the head nod and the eyes feel heavy with sleep. It can also bring on a stroke, which takes its victim as gently as breeze bears a fluff of thistledown.

Then comes a period of false hopes. The loo drops, the air becomes still. From the southern horizon, a black wall begins to advance. Hundreds of kites and crows fly ahead. Can it be . . . ? No, it is a dust storm. A fine powder begins to fall. A solid mass of locusts covers the sun. They devour whatever is left on the trees and in the fields. Then comes the storm itself. In furious sweeps, it smacks open doors and windows, banging them forward and backward, smashing their glass panes. Thatched roofs and corrugated-iron sheets are borne aloft into the sky like bits of paper. Trees are torn up by the roots and fall across power lines. The tangled wires electrocute people and set fire to houses. The storm carries the flames to other houses till there is a conflagration. All this happens in a few seconds. Before you can mention the name Chakravartyrajagopalachari, the gale is gone. The dust hanging in the air settles on your furniture and food; it gets in your eyes, ears, throat, and nose.

Hopes are disappointed over and over again, until the people are thirsty, sweating, dejected, and the prickly heat on the back of their necks is like emery paper. There is another lull. A hot, petrified silence prevails. Then comes the shrill, strange call of a bird. Why has it left its cool, bosky shade and come out in the sun? People look up wearily at the lifeless sky. Yes, there it is with its mate! They are like large black-and-white bulbuls with perky crests and long tails. They are pied-crested cuckoos, which have flown all the way from Africa ahead of the monsoon. Isn't there a gentle breeze blowing? And hasn't it a damp smell? And wasn't the rumble that drowned the birds' anguished cry the sound of thunder? The people hurry to the roofs to see. The same ebony wall is coming up from the south. A flock of herons flies across. There is a flash of lightning that outshines the daylight. The wind fills the black sails of the clouds and they billow out across the sun. A profound shadow falls on the earth. There is another clap of thunder. Big drops of rain fall and dry up in the dust. A fragrant smell rises from the earth. Another flash of lightning and another crack of thunder like the roar of a hungry tiger. It has come! Sheets of water, wave after wave. The people lift their faces to the clouds and let the abundance of water cover them. Schools and offices close. All work stops. Men, women, and children run madly about the streets, waving their arms and shouting, "Ho! Ho!"—hosannas to the miracle of the monsoon.

Once the monsoon is on, it stays for three or four months, bringing frequent rains. Its advent signals the renewal of joy, but after a few days the flush of enthusiasm is gone. The earth becomes a big stretch of swamp and mud. Wells and lakes fill up and burst their bounds. In the towns, gutters get clogged and streets become turbid streams. In the villages, mud walls of huts melt in the water, thatched roofs sag and descend on the inhabitants. Rivers, which keep rising steadily from the time the summer's heat starts melting the snows, suddenly turn to floods as the monsoon spends itself on the mountains. Roads, railway tracks, and bridges go under water. Houses near the riverbanks are swept down to the sea.

With the monsoon, the tempo of life and death increases. Almost overnight, grass begins to grow and leafless trees turn green. Snakes, centipedes, and scorpions are born out of nothing. The ground is strewn with earthworms, ladybugs, and tiny frogs. At night, a myriad of moths flutter around the lamps. They fall in everybody's food and water. Geckos dart about, filling themselves with insects till they get heavy and fall off ceilings. Inside the house, the hum of mosquitoes is maddening. People spray clouds of insecticide and the floor becomes a layer of wriggling bodies and wings. Next evening, there are many more fluttering around the shades and burning themselves in the flames of oil and kerosene lamps.

While the monsoon lasts, the showers start and stop without warning. The clouds fly across, dropping their rain on the plains as it pleases them, till they reach the Himalayas. They climb up the mountainsides. Then the cold squeezes the last drops out of them. Lightning and thunder never cease. In late August or early September, the season of the rains gives way to autumn.

The monsoon does not heed the prognostication of weather prophets or observe the patterns prescribed by the ancients. In May, while papers reported clouds over Sri Lanka and strong westerly winds over Kerala, the skies over Bombay, which should have remained clear for another week or more, were overcast. Gum boots and umbrellas were on sale at the pavement bazaars. The streets were full of urchins in nothing but their shorts. People gazed skyward rather than watch where they were going. "The clouds are too high," remarked the cabdriver who dropped me at the cinema. "In any case it is too early for the monsoon." Two hours later, when I emerged from the theater there was a regular downpour with thunder and lightning. The roads were flooded and glistening with the reflections of street lamps. Most people had been taken unaware. But no one seemed to mind the drenching. Boys splashed about in the dirty water as if it were an alfresco bathing pool.

By the time I returned to Nakshatra Wadi, it had been raining off and on for five days. The peasants reassembled in Trivedi's home. It was warm, damp, and muddy. The change in the expression on their faces was apparent; where there had been tension and despair, there was relief and hope. Sita Ram, the village's gypsy soothsayer, grinned triumphantly and told everyone how he had forecast the rains. "Another few days of this and we can start sowing the summer crop of cotton, rice, and lentils," Trivedi said.

"Not yet," interrupted Sita Ram, and he came out with yet another proverb on the unreliability of rain that falls on one horn of the buffalo but not on the other, which pours for a few minutes and is suddenly gone. "It must drip—zim, zim, zim, zim—till the earth is soaked," he said.

By August, the truant rains have come back to India at last. Wells, lakes, and rivers are filling up. The taps are no longer dry. The water and power problems have ended. So far, the farmers are happy at the abundance of rainfall. If the monsoon continues at its present pace throughout September, the summer crops are expected to be good. It remains to be seen whether they will be enough to banish the shadow of famine that has been looming over us for the last three years and has forced the government to begin buying wheat from the United States this summmer—quite belatedly, some of its critics say.

Trivedi has the last word. "The government has announced big plans for building more dams on rivers and laying out irrigation canals. There is one project to link the Ganges by a canal running over a thousand miles south to the Cauvery. We, too, have made our plans. In the past, we neglected our wells and tanks and let rainwater run to waste. This time we will store it. The drought has been a blessing in disguise."

Weather Enigma | India's most spectacular weather event—the torrential rains of the summer monsoon—comes about because of an extreme temperature difference in the air over land and sea. Or so goes the standard explanation of the phenomenon. As the sun "moves" higher in the cloudless sky of May and June, it heats the atmosphere over the Indian plains. The theory is that when the hot air rises and leaves a vast low-pressure zone below it, enormous amounts of warm, wet air rush into the breach from the Indian Ocean and the Bay of Bengal. These winds continue blowing northeast across the subcontinent. Along the way, their clouds may dump water on some places and pass over others, but the real downpours occur when the winds encounter the high Himalayas in northern India and, as a consequence, rise to cooler altitudes, where their vapor condenses into water. Much of the wind is then deflected toward the northwest and travels along the Ganges and the barrier formed by the mountains.

Surprisingly few studies have been done to explain why rainfall is abundant during some summer monsoons and not in others. Dr. Reid Bryson, director of the Institute for Environmental Studies at the University of Wisconsin, relates the drought of recent years in India to long-term climatic changes. Dr. Bryson is one of those scientists who believe that the earth has entered a new cooling age and that in such periods the world's deserts normally expand southward as the Arctic gets colder. Because of the patterns of worldwide air circulation, the atmosphere of the deserts is characterized by dry "sinking air," which spreads in all directions and blocks the passage of the monsoon winds. Indian scientists have said that the Indian Desert has been growing toward the southeast in recent years (it now seems to extend right to the suburbs of Delhi, one meteorologist reports) and, as a result, Dr. Bryson believes that monsoon failures may be more common in the years ahead, unless climate modification is possible.

Dark Clouds of Inspiration | It is not surprising that much of India's art, music, and literature is concerned with the monsoon. Paintings depict people on rooftops looking eagerly at the dark clouds billowing out from over the horizon, with flocks of herons flying in front. Of the many melodies of Indian music, Raga Malhar is the most popular, because it brings to mind distant echoes of the sound of thunder and the pitter-patter of raindrops. It brings the odor of the earth and of green vegetation to the nostrils, the cry of the peacock and the call of the koel to the ear. There is also the Raga Desha, which invokes scenes of merry-making, of swings in mango groves, and the singing and laughter of girls. Most Indian palaces of the past had specially designed balconies from which noblemen viewed the monsoon downpour. Here they sat listening to court musicians improvising their own versions of monsoon melodies, sipping wine and making love to the ladies of their harem. The most common theme in Indian songs is the longing of lovers for each other when the rains are in full swing. There is no joy greater than union during monsoon time, no sorrow deeper than separation during the season of the rains.

An Indian's attitude toward clouds and rain remains fundamentally different from that of the Westerner. To the one, clouds symbolize hope; to the other, they suggest despair. The Indian scans the heavens and if cumulus clouds blot out the sun his heart fills with joy. The Westerner looks up and if there is no silver-lining edging the clouds his depression deepens. The Indian talks about someone he respects and looks up to as "a great shadow," like the one cast by the clouds when they cover the sun. The Westerner, on the other hand, looks on a shadow as something evil, and refers to people of dubious character as shady types. For him, his beloved is like the sunshine, and her smile a sunny smile.

Monsoon is the subject of many of the most beautiful compositions by Indian poets. Amaru (seventh century, A.D.) described its advent and the thoughts of love it rouses.

> The summer sun, who robbed the pleasant nights,
> And plundered all the water of the rivers,
> And burned the earth, and scorched the forest-trees,
> Is now in hiding; and the rain clouds,
> Spread thick across the sky to track him down,
> Hunt for the criminal with lightning-flashes.

> Where are you going in the dead of night?
> "To meet my lover who is life and death to me."
> And are you not afraid to walk alone?
> "How can I be alone? Love keeps me company."*

*Translated by John Brough. Poems from the Sanskrit; Penguin.

A Report from the Majority of the World
BY JAMES P. STERBA

Nestled under 4,315 coconut palm trees somewhere between the discovery of fire and the beginning of Armageddon, but nearer to both than the minority of men educated enough to have looked up either in a library, is Begadjah (pronounced ba-GOD-ja). It is five motorbikes, eighty-nine radios, one blacksmith; it is several thousand years beyond the Stone Age, a half-step out of subsistence, three years beyond hunger and malnutrition; it is thus a success story. Begadjah is producing enough "miracle" rice to feed itself today, and it is producing enough babies to make itself hungry again a few years or a few decades from tomorrow. The "green revolution," perhaps the most important development in the last half of the twentieth century, has made a mockery of hunger in Begadjah. The question is whether the Begadjahs of the world will eventually make a mockery of the green revolution.

The smoke floats slowly upward from the morning cooking fire to the red tile roof, then slowly fills the room with a haze that irri-

From *The New York Times Magazine,* September 5, 1971.
Copyright © 1971 by The New York Times Company.
Reprinted by permission.

tates the eyes of the small girl trying to heat water for tea. The wood is still a little green and the rice straw is slightly damp. The matted reed walls that enclose the kitchen do not keep out the dampness of the chilly morning fog. The floor is dirt. The girl's knees rest on a bed of straw. The room is dark except for the embers of the fire and a tiny naked flame atop an oil lamp. The oil would make the straw and wood burn, but it is too expensive for such purposes. A baby is held snugly to the girl's bosom with a broad cloth draped over her shoulder and tied around her waist. The girl blows into the embers now and then, leaning forward slightly, trying to coax out a flame and at the same time keep the curling smoke from the baby's eyes.

Outside, a woman sweeps the dirt front yard with a broom made of palm-leaf slivers. In back of the house, a naked boy raises water in a bucket from an open well, scoops it from the bucket with a coconut shell, and pours it over his face and shoulders. Down the path, neighbors are bathing in the river and relieving themselves in small holes on its banks. Village roosters have been predicting the sunrise for several hours, but at 5:30 A.M. they remain false prophets. It will be at least thirty minutes before the first bright rays of the sun pierce the mist and spotlight the blue-green slopes of the volcano that silently belches white steam in the distance.

There are at least thirty minutes for the banana and papaya trees to swim in the morning dew. They are laden with ripening fruit this time of year, but there will be no bananas or papaya for breakfast in Begadjah. The fruit is too valuable to eat. It must be sold, and some of the village women are already beginning to pad by, bananas in reed baskets wrapped in cloth slings on their hips, going to sell the fruit and buy the day's food at the marketplace a mile down the dirt path and across a paved road. The equatorial sun will make the tar on the paved road sizzle by late morning, and most of the women in Begadjah wear no sandals. But this is only one of the reasons for going to the market early. Today, there is a special reason—the rice harvest officially begins as soon as the dew evaporates.

It is one of the most important days of the year, and Djojodi-kuromo, the fifty-five-year-old chief of one of Begadjah's eight hamlets, has been up since 4 A.M. preparing it. He and the other hamlet chiefs had met with Josopanitro, the sixty-year-old village chief, a few days ago and decided that today was the day. Then last night, before attending the celebration of the birth of his neighbor's sixth child, Djojodikuromo relayed the message to his neighborhood chiefs: The goddess of earth would be asked to guide the harvest at five this morning in the usual simple ceremony.

Under the light of bamboo torches, Djojodikuromo led a small procession of villagers carrying bundles of food wrapped in banana leaves to a nearby rice field. One bundle was placed in the middle of the field. The others were placed at the edges as symbolic offerings to the goddess.

The golden rice stalks were carefully snipped with a bamboo-handled blade from the middle of the field. Three bundles were picked like this and placed in a new *selendang,* a cloth reserved for newborn babies and the goddess, represented by the rice. Then a woman lifted the bundles like a swaddling infant and carried them in silence to a special resting place in the village. Offerings of food would be placed before the bundles daily for the duration of the harvest.

Thirty minutes after daybreak, the tiny open marketplace is jammed with jabbering women, some sitting on their haunches with large cuds of tobacco stringing from their mouths, others kneeling on burlap mats in front of their specialties—peppers and onions, pottery and coconut-shell water scoops, vegetables, cloth, soybean cakes and biscuits, rice, oil. For the women who buy food here or at more distant markets daily for the 3,838 mouths in Begadjah, morning marketing is a pleasant chore, the social hour, a time to swap gossip. Refrigeration would destroy it, but that is not a worry. Begadjah has no electricity and no expectation of getting any soon. Even if it came, no one could afford a refrigerator. An icebox? No one can afford an icebox, either, let alone the daily cost of ice that would have to come from the city of Solo, twelve miles up the road. Except for chilly mornings, the closest the people of Begadjah get to cold is Popsicles. A few years ago, a man from Solo began delivering them to small boys who buy them for two rupiahs (about a third of a penny) and sell them for two and a half rupiahs (half of a penny).

For five rupiahs (a penny) shoppers in the market can buy a

cup-size bowl of soup or a handful or flower petals for an ancestor's grave. Eggs cost three cents, but most villagers don't buy them very often. They are too expensive. Most of the eggs laid by the chickens and ducks of Begadjah are sold to a man who comes from Solo.

Four women sell medicinal roots, seeds, and herbs, which they will blend on the spot for a price relative to the affliction. A penny is standard for a prescription. Business is brisk this morning, because after eight or nine hours of backbreaking work cutting rice in ankle-deep mud under a blazing sun there will be no shortage of aches and pains at sundown.

In front of the market, near the paved road, sits a woman minding six chickens fluttering in the dust, trying to escape the twine that binds their legs. It is doubtful that anyone in Begadjah will buy one; at forty cents, they are too expensive. Chickens, like fruit and eggs, are for selling. And when the right bus shrieks to a halt, the chickens will be tossed on top for the ride to Solo, where rich people can buy a whole one roasted for seventy-five cents. Seventy-five cents will buy three days' food for a family of six in Begadjah. Nothing special—rice, greens, dried fish, soybean cakes called *tahu* or *tempe*. No meat, it's too expensive. The average villager here eats a piece of meat about the size of an ice cube, fat included, about once every ten days. Which explains why there is only one woman selling meat in the market. She sits in the back with a few slabs of goat meat tucked into a basket, the goat's head and cakes of its drying blood laid out on a piece of burlap in front of her. Flies prefer her company. Dogs glide like sharks around her.

Expensive items—almost anything over a quarter—can be bought on credit here, two cents down and two cents a week. Clothes fit into the expensive category. A piece of hand-dyed traditional batik cloth for a sarong—a skirt worn by both men and women—can cost two or three dollars. A sarong that expensive might last five or six years, but it cannot be purchased in this market. Nothing here sells for more than eighty cents.

Men in the market are rare. Across the paved road sit three who are resting after carrying one-hundred-pound bundles of firewood six miles on their shoulders to sell. Toward the back of the market is the man who rents space to the women sellers at rates ranging from three to twenty cents a day. The spots under the shade of woven palm leaves are the most expensive. Another man has come with a bundle of leaves to sell. Begadjah has no paper or plastic bags, so everything is wrapped in leaves. Banana leaves are preferred for strength, but a man can sell other large tropical leaves here. He can spend all day gathering them and tying them into bundles the size of bushel baskets, then sell two bundles here for a dime. It is always something to fall back on.

For less than a penny, the tobacco sellers at the market will blend betel nut, betel leaves, and lime into a supposedly delightful chew, the red juice from which stains both the women chewers' mouths and the trail home, which is marked by tiny red Rorschach-like patterns every twenty feet or so. The plug of tobacco that accompanies this mixture serves as a sponge, both holding in the juice and cleansing the mouth of some of the stain. By dangling part of it between the lips, the chewer can prevent the juice from dribbling down the chin.

The penny chew is one of Begadjah's few luxuries, and a visit here allows one to discover the great proliferation of luxuries that rich people (those who make more than a dollar a day) take for granted. For example, garbage is a luxury, and Begadjah doesn't have any. The people here simply cannot afford to throw anything away. Virtually everything has at least a second use, and most things have a third or fourth. Coconut husks can be used for fuel. Cow dung is a fertilizer, as most of the world's farmers know. It is also used here to strengthen homemade bricks. Hair combings are hoarded like treasure. A small handful can bring thirty cents. Tin cans are rare and can be sold. Bottles are rare, and a broken one is a minor tragedy. Paper is precious. The act of writing on a piece of paper is an act of outrageous waste for most people here. The question of what to do with old newspapers doesn't arise because there aren't any. Paper is for permanent records and school books, and there is a shortage of both here. There are platoons of professional cigarette-butt pickers in Jakarta. No such job opportunities exist here, for each man saves his own. The common man's smoke in Jakarta, Indonesia's capital, is a *kretek,* a factory-made cigarette laced with aromatic cloves. In Begadjah, a kretek is a luxury.

The bicycle is threatening to become Begadjah's family car, but at the moment it remains a luxury item. There are 768 families in Begadjah and only 174 bicycles. A motorbike—there are five in the village—puts one into Begadjah's Scarsdale class; a horse cart or a cattle cart—Begadjah has one of each—does the same. Automobiles? Well, most of the traffic through Begadjah is bicycles, motorbikes, trucks, horse carts, and buses. People here still stop and look at the automobiles that go by on the paved road.

The world of Begadjah, Central Java, Indonesia, 1971, is a slow-motion world of oil lamps and small change, bare feet and leathered hands. It is a world in which time seems irrelevant, and one gets the ludicrous notion that if the world ended tomorrow the people of Begadjah wouldn't hear about it until sometime after the first of the year. There are eighty-nine battery-powered luxury items called radios in Begadjah, and some people might listen to the news. But they probably wouldn't pay much attention because the radio world is not their world any more than the world of light bulbs and paper bags. Though word of Richard Nixon's forthcoming visit to China has been bouncing around the world, no one in Begadjah has heard of it. But then, no one in Begadjah has heard of Richard Nixon, either.

Not that Begadjah is out of the mainstream. Quite the contrary. The average village here may be fuzzy about that minority of people who drive cars, fly in planes, start wars, take diet pills, go to high school, make or even read news, but he can probably feel perfectly secure in believing that he knows what the majority of human beings are doing because they are doing the same things that he and his neighbors are doing. He could raise his arm, point to his neighbors in the rice fields who are proceeding through life at a 90-degree angle and say, "This is the way the world lives." He would be right.

And these are not bad times in Begadjah. Times have never been better. Begadjah doesn't seem to have had any good old days. Josopanitro, the village chief, was born here in 1911 and has lived here ever since, and he can't remember any:

"We just obeyed orders under the Dutch. A few of them were nice to us, but most of them lived in town and didn't want to have anything to do with us. The land was supposed to be ours, but they used it to plant sugar. They paid us a little money for it. They paid us to work on it, but not much."

That's all he could think of to say about three hundred years of Dutch colonial rule, except that the Dutch weren't so bad compared to the Japanese, who invaded in 1942.

"We were all afraid of the Japanese. They gave fierce commands and everyone had to work—women, children, even sick people. If they saw us not working, they would hit us with the bottoms of their guns. Even if we tried to rest for a minute, they would hit us. We had to give them half our rice. No one had enough to eat."

When a young band of Indonesians, led by Sukarno, proclaimed independence in the wake of the Japanese defeat in 1945, everyone in Begadjah was excited, Josopanitro recalled.

"We were told to make flags, but there was no cloth. Our clothes were made of burlap and goatskin. When someone died, there was no cloth to wrap the corpse. But there was a little paper then, so we made flags out of paper." The joy was fleeting because the Dutch soon came back, this time with many soldiers.

"They had guns, and the people here only had bamboo spears, but we controlled the night and they only controlled the daylight. They took all of our valuables that they could find, but we hid many things so they could not find them."

Djojodikuromo was captured once and held for seven days.

"They asked me if I had seen any Indonesian soldiers, and I said no. So they took me to their compound and tied my feet with barbed wire and threw me in the W.C. Each night they would bring me out and ask me where the freedom fighters were. I knew all the time, but I wouldn't tell, so they beat me with their guns. There was blood all over, but I didn't tell."

The Dutch finally let Djojodikuromo go, gave up, and went back to Holland. And Begadjah, under Sukarno's Indonesia, was finally independent. But still hungry.

It was a condition that didn't seem to change much over the next fifteen years, despite the flood of Sukarno's rhetoric and the giant, expensive monuments and buildings that went up in Jakarta. Hardly anyone ate rice in those days. The staple diet was manioc roots. Children's bellies puffed from malnutrition.

No one likes to talk about what happened next. Indonesia got into the record books as perpetrator of one of the worst bloodbaths in the history of man. The powerful but impatient Communist party of Indonesia leaped for power on the night of September 30, 1965, but a young army general named Suharto grabbed it first. Communists and anti-Communists, fanatic Moslems and loyal nationalists, friends and enemies then engaged in a slaughter that reduced Indonesia's population by 300,000.

Djojodikuromo hid in piles of rice straw during those days. He slept in a different straw stack each night. As a hamlet official, he had been told that the Communists would kill him if he didn't join them. Josopanitro hid in Solo for two months. He didn't want to join, either. Mohamad Marzuki, the village religious leader, hid in the tomb of Kjai Djalak, a missionary who brought Islam to Begadjah in the seventeenth century. The villagers had promised themselves that they would build the tomb over the grave as an offering if they lived through the Japanese occupation and the war for independence. It was a good hiding place in 1965. The Communists would come in from a village they controlled about three miles away and ask people to join them. Josopanitro said thirty-six people in Begadjah joined.

"They were arrested and put in jail," he said. "Nobody was killed here. Not here." One hears the same phrases all over Indonesia these days.

After that, Begadjah settled into the present, an era of quiet but relatively pleasant desperation, thanks to a Christian Chinese missionary doctor who started a development program, a president who prefers the production of food over the erection of monuments, and, of course, the goodness of earth.

It is a comforting quiet, one that no one here seems willing to tamper with. Indonesia's July 3 national election, the first in sixteen years, was a three-hour affair here without incident and without soldiers. Apparently the people voted the way they wanted to. The government-backed party was second here, not because people rebelled but because consistency is a virtue and most of the people voted this time the same way they voted sixteen years ago. Begadjahans do what they are told, but, though the government message was clear in other regions, no one seems to have told the people here how to vote.

The Indonesian Nationalist party has always been strong here. And the government-backed party (which is billed as a "nonpolitical, nonparty development organization"), called Golkar, was apparently not very active in Begadjah during the campaign. All government officials, including those at the village level, were ordered to join Golkar or face losing their jobs and the income from the land that goes with the jobs, but the village officials in Begadjah said that although they joined Golkar they didn't tell the people how to vote. The dormant Nationalist tendencies prevailed.

The ceremony in Begadjah's rice field this morning was a ritual of appreciation as well as hope, for rice is the village's great success story. Begadjah is caught up in the green revolution—miracle rice, two harvests a year, from 450 tons in 1966 to 860 tons last year, from 2 tons per hectare to 4 tons per hectare. And *that* is something, because it has meant that for the third year in a row there has been enough to eat in Begadjah.

But, although everyone has felt the impact of the doubling of production in four years, a good rice harvest does not mean well-being for everyone in Begadjah. Fewer than half of the family heads own land. The rest work as laborers, and outside the planting and harvesting seasons there are few jobs for which a man can be paid enough to support a family.

There are fifteen small weaving factories in Begadjah where cheap thread bought in Solo is spun onto spools and then woven into a type of cheesecloth that is used for wrapping corpses, among other things. But the pay for even the best weavers is only a penny a meter, hardly enough to feed a wife and five or six children.

Sutarno, the twenty-five-year-old village blacksmith who learned his trade from his father, can support himself and the girl he is about to marry by turning out the two most essential tools in the village, sickles and hoes, but even when he is busiest, he can hire only two temporary helpers.

Kromosentono, sixty-five, is one of seven brickmakers in Begadjah. With two helpers, he can mold three hundred bricks a day and make nearly a dollar. But there are two problems with bricks: They can't be made in the wet season because they won't dry, and sometimes months will go by without anyone's buying any. But Kromosentono is fortunate. He has a third of a hectare of rice land as well.

To make it in Begadjah, a man must own land or have the use of land. There are 185 hectares availabe. Farmers own 154 hectares in plots of less than half a hectare, about an acre and a quarter. A man can squeeze by on half a hectare. He might even do well, especially now with miracle rice. One good harvest and he can afford to buy a few chickens, perhaps even a pig.*

Eighteen hectares in Begadjah are government land, used as salaries for village officials. Josopanitro, the village chief, is given the use of five hectares. He is a wealthy man. Mohamad Marzuki, the religious leader, is paid one hectare. He has five bicycles, a large house with a new addition, two gold rings, and a vegetable business on the side, and he smokes kreteks in a polished bone cigarette holder. His wife has gold teeth. All the village officials in Begadjah—the hamlet chiefs, the irrigation man, the agriculture man, and the assistant village chief—have made it.

The government also holds thirteen hectares for village development projects. Two of these hectares were given for twenty-five years to the Christian doctor's development group as payment for an elementary school it built three years ago. The rest is rented yearly, with profits going into the village treasury or to maintain the seven irrigation locks, twelve bridges, and other such hardware in the village.

But what of the majority who don't own land?

The man who sells soup for a penny a bowl is doing well.

Sulastri, who is not sure if she is under or over thirty, runs the only snack shop in the region, across the paved road from the market. Few of the people of Begadjah are her patrons because they can't afford her prices—two cents for a cup of tea or coffee.

---

* Although an oink is as offensive in Islam as Bugs Bunny would be in the Bible, Begadjah has 652 pigs at the moment. Their owners explain them by grinning and saying, "I'm only a statistic Moslem." There is a ready market for pork—3 million ethnic Chinese—in Indonesia.

Her customers are travelers, and with the occasional money sent by her husband, who is a soldier in Sumatra, she is doing well.

Tedjosuwarno, at twenty, has no problems. He slept through the rice ceremony that his father, Djojodikuromo, presided over this morning. He never seems to work, yet he probably has the brightest future in Begadjah. He is an artist, a registered *dalang,* a master of the *wajang kulit,* the traditional Indonesian puppet shadow play. He is a graduate of the rigorous dalang school at the sultan's palace in Solo. The others are all twenty-five or older; he lied about his age to get in. Now he charges $15 to $20 for an all-night performance, and he gives ten to fifteen a month. He dreams of replacing Ki Narto Sabdo, who makes $200 a night, as Indonesia's best dalang. But even at $15 a night, Tedjosuwarno has made it.

Many of those who haven't made it leave between harvests for Indonesia's cities, where they live for months in festering squalor, sleeping one hundred to a room in a dirt-floor hostel and feeling extremely lucky to get a job pedaling a three-wheeled *betjak* taxi or carrying soup or fruit or sisal mats or plants endless miles every day for thirty cents in sales. If they live frugally, they will be able to save half of that and return to Begadjah in four to six months as men of temporary respect.

Sarman, who is thirty-four and has six children, used to go to Jakarta every year to sell balloons. He would buy one hundred balloons for 35 rupiahs, blow them up, and sell them for one rupiah each.

"On a good day, I could get 150 rupiahs [40 cents]," he said. "I would always leave for Jakarta on a lucky day after the fasting month. When I would save 8,000 rupiahs [$21], I would come back to Begadjah. Sometimes it would take four months. Sometimes six."

Asked if he liked Jakarta, Sarman looked puzzled at first, then said, "When I travel I must be glad because if I am not glad I might get sick."

Sarman cannot go to Jakarta any more because so many village men like him have crushed into the capital in recent years that the governor has banned them from entering the city unless they can prove they have a steady job. It is an impossible ban to enforce, but Sarman doesn't want to take the chance. This year after the harvest he is planning to go to Palembang in south Sumatra. It is more than twice as far, but he has heard that a man can make good money as a street vendor there selling fruit with sugar.

Everyone thinks education is important for Begadjah's children, but there are few tangible bits of evidence that show why. Some five hundred students attend elementary-school classes in Begadjah daily, but there are a few hundred more children for whom there is no room, no time, or no motivation to attend school. Far less than half of those who finish the six elementary grades go on to high school.

Schoolwork can be perplexingly difficult after the first two grades because it is taught in what is essentially a foreign language: Indonesian. Nobody in Begadjah speaks Indonesian unless he has to, and only about half the people can speak it at all. The everyday language is Javanese. Children grow up rarely hearing Indonesian, so the first two grades are taught in Javanese, and Indonesian is introduced as a language in the third grade. The fourth, fifth, and sixth grades are taught completely in Indonesian, but as soon as school lets out for the day, the pupils revert to Javanese. And as soon as he finishes elementary school, the Begadjah child starts forgetting the official language of Indonesia.

All this can be very discouraging, and if a student conquers it, he can go on to high school, graduate, and face even more discouragement. Edi Suradji graduates from high school this year. He doesn't have the faintest idea where he can get a job, and he says none of his friends at the school in Solo do, either.

Edi Suradji has more immediate problems. His eyes are red and inflamed from an infection that nearly everyone in Begadjah seems to be catching. There is no medicine. If it gets too bad, he can go to the Christian clinic, but he doesn't want to. The Christian clinic is mostly for having babies.

Begadjah's infant mortality rate has dropped drastically since the clinic opened. There a woman can have her baby under the supervision of two nurses for $5. It is well worth the price, and families save for months to pay it because babies are evidence of well-being in Begadjah, despite the birth-control advice the clinic has been dispensing lately and the family-planning posters that have been tacked to village trees.

"We have as many children as God will give us," said Sarman, the father of six. "We are told by the posters that the more children we have the more difficulties we have. Before, when we didn't eat such good food, women couldn't have as many children as they can have now. You see, destiny is in Allah's hands. Maybe if we only have one baby it will be difficult. Maybe if we have seven babies it won't be difficult. It depends on Allah."

Begadjah is racing to fulfill man's destiny on earth at a clip of two or three babies a day. China, India, and Pakistan have nothing on Begadjah, for it is positioned well. It is in the middle of the most populated region of the most densely populated island in the world, Java. And it is in the middle of Indonesia, where no one is quite sure whether there are 115 million or 123 million people, and where the minister of agriculture reported the other day that despite miracle varieties, the production of rice is still being topped by the production of babies.

Begadjah might be famous one of these days. One can almost picture the newspaper editors puzzling over the dateline for the world's last great story. Washington? Moscow? Not a chance, even though someone there will undoubtedly try to take the credit. The dateline will probably be bestowed on a place like Begadjah. How would the story begin?

Special to The New York Times

BEGADJAH, Indonesia—Man's life on earth ended today. Experts, roused from their sleep, declined to comment. But one local man, concluding an all-night celebration of the birth of his seventh child, said: "Allah will provide."

We Are All Developing Nations
BY BARBARA WARD

In the coming months, as in the past year, one of the most complex and difficult problems confronting the West is its relationship with the billion and more human beings who live in the uncommitted, underdeveloped world.

Among all these anxious, seething peoples there is a gap in understanding of the West's position—and in sympathy with Western analyses of the world's ills—that undoes much of the good that specific Western policies are designed to achieve.

Can the gap be defined? Some elements are, of course, well known. The African's passionate concern with colonialism and neo-colonialism springs from his knowledge that racial domination still is a fundamental social and political fact in southern Africa. At the Belgrade meeting of uncommitted nations it was, significantly, the Asian leaders who steered the conference away from obsessive concentration on "imperialism."

In the economic sphere, it is another incontrovertible fact that while the West continues to increase its wealth, the uncommitted peoples fall further behind. When in their November meetings the

Atlantic powers accepted the goal of adding $500 billion to their annual national income by the end of this decade, they incidentally made known an actual acceleration in the rate at which the rich are leaving the poor behind.

Yet such well-known and documented stumbling blocks as these are not the whole story. In the relations among states, psychological reactions have a profound influence, nowhere more sharply than with states aware down to the last nuance of a newly found independence. Emotions and prejudices cluster around the central political and economic facts of these relations, distorting them, clouding them, sometimes standing them on their heads. If one wanted a shorthand definition of the particular malaise that hangs over today's contacts between the West and the uncommitted lands, one might say that, while we see them as "underdeveloped," they are in a fair way to seeing us as "overdeveloped," and the psychological gap, like the economic gap, is tending to widen.

Take the political issue. Most developing lands today inherited their political and administrative structures from the Western colonial powers. After decades of largely autocratic rule, they were put through a relatively short course on a constitutional system that had evolved through five or six centuries of increasingly sophisticated politics in the West.

Some countries were lucky. The Indians had half a century in which to master the intricacies of divided power, parliamentary control and opposition, administrative procedures, checks and balances, and decentralization. At the other extreme, the wretched Congolese galloped through nine months of political training at the national level and collapsed at the starting line.

It is not, therefore, surprising that in the past decade virtually all the underdeveloped ex-colonial lands have retreated from full representative, constitutional government—to military autocracy, as in Pakistan, or to single-party rule with varying degrees of authoritarianism, as throughout emergent Africa. The pressures that dictated the change were largely the same: nation-building in the midst of tribal differences, economic mobilization against a background of total poverty, troubled frontiers, conflicts envenomed by the cold war.

The change need not have undermined relations with the West, for the Western powers might, from their own experience, have measured the difficulties under which the new states operate. After all, Western governments, too, have been known to revert to more forceful rule when crises seemed to threaten the fabric of the state. The American South, Northern Ireland, France ruled by emergency decree, all represent similar responses to similar pressures.

The malaise springs rather from the fact that so many Western critics seem to have forgotten their own compromises with the maintenance of full and elaborate constitutional government. They have led a chorus of blame and criticism over the "backsliding" of the underdeveloped lands and have passed over in silence their own departures from pure principle.

When, for example, southern senators lecture African leaders on the evils of single-party government; when the British press denounces deportations in West Africa at precisely the moment that a Cypriote archbishop is in forced exile in the Seychelles; when no allowances are made for the turmoil of early independence; when dictatorial rule is attributed to some local, specialized form of original sin, then the feeling grows irresistibly that a gulf of misunderstanding separates the sophisticates of the West from the struggling peoples of the new lands. One is driven to feel even that the Communists, with their straightforward preference for strong government and direct rule, may be nearer in experience, and therefore in sympathy, to local leaders struggling for the first time with the realities—not the dreams—of independence.

A similar gap between a feeling of overdevelopment and underdevelopment exists in the economic relations between uncommitted countries and the West.

The minutiae of Western economic operations seem unutterably complicated to relatively inexperienced officials. Scores of documents to cover a single transaction, Congressional procedures and checks, which can delay an aid program by eighteen months, the infinity of detailed information demanded from nations with only the most rudimentary statistics—all these are compared with the usual Soviet procedure of opening a line of credit with a minimum of technical fuss.

The fact that much of the Western pattern of negotiation is designed to protect both parties and to check waste is overlooked; the fact that Soviet aid is usually more expensive in the long run has not yet been experienced. Meanwhile, Western methods seem alien and "overdeveloped."

Nor is it simply a matter of procedure. The Western world market is an arena of incredible sophistication in which vast transactions are determined by marginal changes in current or prospective prices; in which a wide variety of interest rates applies to different types of capital transactions; in which speculation and price fluctuations lend a constant tremor of uncertainty to the developing economy's sales of raw materials; in which—in markets, in tariffs, in investments—the cards seem to be permanently stacked in favor of the developed lands.

The prospect of a unified Atlantic economy of the rich seems to accentuate the risks. Again, in comparison, Soviet bulk purchases or Soviet long-term loans at marginal interest rates have a deceptive simplicity.

Above all, the gap between the very rich and the very poor is abysmally deep and growing deeper. The collective national income of the billion people who live in the uncommitted and developing lands may be on the order of $130 to $135 billion. The national income of the 185 million souls in America alone is more than $430 billion. In the Western world as a whole, some 800 million people enjoy something like $1,000 billion. At this point, one must realize the paradox that precisely those bold and ambitious policies for Western growth that are part of the process of checkmating communism in Europe can aggravate the alienation and resentment of the developing nations.

If they see another $500 billion added to the West's annual wealth in the next decade, while their own national incomes do no more than possibly keep pace with their rising populations, then that continuous impoverishment of the already poor—which Marx forecast falsely for Western society—may reappear as a brutal fact on the international scene and inject an element of revolutionary despair into future relations between the overdeveloped and the developing worlds.

FOOD, RESOURCES, AND NATIONAL DEVELOPMENT

Even in the cultural sphere—in which, at the popular level, Western influence is strongest—there are dangerous gaps and misunderstandings.

It is true that many aspects of the "American way of life" have conquered the world. T-shirts in Moscow, Hawaiian shirts in Buenos Aires, and blue jeans the world over are symbols of the new informal "Western" style. "High Life," a popular song of Ghana—"What a girl wants is a Jaguar [a sports car], a fridgeful [a refrigerator full of frozen foods], and a Been-to [a young man who has 'been to' England or America]"—provides the best summary of the first shy beginnings of the mass-consumption economy.

Yet, in the new nations, the mass of people determines attitudes far less than the few young intellectuals who, just because they are so few, find themselves in positions of power almost before they have left their universities. Among them, reactions are much more ambiguous. Western entertainment is both loved and hated. Its slickness, its gloss, its competence compel attention. But the emptiness and triviality of much of the content create a revulsion.

In Western Nigeria, the television service, which pipes in from a British company the usual quota of Westerns and police dramas, may sell the goods in Lagos. But at Ibadan University, the students of today—who will be leaders of Nigeria tomorrow—denounce the cultural betrayal of their people. They see improved means devoted to unimproved ends—a vast elaboration of technical competence devoted to an unworthy product.

This form of overdevelopment, which some call decadence, is contrasted with the constant Soviet underlining of Culture with a capital C with pictures of rapt people watching ballet or jolly peasant dancers re-creating the popular culture of the villages.

When President Nkrumah visited Moscow last summer, the Russians arranged to have the cast of one of Ghana's most successful folk plays, *Obadzeng,* accompany him. It played before applauding audiences, and the Ghanaians were flattered by the contrasts drawn between their simple, direct folk art and the commercialized and basically trivial entertainments of the West.

In great measure, this miasma of misunderstanding, suspicion, and hate-love clouds the vision of the developing peoples when they look at the West today. If it is true that we underestimate their political difficulties, misunderstand the nature of their economic dilemmas, and often underrate their cultural pretensions, it must be said that they as radically misunderstand and distort the attitudes of the West.

Weary of our political sermonizing, they forget their own profound stakes in the great Western traditions of freedom and self-determination, traditions that were the mainsprings of their own drives to independence and which defend that independence now it is attained. Only the existence in America of a super-power *interested* in their survival prevents them from being swallowed up by the thrusting empires of the East.

This is the first century in which small nations enjoy the right to separate existence, and the only reason for their new status is the West's decision to use its overwhelming power to support, and not to swamp, the weaker brethren.

Similarly, their intense concern with their own poverty and with the worldwide contrast between rich and poor leads them to neglect the staggering revolution that in a couple of decades has overtaken the West. Until the day before yesterday, relations between the developed and underdeveloped nations turned on pure Western self-interest. Capital went out to earn large profits in backward lands by using up local resources and exploiting reserves of cheap, untrained labor. This was the essence of "imperialism" in the classic Marxist sense.

It has now been totally reversed. Westerners are ready to transfer large sums of capital in the expectation of no immediate return, to build up local competitors, and with the express aim of training and developing local labor. Lenin has been stood on his head—yet cries of "neo-colonialism" still echo from the underdeveloped lands.

One could extend the list of misunderstandings and misjudgments to every field. Taken together, they are perhaps the most formidable barrier to cooperation between the West and the uncommitted lands, for they add an extra edge of dislike and resentment to such concrete issues as colonialism or economic need and create a settled habit of misjudgment that undoes much of the good that individual policies and acts might create.

Is there any way out of the morass? Concrete policies are, of course, vitally important. A speedy end to colonialism in southern Africa would transform the outlook of African leaders. Generous, sustained aid from the West along the disinterested lines laid down by President Kennedy would have a cumulative effect in allaying suspicions and increasing goodwill.

Yet even such advances might leave much of the malaise intact. It lingers on in Asia in spite of virtually complete independence from the West. Aid is already generous and still the cries of "neo-colonialism" are raised. Something more is needed to span the psychological gap between the very rich and the very poor, between the overdeveloped and the underdeveloped, between the wealthy North of the world and the developing South. It is, perhaps, in this geographical contrast that one can find a possible clue to a solution.

Very often in human affairs a relationship undermined by profound emotional misunderstandings cannot be sorted out grievance by grievance. It can be improved only when a sort of psychological mutation occurs and each protagonist begins to see the other in a wholly new light.

A typical example is the swing from enmity to friendship that takes place when—as with postwar Germany or Japan—nations in a system of alliances change sides. The old quarrels are not settled. They are transcended in a new way of looking at the total relationship.

Such a mutation could perhaps take place today if both overdeveloped and underdeveloped societies could learn to look at each other with a quite new perspective. Such a perspective in fact exists.

If one looks at the human race as a unity, it is clear that mankind as a whole is undergoing the most profound revolution in its way of life since the beginning of settled agriculture and the invention of the wheel. Science and technology have unleashed forces that are certain to modify every institution and relationship, to reshape every economic system, and, by their fundamentally experimental character, to launch every society upon a flood of change.

In the North this transformation began first and has proceeded farther. It has brought vast gains in wealth and created for the first time physical availabilities and resources that open up a new world of human choice. For the first time, to give the simplest instance, all mankind can be fed. But the scientific revolution has left unsolved many of the most poignant problems of human existence and has aggravated others—for example, the problems of city-dwellers in the vast megalopolises of the future.

In the underdeveloped South the same onslaught of science and technology has begun. The period of wider resources and wider choice still lies ahead, but already it is clear that the results of the new revolution will not be much different from those in the North—some problems, mainly physical, will be solved; others will be unchanged; some will be aggravated.

Much that each region finds disagreeable in the other springs from the effort to cope with wholly new forces unleashed on society. The West's cultural uncertainties, for instance, reflect the dilemmas of the first epoch in human history to experience, as a result of technological change, the phenomenon of mass leisure. The developing lands' political uncertainties reflect in turn the new imperatives of national growth and modernization.

In short, overdeveloped and underdeveloped alike are caught up in a continuous revolution—the revolution of science and technology. It is a revolution that engulfs them equally in a torrent of change, which they cope with as best they can—fumblingly, mistakenly, hopefully, courageously. It is a revolution in which, given a frank recognition of their common destiny, they can aid each other, not only by the economic assistance of North to South, but by a joint assessment of the errors that have been made and can be avoided, and by a joint exploration of the problems that beset *all* humanity in the nuclear age.

For the overtones and undertones of "overdevelopment" and "underdevelopment" we should substitute a more exact and human definition—that of development itself as a process in which all the peoples of the world are involved. Those who started first have the advantages and the disadvantages of pioneers. They are richer but they have made painful, costly, even devastating mistakes. Those who started later can be helped as much by the mistakes as by the generosity of those at the head of the column.

In short, all the nations of the world are developing nations.

None can evade the consequences of the greatest cycle of change in human history.

Compared with the scale of this challenge, the differences between overdevelopment and underdevelopment sink into unimportance. The fundamental fact is a shared experience, a solidarity of learning and doing, a single revolution in which humanity as a whole is irreversibly engaged.

The World Is Running Out of Raw Materials
BY WALTER SULLIVAN

Those who wish to dramatize the population explosion point out that, if present growth rates continue, the mass of humanity in a few centuries will exceed the entire mass of the earth. What that shows, of course, is that there is a limit to the population that this planet can support. But what is that limit?

At a recent committee meeting of the American Association for the Advancement of Science a leading government scientist pointed out that there has never been a broad scientific study of this essential problem in all of its ramifications.

The psychic effects of crowding are often mentioned. It is known that some mammals under crowded conditions undergo hormonal changes that cut their birth rate. But if we can make the deserts bloom and thin out our more congested cities, we can greatly increase world population without this becoming a limiting factor.

Perhaps our political institutions are incapable of bringing about such a revolutionary redistribution of the population. This is uncertain, but what is definitely known is that the raw materials needed to support modern civilization are limited.

If we are to rebuild our economy, irrigate the deserts, industrialize the underdeveloped nations, vast amounts of energy will be required and, unless we can harness the power of the hydrogen atom, that energy depends on limited supplies of fuel.

To what extent, then, is world population limited by our finite reserves of fuel, metallic ore, and other raw materials? A book recently published by Dr. Charles F. Park, Jr., professor of geology and of mineral engineering at Stanford University, indicates that the world population may already be far beyond the level that, in the future, could be supported by this planet's resources.

Dr. Park's analysis is featured in the current issue of *Focus,* a publication of the American Geographical Society. It is entitled: "Affluence in Jeopardy."

He says that we have taken false comfort in the argument that ample mineral resources lie under the sea or deeper in the ground. The world is already beginning to run short of some materials of great importance to a technological society, such as mercury, tin, silver, and cobalt. The big drain, however, will come if and when the world population reaches its projected level for the year 2000 (roughly double that of today) and the nations of Asia, Africa, and South America become fully industrialized.

In 1967 the United States had a per capita consumption of about one ton of iron. If global consumption reaches that level by the year 2000 and the population has doubled, the world's annual demand for iron will be twelve times what it is today.

In 1967 the American per capita use of copper was eighteen pounds. If, by the year 2000, world requirements reach this level, the global demand will be eleven times what it is today, which Dr. Park, as an ore specialist, calls "staggering."

If the same formula is applied to lead, the needs will rise sixteenfold. As it is, readily accessible lead ore in this country has fallen to such a level that most lead for American industry has to be imported. By the year 2000, according to Dr. Park, it "would be a difficult and probably an impossible task to obtain the indicated amounts of copper and lead."

Furthermore, he points out, these projections do not allow for any increase in per capita consumption by highly technological societies, such as that in the United States. Such stagnation is highly unlikely.

Those who believe atomic energy will prevent disastrous poverty, starvation, and civil unrest during the coming century note that cheap electric power could be used to desalt seawater, irrigate the deserts, and extract minerals from our waste materials. Our daily refuse would be sent to special plants for sorting by electric and other means, instead of being buried, burned, or dumped at sea.

Dr. Park concedes that iron could be salvaged in this way, but he despairs of recovering such critical substances as silver and mercury. Some 31 percent of American silver consumption (46.5 million ounces) goes into photographic film. The second most important industrial use is in electrical and electronic equipment (24 percent). Other uses include silverware and jewelry (17 percent), brazing alloys and solder (12 percent), and batteries (7 percent).

Mercury is used in temperature and pressure recording devices. Such substances, Dr. Park argues, are irretrievably lost in the vast amounts of daily refuse. "One cannot conceive of the reclamation of mercury from broken thermometers."

He also is pessimistic about the role of substitutes for scarce substances. Mercury is unique in being the only metal that is liquid at room temperature. It is possible, however, that photosensitive plastics may someday replace the silver nitrate used on film. Aluminum, which is comparatively plentiful, can replace many uses of copper. There are substitutes for some uses of cobalt, but only cobalt is suited to the making of permanent magnets.

Thus Dr. Park argues that the popular concept of a constantly expanding economy and an upgrading of other nations to our living standards is a sure path to disaster unless radical checks in population can be achieved. Ocean resources and deep-lying deposits can be exploited but only at high cost, not only in dollars, but in energy, and our fuels are limited.

He scoffs at the export of people to other planets as impractical. Some believe mineral resources on the moon can be brought to earth, but this will depend on whether the moon has undergone the internal heating and differentiation that, on earth, has extracted from the primordial mixture of materials the veins of pure ore found on earth.

His argument also leads one to conclude that the long-term destiny of mankind depends not only on halting the growth of population, but on learning how to extract energy from the fusion of hydrogen isotopes. This fusion releases the unruly power of the hydrogen bomb.

Those in this country and abroad seeking to harness the fusion reaction are optimistic, but the solution to this problem is not in sight. Success would provide ample energy for the remaining lifetime of the earth and should enable man, under wise leadership and assuming some method of population control, to work out ways to live in equilibrium with his environment and its resources.

Technology to Be King
BY ROBERT K. PLUMB

Man is standing at the gateway to a new era of civilization.

In the next hundred years the earth's population will multiply at least two to four times. Technology can feed, clothe, and shelter these people adequately and in some cases well.

There will be no shortage of minerals, meals, or metals. Machine civilization will spread over the earth and it can provide for all from the most common substances: air, seawater, ordinary rock, and sunlight.

Only one possible raw material shortage is foreseen—brain power. Educated men and women are needed to plan and design, to construct and operate the machine civilization that will care for the startling increase in world population expected by the year 2050.

Brain power is the key. Education, government, and industry must meet in a deliberate and sustained effort to sense the future and to plan for it. There is a chasm that technology must hurdle:

Raw materials and food already are running short just as the earth's population starts its greatest increase—from 2.6 billion persons in one hundred years. Possibly more.

Drafted by Savants | These conclusions are part of a "speculative projection" on the world that has been drafted by faculty members of the California Institute of Technology. The projection, a glimpse into the twenty-first century, has been presented at private conferences.

The findings have been discussed in the boardrooms of twenty-seven of the nation's leading corporations in the last few months. During the summer the principal officers of eight other corporations will hear the data on which the conclusions were based and will discuss them.

One conference was held at the University Club here last week for newsmen. California Institute of Technology faculty members present were Dr. James F. Bonner, professor of biology; Dr. Harrison S. Brown, professor of geochemistry; Dr. John R. Weir, associate professor of psychology, and Robert V. Bartz, director of the Industrial Associates Program of the institute.

The California report on world resources is designed to complement regular studies made by individual industries. Long-term trends and prospects, beyond the conventional business purview, are the substance of the study. Thus oil companies heard reports on the exhaustion of the world's oil and gas pools; steel companies heard about the time when iron ores are gone; utilities about the time when nuclear fuels will be about the only available sources of electricity.

Production Is Qualified | The predictions apply only if world catastrophe is avoided. Technology can ease but it cannot solve political and economic problems, the scientists reported.

Speaking for the physical sciences, Dr. Brown speculated that the population of the earth would probably increase to between 5 and 10 billion persons by the year 2050. There conceivably might be a ten- or fifteenfold increase, however; a fifteenfold increase would put the world population a century in the future at more than 30 billion.

Industrialization will spread rapidly, Dr. Brown predicted, more rapidly than it did in the United States and in Europe, because the "know-how" is already present: Each part of a factory will not require invention, since designs and methods of operation are already known.

The per capita demand for raw materials at the "American level of industrialization will increase rapidly," Dr. Brown predicted. Now, eight tons of steel are in use in the nation for each individual. In a century this might increase to one hundred tons. The amounts of other materials in use will similarly increase.

At the same time, he said, the present raw materials are being used up rapidly. Our ancestors picked up crystals of copper and pieces of coal on the surface of the earth. Now we have to follow coal seams farther underground and drive deep, even under the oceans, for oil. Nations that are not now industrialized will find that their industry must be based on leaner ores, poorer fuels. But our highly complex industrial processes can use low-grade raw materials.

As the population grows, Dr. Brown predicted, machine civilization will have to make use of the most common and abundant raw materials—air, seawater, ordinary rock, and sunlight.

Many of the techniques are now known and others will be developed, he predicted, for utilizing low-grade mineral ores, then ordinary granite, and finally ordinary rocks.

It works this way: Studies at the California Institute of Technology disclose that the average ton of granite contains about four grams of uranium and twelve grams of thorium. These two materials can be used in nuclear reactors (if so-called nuclear "breeding" reactors work) to release the equivalent of the heat from fifty tons of coal for each ton of granite. This is enough heat to extract metals even though they are of very low concentration from the granite, and to leave the excess energy to distill seawater, power factories, and provide a basis for a machine civilization that uses only rocks as a raw material.

Dr. Brown drew up a possible plan for the provision of an energy equivalent to the annual burning of 70 billion metric tons of coal for a population of 7 billion persons living a century in the future at the "American" level. Half the energy would come from nuclear sources, one-fourth from solar energy, another fourth from synthetic liquid fuels made from rocks and from water power and wood. (This energy balance allows for the equivalence of 2.7 billion tons of wood to be turned into lumber and paper each year.)

The Processing of Rock | Dr. Brown envisioned the time when great factories around the world could process rock much as oil refineries now process crude petroleum: The factories would operate on the energy from the radioactive materials in the rocks and would pour out a steady stream of metals and other chemicals. The factories would end the present role of mineral resources in world economy and politics.

All this, Dr. Brown emphasized, is a prediction for a period "in the absence of a world catastrophe." And he stressed that machine civilization itself was very vulnerable. If many highly complex factories must work together to provide for civilization, then the system can easily be put out of order. We are now approaching such a "point of no return," he warned.

Furthermore, he said, a civilization based on the utilization of common raw materials—air, seawater, ordinary rock, and sunlight—could not be restarted if anything should happen to it. The rich raw materials needed to make the complex factories to process very lean raw materials would not be available.

Nevertheless, Dr. Brown emphasized that the machine civilization could free man from dependence upon present raw materials if brain power were present and if the planning was done in time.

Food presents no insoluble problem according to Dr. Bonner. His studies indicate that improvements in conventional agriculture can greatly increase the world food supply and that eventually nonconventional food production techniques will feed any expected increase in world population "if we look beyond the limits of our present agricultural systems."

Brain Power Held Key | Dr. Weir emphasized that brain power was the key.

"As we expend more and more money in the extraction of materials from lower and lower grade ores, we meet an ever-increasing need for more skilled manpower, for more trained scientists and engineers," Dr. Weir said.

"So in a very real sense the critical limiting factor on the world's resources is not materials, energy, or food, but brain power," he asserted.

Already we have a shortage of engineers and scientists; this will certainly get worse in the future, he said. The big problem is the waste in the development of intellectual talent. Half the capable young men and women are not educated, one-third of the exceptionally talented are not educated, he said.

Fortunately, Dr. Weir emphasized, manpower is the only one of the resources of the earth today that is replenishable. If the population is to increase, then the number of young men and women to be educated must increase.

To reduce the waste of talent, Dr. Weir recommended that society make conscientious effort to identify talented young scientists and engineers early and to encourage them to get an education. Also, he suggested that we improve methods of teaching so that creative thinking can be stimulated in the talented. He urged, too, that ways be found to teach "difficult" subjects to persons who do not possess the ability to learn them with present teaching methods.

The brain power to meet the demands of machine civilization, where increasing population is multiplied by increasing demands (under conditions where raw materials become scarcer), can be trained only if everyone—education, government, and industry—rises to the challenge, Dr. Weir emphasized.

Companies and corporations (all affiliated with the institute through its Industrial Associates Program), whose officers have participated in the conferences to date are: Aerojet-General, Avco Manufacturing, Beckman Instruments, Byron Jackson, Convair, Douglas Aircraft, E. I. du Pont de Nemours, G. M. Gianini, Gilfillan Brothers, Gulf Oil, Hercules Powder, Hughes Aircraft, Hycon Manufacturing, International Business Machines, Lockheed Aircraft, North American Aviation, Ramo-Wooldridge, Rand Corporation, Richfield Oil, Shell Oil, Socony-Mobil Oil, Standard Oil of California, Standard Oil of New Jersey, Texas Company, Union Carbide and Carbon, Union Oil, and Westinghouse Electric.

The series of conferences will be concluded this June and September in meetings with eight additional companies: Bendix Aviation, Continental Oil, Dow Chemical, Elgin National Watch, Ford Motor, Great Lakes Carbon, Stanolind Oil and Gas, and United States Steel.

PART 3

ENVIRONMENTAL POLLUTION

It is ironic that as man has mastered his physical environment he has lost many of the benefits of that accomplishment in the rising costs resulting from pollution. As the realization of that fact has dawned upon him, man has found a culprit in the very mechanical technology that brought him control over his environment. But that is a delusion. Man has only himself to blame. He has long been a reckless exploiter of nature. Moreover, he has been insensitive until recently both to costs that are not usually expressed in monetary terms and to the cumulative character of both social and economic costs.

The first article in this section, "That 'Hellish and Dismal Cloud,'" describes how our increasing intensity of environmental usage has raised the degree of contamination of the air to an almost prohibitive level. George H. T. Kimble goes beyond description, however, to provide an analysis of the problem and some suggestions on what can be done about it.

Cumulative though environmental pollution often is, the second article in this section indicates that pollution can occur with catastrophic abruptness. Thus the beautiful oceanfront of Santa Barbara, California, was suddenly inundated with raw petroleum. The accident of an oil well blowout is tragic enough. Equally disturbing is the power of vested interests and the inertia of government in resisting the application of environmental protection measures.

The transportation of oil can be an environmental threat whether it occurs over land or over sea. The great debate on the wisdom of constructing the trans-Alaskan oil pipeline is examined by Thomas Brown, in "Our Arctic Will Never Be the Same: That Unstoppable Pipeline," with unusual objectivity. It is gratifying to learn that the attacks of conservationists on the project have led to improved design and to a cleaning up of environmental messes left by oil exploration companies. The issue, however, is far more complex than conservation alone. It is deeply entangled in national economic policy, questions of states' rights, international politics, and the energy crisis of the nation. In such a context it is not unlikely that the need for environmental protection might be thrust into the background.

It comes as something of a shock to learn, in "We Are Killing the Sea Around Us," that an area as vast and as deep as an ocean is not immune to pollution. The view of the oceans as dumps of seemingly unlimited capacity reflects ignorance more than anything else. Of course, without the help of scientific discovery we could not know how poisons dumped into the seas can become concentrated in certain plant or animal species, which can then transmit the lethal effects back to man. Nor is it self-evident that poisons in the sea can retain their potencies indefinitely. The accumulation of knowledge has coined a new aphorism: Diffusion is no solution to pollution. The growth of knowledge has also complicated the administrative problem in environmental control. The movements and concentrations of pollutants in the seas are threats to all nations bordering upon coasts; effective controls require the utmost cooperation from all nations exposed to the risks.

A partial solution to the destruction of the seas lies in the recycling of waste material. As LaMont Cole points out in his article on "What to Do with Waste," waste is a state of mind, for much of it can just as accurately be regarded as a resource. The numerous uses for the refuse with which we litter our environment, as he observes, await only some imaginative adjustments in our conceptions of economics.

Part III closes with another symposium organized from scattered accounts of seminars and interviews. The discussion is addressed mainly to the question of population increase as a cause of pollution and other undesirable effects on the quality of life. Two positions are noticeable in the remarks. One attributes the determining influence to a single factor, population increase, on a wide assortment of outcomes. The other adopts a more comprehensive view toward causation; it recognizes that social problems are products of numerous influences. In this view population control is but one of several tactics needed to deal with threats to environmental quality.

That "Hellish and Dismal Cloud"

BY GEORGE H. T. KIMBLE

Air pollution is as old as fire. For thousands of years smoke haze has hung low by night over the villages and fields of the Middle East, as it still does in almost all parts of the world where farmers burn brush and grass for the fertilizing ash they yield.

For well over one thousand years Britain and her European neighbors have been using soft coal as a fuel and so feeding the air with increasing amounts of soot and gases. As long ago as 1306, in the reign of the English King Edward I, a royal proclamation prohibited the use of coal while Parliament was in session, so bad was the pollution.

By the seventeenth century London's fogs had become so dirty that John Evelyn, the diarist, was compelled to protest against the "hellish and dismal Cloud" that enveloped the city periodically and affected the inhabitants to such an extent that "catarrhs, phthisicks, coughs and consumptions rage more in this one city than in the whole earth besides."

The recent introduction in Congress of a bill giving enforcement powers in air-pollution cases to the federal government was a sharp reminder, if one were needed, that we are dirty people. We spend fortunes on detergents, toothpastes, and cleansing creams; we keep battalions busy taking care of our trash, and there is not a place in all the land where the voice of the suds-seller is not heard. But we are still dirty, for we dwell in the midst of dirty air—air that grimes our public buildings, that impairs the beauty of our skies and earth, that undermines our health and shortens our lives—air that we ourselves have dirtied.

Today, on this continent alone, at least ten thousand communities, representing a population of more than 100 million, are now seriously affected by pollution. In South America, Africa, Asia, Australia, and Europe there is hardly a city of any size that is stranger to irritating haze and industrial "fallout."

Nor is it merely the cities of the earth that suffer in this fashion. City-made pollution is no respecter of city limits; it goes where it is borne by the wind. Frequently it is borne many miles, as any New York suburban housewife knows, and as anybody can see by observing the movement of factory smoke downwind on a quiet evening. We also need to remember that many rural areas make their own brand of pollution. Half the farmers of the world continue to burn brush and grass during the dry season, and almost as many continue to plow up land that takes flight in the slightest breeze. When I was in New Zealand during World War II, it was periodically possible to write one's name in the dust that had been carried from the dried-out wheatlands of Australia, more than twelve hundred miles away.

No less modern, and more sinister, is the growing toxicity of the air. Until recent times the prime cause of air pollution was the excessive and grossly inefficient combustion of coal. Although there is still plenty of this kind of pollution, the prime cause of pollution in most large cities today is the emission of gases and solids from internal combustion engines and from industrial plants. Automobiles are generous contributors of nitrogen oxide and carbon monoxide (in London they contribute about two thousand tons of the latter daily; in New York and Los Angeles upwards of ten thousand tons). Metallurgical plants contribute such toxic substances as hydrofluoric acid, sodium and calcium fluorides, and, often, arsenical compounds. Chemical and petrochemical plants contribute hydrogen and sulfide, chlorine, sulfur dioxide, and, often, compounds of selenium, tellurium, and beryllium. Other poisons injected into the air of our industrial cities include sulfuric acid, hydrochloric acid, and compounds of zinc and lead.

The damage done by these pollutants is compounded by the chemical reactions that frequently take place once they get into the air. In many cities it is these secondary pollutants, as they are called, that are the real villains of the piece. In Los Angeles, for instance, some of the most harmful ingredients of the smog are those produced by sunlight working photochemically on the hydrocarbons that are present in fumes from incompletely burned fuel.

To make matters still worse, the world now has to reckon with pollution from radioactive debris. Although there are differences of opinion concerning the territorial extent of the danger arising from this source—to say nothing of the immediacy of the danger— nobody doubts that the danger exists. The first thing the British Atomic Energy Authority did when radioactive debris escaped from its plutonium plant near Carlisle was to quarantine the nearby farms and prohibit the sale of their produce, because soil, grass, cattle, and mule had all become contaminated.

A third feature of air pollution that is comparatively new is the sheer bulk of it. During last winter's London smog, smoke and sulfur compounds were being poured into the air at the rate of thousands of tons a day. At its worst, the smog is believed to have contained between six hundred and one thousand tons of smoke particles alone. In the Ruhr valley of Western Germany the daily fallout of ashes and soot is put at 1 million tons; that of sulfur dioxide at 4 million tons. Even in so comparatively clean and pleasant a place as Puget Sound, several thousand tons of industrial wastes daily become airborne.

The full cost of air pollution to the communities producing it—to say nothing of those that simply "catch" it from their neighbors—has never been calculated and is probably incalculable. Such attempts as have been made to put a price on the damage it does to property, crops, cattle, and materials indicate that, in the United States alone, it may be as high as $12 billion annually, or more than $60 per person. But clearly nobody can put a price on the four hundred lives lost in the 1962 London smog—let alone the four thousand lives lost in the smog ten years earlier—or on the loss of health, temporary or permanent, suffered by thousands more. Nor can anybody weigh the deprivation of beauty, happiness, and comfort that pollution imposes upon those who have to live with it.

What is being done about the problem? A great deal, as any citizen of St. Louis, Pittsburgh, and Los Angeles will be happy to tell you. St. Louis has almost forgotten what bad smog is like since it prohibited, in the late 1930's, the use of certain types of soft coal. Pittsburgh, though later in taking legal action against the polluters of its air, can likewise point to visible gains, not the least of which is the ability of its people to see the city about twice as often as they could twenty years ago.

In Los Angeles County, notwithstanding its phenomenal growth (from 3,900,000 people and 9,800 industries in 1948 to 6,500,000 people and 16,000 industries in 1960), the volume of contaminants entering the air from stationary sources is less than half what it was fifteen years ago and about five thousand tons a day less than it would have been but for the control measures taken in the interval. Even London believes it is getting to the point where it can see daylight, for since the Clean Air Act was passed in 1956 the average concentration of smoke over the city has been reduced by roughly 40 percent.

Of course, much more can be done, as speaker after speaker at the National Conference on Air Pollution pointed out in Washington last December. Our lawmakers can prohibit the open burning of trash in backyards and city dumps, including the burning of junked cars, tires, batteries, and so on; and they can enforce the use (as they are beginning to do) of "afterburners" on all gasoline-fired vehicles. Our chemists can go on applying their wits to the problem of trapping the gases and solids that escape from engine exhausts and commercial and industrial plants of every kind. Our city planners can make better use of their chief tool of pollution control, namely zoning.

Perhaps the meteorologist can do something about it, too. Given enough heat and air movement, any unwanted accumulation of airborne gases and solids can be dispersed. During World War II, when round-the-clock aircraft patrols were frequently necessary, many British airfields were kept open in thick weather by firing gasoline fed through perforated pipes laid along the edges of runways. The intense heat generated by the flames evaporated the unwanted moisture in the air and so increased visibility.

The cost, needless to say, was considerable. Fifteen million gallons of gasoline were used over a period of two and a half years in bringing in twenty-five hundred planes. Quite clearly, no commercial airline could afford to expend six thousand gallons of gasoline per plane per landing. More recently, unwanted water particles and other solids have been dispersed on an experimental basis by means of the "seeding" technique: that is, by spraying the air with silver iodide or some other nucleating agent.

But will air pollution ever be eliminated completely? I very much doubt it, for two reasons. First, everybody is a polluter of the air, whether he is only a cigarette smoker or a leaf burner, and it seems as unlikely that we can ever legislate effectively against universal "sin" as against universal selfishness, a species of which air pollution is.

Second, not every part of the world is fitted, atmospherically, to cope with air pollution. What makes it the habitual and serious problem it is in a place like Los Angeles is not so much the fact that the county has 3 million vehicles and sixteen thousand industries as the fact that there is not enough rainfall or wind to clear away the resulting impurities. For southern California lies close to the heart of one of the most persistent high-pressure (or anticyclonic) systems to be found anywhere on earth.

Such systems are generally notable for three things: their aridity (the air in them spends most of its time subsiding, that is, warming up and so becoming drier); their "airlessness" (the winds are at best light and near the center are often impalpable), and their inversions (that is, the existence in their lower layers of a temperature gradient that is the inverse of the normal one, since the temperature increases with height). The aridity means that there is seldom any rain to wash the impurities out of the air; the airlessness that there is seldom enough wind to displace them horizontally; the inversion that there is virtually no chance of displacing them vertically.

Of the three features, the inversion is the one that gives Los Angeles the most trouble, because it closes the only escape hatch for the impurities. These impurities can no more rise into the warm air that lies above the colder surface air than a plume of cigarette smoke can rise above the ceiling of the room in which the smoker sits. Besides building up an ever-greater accumulation of themselves just under the "ceiling" of the inversion, these suspended impurities act as heating surfaces for the incoming rays of the sun, and so raise the temperature of the air around them, thereby reinforcing the "ceiling." It is largely because of this that a Los Angeles smog is hard to budge once it has become established. And the longer it lasts, the higher the concentration of toxic impurities becomes, with all the attendant hazards for the smog-bound.

Theoretically, it should be possible to destroy the ceiling by heating the air below it, but the cost of doing this would be considerable, since it would take all of 3 million megawatts to raise the air temperature above the city by as little as 2 degrees F. an hour. Theoretically, too, it should be possible to disperse the impurities by blowing them away, but here also the cost would be considerable, since the ventilating plant would have to generate at least 250,000 tons of fresh air a minute.

True, the meteorologist may one day lick the problem by stopping the inversions from forming, that is, by controlling the circulation of the atmosphere to the point where he can shift an anticyclone as soon as he sees it beginning to form in the Los Angeles area. The only trouble about this, though, is that San Francisco might get the shifted system and the smog that goes with it. On second thought it might be cheaper and more satisfactory all around to shift Los Angeles, which as any geographer knows, should never have been built where it is in the first place.

Santa Barbarans Cite an Eleventh Commandment:
"Thou Shalt Not Abuse the Earth"
BY ROSS MACDONALD AND ROBERT EASTON

Life in Santa Barbara today is somewhat reminiscent of civilian life in a war zone. When oil from a blown-out offshore well flooded the city's beaches early this year, many residents were reminded of the oil from torpedoed tankers that came ashore on the East Coast in the forties. Others were reminded of the Torrey Canyon disaster of March 1967, which devastated the coast of Cornwall, England, with oil from a grounded tanker. But Cornwall's case stemmed from a single accident. Santa Barbara's predicament is continuing—it lives under constant threat of further oleaginous invasion from the sea.

And what happens out there, oilwise, on the continental shelf off Santa Barbara is beyond the control of local citizens. That is largely in the hands of the federal government, and because of government secrecy it is difficult to get hard information.

What citizens are afraid of is that, when the chips are down, Santa Barbara will be sacrificed to the government's appetite for oil revenue and its long-term policy of favoring the oil industry at the expense of everyone else.

The sacrifice seems to be proceeding. Oil is still leaking into the Santa Barbara Channel as a result of the January 28 blowout, though at a reduced rate. As wind and tide determine, it revisits local beaches and reblackens the harbor. Beach users equip themselves with special shoes or a can of cleaning fluid. Such sports as boating, fishing, and bird-watching are not what they used to be. The tourist trade has fallen off sharply. At noon on Sunday of the Labor Day weekend not a single swimmer could be seen in the ocean off East Beach, formerly one of the most popular public beaches in California.

The oil industry has denied or minimized these continuing effects of the continuing spill. Union Oil's company magazine recently proclaimed that "Santa Barbara's beaches are back to normal." An American Petroleum Institute official, Kerryn King, did admit that he saw some oil on a helicopter tour of the beaches on Labor Day. But he insisted that it came from "natural oil seepage rather than from the leak in the area of Union Company's Platform A" (the designation of the drilling operation five and a half miles offshore where the blowout occurred).

Actually, as the Santa Barbara *News-Press* pointed out on September 3, "all Santa Barbara County beaches—and some (nearby) Ventura County beaches—are vulnerable to oil pollution from time to time from leakage in the Platform A area." Yet in this same area, within two-thirds of a mile from Platform A, the Sun Oil Company was planning last month to install another platform, 200 feet high (the average height), with a capacity of sixty wells.

(Original Department of the Interior plans for the Santa Barbara Channel resulted in the leasing of seventy-one tracts, each tract capable of containing one or more such platforms, or comparable subsurface or bottom installations—each platform capable of drilling and servicing sixty wells. The potential total is thus more than 4,000 offshore wells. In the past, according to Interior Department statistics, a blowout rate of 2.5 per thousand wells has held true. Over the next few years, if government and industry persist in their plans for a forest of oil installations in the channel, Santa Barbara can anticipate perhaps ten repetitions of the January 28 blowout.)

A blowout, according to Webster's, is "an uncontrolled eruption of an oil or gas well due to excessive natural pressure." It is like a tap that you can't turn off. As Robert R. Curry, a geologist and geophysicist, explained to the U.S. Senate subcommittee on water pollution, blowouts occur most commonly during the drilling or completion of an oil well. When the pressures in the drill hole from above are less than the pressures on the oil-bearing strata below, oil and gas can erupt with terrific force.

This is what happened in the blowout at Platform A, according to the official U.S. Geological Survey report. In the process of pulling up the drill pipe from a total depth of 3,479 feet, the drillers lost control of the pressures from below. These are ordinarily balanced from above by the weight of "drilling mud," a chemical fluid of high specific gravity that fills the hole as it is drilled. But when this balance was disrupted, drilling mud and gas began to pour out of the top of the well.

"The rig crew," the official report continues, "made unsuccessful attempts to control the flow. Within a few minutes it was decided to drop the drill pipe in the hole and close the blind rams on the blowout preventer (a hydraulically operated valve device that closes and plugs the top of the hole). This action effectively controlled the flow of mud and gas from the casing of the well." Unfortunately, the casing went down only 238 feet below the ocean floor. Gas and oil from a much deeper level forced their way up outside this casing and through the fissures in the ocean floor. "Soon after flow from the wellhead was contained, gas and some oil began to boil up through the water near the platform," said the report. Now the well was completely out of control, or "wild," as the oil men say.

When the well on Platform A blew out, according to a worker on the platform, a jet of gas and drilling mud rose over 100 feet in the air. The following day, when newsmen first went out, the sea around the platform was thickly covered with crude oil bubbling with gas.

Drilling and pumping continued from floating rigs and from fixed platforms nearby. A Union Oil vice president assured the city fathers that the spill would be capped and under control within twenty-four hours.

Once started, a major spill tends to go on for a while. A recent gas blowout off the Australian coast ran for a month before the

Houston wild-well control specialist, Red Adair, got it capped. At Platform A, the upsurge of oil and gas through the fragmented and fissured ocean floor had rendered useless all the regular safety devices, as the government reported. Apparently the only way to stop it was to get together enough drilling mud and cement to fill the hole and once again balance the tremendous pressure from below. To gather the necessary thousands of tons of material would take some days.

Meanwhile, the crude oil was surging up into the channel and spreading over hundreds of square miles. As with everything else concerning the spill, there were and are differences of opinion about the amount of oil spilled. Union Oil's initially quoted estimate of 5,000 barrels a day was later withdrawn and lowered to 500 barrels a day. A scientist with General Research Corporation, Alan A. Allen, who inspected the channel every day from the air, estimated the minimum flow at 5,000 barrels a day, or more than 2 million gallons in the ten and a half days before the well was plugged.

During the first five days the wind favored Santa Barbara and kept the oil off its beaches, though a mile of beach to the south was heavily tarred. Secretary of the Interior Walter Hickel overflew the channel and requested the oil companies to suspend drilling operations. But the following day, in a curious display of uncertainty and bad timing, he suspended the suspension and told them they could resume drilling.

That was a blue Monday. The wind changed, and the oil surged onto the white beaches. It entered the harbor, which is for many the living heart of the area, and blackened the hulls of nearly eight hundred boats. Yachtsmen and fishermen stood on the pier and watched the blackness take it all. Some of them were crying.

They seemed to feel that something beautiful had been destroyed. The worst of it was that the horror kept recurring, and the oil came in on nearly every tide for weeks and months. The boats had to be cleaned and re-cleaned. Some of the glass hulls whose gel surfaces were impregnated with oil could be restored only with great difficulty and at great expense.

After the well had been plugged, we asked an oil geologist (who insisted on anonymity) how he accounted for the continuing leakage around it. He reasoned that the Union Oil hole, now plugged, had connected two pools of oil, one at a depth of more than 3,000 feet, the other at 200 or 300. High pressure in the deep pool had forced oil up through and around the uncased walls of the plugged hole and pressurized the shallow pool. Oil from the shallow pool, he believed, was bleeding up through the fissures and loose sand of the ocean floor and rising to the surface.

Making an aerial survey of the channel, we circled Platform A and could see oil welling up in multiple leaks along an east-west front of about a thousand feet. Wherever we flew in the channel we saw oil. Anacapa Island, a national monument and wildlife sanctuary, was completely surrounded with the stuff. Along 45 miles of mainland beaches south of Santa Barbara the high-tide line was thickly marked in black. (Eventually the oil slick spread over 200 miles and affected the coast as far south as the Mexican border.)

The only living things visible on the beaches were oil-damaged birds and the Union Oil clean-up crews. The latter had an unenviable job, because their work was never finished. They would clean a patch of beach with their heavy equipment, trucking away or burying or burning the tarry debris. Then the tides would come in, bringing more oil, uncovering buried tar, rendering the beaches again unusable.

Flying over Santa Barbara Harbor, we could see another exercise in futility. Hot-water sprayers were being used to clean the rocks and seawalls. The softened oil would run down into the water and then come back in to give the intertidal life another bath of oil—provided they had survived the hot-water spray.

Oil blowouts are much more common than is generally realized. During 1968 alone, wild-well expert Adair was called in to control forty blowouts, worldwide, eleven of which were offshore. When the Adair company was brought in on the Santa Barbara spill, one of the employees reported that "blowouts have become so common in the offshore fields of Louisiana that they scarcely rate notice in the newspapers." In this connection, geologist Robert R. Curry had warned the U.S. Senate subcommittee: "Santa Barbara offshore exploration and production could yield a higher frequency of spills related to blowouts than in the Gulf Coast because of Santa Barbara's deeper water, greater density of faults and fissures, greater tectonic activity, and paucity of subsurface geologic knowledge."

Even if the city should be preternaturally lucky and have no further blowouts, it faces an alarming future. This is earthquake country. In the summer of 1968, University of California scientists reported sixty-six earthquakes epicentered in the Santa Barbara Channel. Geologists have repeatedly warned of the danger of earthquake ruptures or tidal waves releasing undreamed of spills of crude oil. Arthur L. Sylvester of the University of California recalled an 1812 tidal wave in the channel that reached the height of 50 feet. "One big quake," added Curry, "—and one is coming—and we might have to write off the southern California coast as a total loss for decades thereafter."

Too bad, the Department of Interior says, in effect, as it authorizes more platforms and further drilling. Perhaps we should not have sold leases in the Santa Barbara Channel—former Secretary of the Interior Stewart Udall now admits that it was a serious mistake, "a conservation Bay of Pigs"—but once done the mistake cannot be undone. The oil companies own the leases, says the Department of Interior, and it would be uneconomic to buy them back. But we'll protect Santa Barbara by tightening up the drilling regulations.

Unfortunately, as Santa Barbarans know, their earthquake-faulted channel does not always obey government regulations. They see their environment and ecology threatened with destruction. They are determined to resist this, even if it means, as it does, changing the policy of the United States Government.

The resistance movement has radicalized the community. Militant citizens have sat down in front of oil trucks, picketed their oil-tinged chamber of commerce, and persuaded their county supervisors and city council to obey an "eleventh commandment." This commandment, according to its author, the Santa Barbara historian Roderick Nash, is "an extension of ethics to include man's relationship to his environment: Thou shalt not abuse the earth."

Nash presented his eleventh commandment in a lay sermon. It gave the aroused community an ideology and a creed and attracted national attention.

Concerned people throughout the country have become aware that the Santa Barbara spill and its aftermath are setting a national precedent for good or ill. George B. Hartzog, Jr., director of the National Park Service, said: "In the recent disastrous oil incident at Santa Barbara, the wide acceptance of the idea that the ecological consequences far outweighed the economic implications suggests that ecology has finally achieved currency."

The stakes are high, both locally and nationally. The Santa Barbara environment, with its public beaches and parks, its civilized amenities and its natural attractions, has some claim to be treated as a natural resource. Two of the offshore islands are national monuments, and five of them have been proposed for inclusion in a new national park. Bills to create this park and, complementing it, a channel marine sanctuary and undersea wilderness area have been introduced in Congress. Hundreds of thousands of people annually have been accustomed to use the channel and its shores for swimming, boating, fishing, bird-watching, and skin-diving.

Over against these people and their interests, and over against Santa Barbara and its sister communities, is balanced the rather large fact that the channel happens to cover one of the richest oil fields in the world, adjacent to one of the richest and most oil-hungry markets in the world. With its superabundance of automobiles, industrial complexes, and airports, California probably uses more gasoline and oil per capita than any other comparable area.

It is also an oil-producing and oil-refining state, and one in which the oil industry has great economic and political power. Oil has been pumped out of the ground near Santa Barbara since the beginning of this century. On the beach and tidelands off the nearby town of Summerland, the state government is still spending scores of thousands of dollars cleaning up the filth and wreckage left in the wake of an oil strike which occurred before World War I.

The first major modern breach in the Santa Barbara Channel "sanctuary" occurred in the early 1950's, when the state of California opened to leasing some of the offshore tidelands it controls. These state tidelands extend offshore to the three-mile limit; the federal government controls most of the rest of the 25-mile-wide channel; local governments have no jurisdiction in the channel, as a seagoing local judge learned when he was sprayed with a hose for venturing too near to Platform A.

Partly because they were drilled in shallow water and more stable formations and partly because California state drilling regulations were tougher than federal, the oil wells in the state tidelands have caused no major spills. State leases are in any case a diminishing threat. Their oil is almost exhausted. Their wells are being phased out, and the platforms will be removed.

Their very presence, of course, encouraged offshore exploration for oil in federal waters—exploration which apparently located an immensely rich oil pool. The prospect that this pool might be drained by the wells in the state tidelands was one reason the federal government decided to open up the offshore field beyond the three-mile limit.

The oil companies which explored the channel field have not released estimates of the oil reserves they found. Some observers think it is at least as rich as the billion-barrel Ventura Avenue field on the mainland of neighboring Ventura County. At current prices, each barrel pumped is worth about $3.50 at the wellhead. The oil companies' judgment of the value of the field can best be measured by the approximate $100 million they spent on exploratory development before February 6, 1968, when they paid the federal government $603,204,284, a record sum surpassed only by the recent lease auction in Alaska. The United States Treasury is being paid additional royalties at the rate of one-sixth field price a barrel of oil produced and is looking forward to receiving more.

Both government and industry take the position that oil production and local environmental values can be made compatible. Santa Barbara and its allies, nationwide, take the position that here, if anywhere, oil and environmental values are incompatible. So the battle lines have been drawn.

It was late in the day for the people of Santa Barbara to take a stand. Supervisor George Clyde, the impassioned and scholarly Santa Barbara County official who has fought the oil invasion most effectively, recently admitted that the Board of Supervisors should have taken a stronger anti-oil position prior to the fall of 1967. It was then that the Department of Interior abandoned its long-term policy of protecting the channel and announced its intention of selling oil leases there.

Encouraged by a citizen protest led by Fred Eissler of the Sierra Club, the supervisors took some delaying action. They asked then Secretary of the Interior Udall to give some time for study. Udall granted forty-five days, but was under Budget Bureau pressure and impatient of further delay. As the supervisors were still trying to persuade the government to grant them a public hearing the first oil platform was at sea and on its way to the channel.

Eissler is a tall, raw-boned Santa Barbara high school teacher. As a national director of the Sierra Club, he had corresponded with Secretary Udall while the latter prepared to make his decision on the fate of the Santa Barbara Channel. Afterward, Eissler revealed how the secretary and his aides arrived at their decision.

Eissler produced copies of two memos written by Stanley A. Cain, a botanist and ecologist who was Udall's assistant secretary for fish, wildlife, and parks. Cain's first memo (August 7, 1967) argued in favor of making the Santa Barbara Channel a marine sanctuary. But within a few days, after discussions with the Budget Bureau and with J. Cordell More, Udall's assistant secretary in charge of mineral resources, Cain went over to the other side.

The overriding consideration appears to have been financial. Lease money from the Santa Barbara Channel would help to balance the budget. Cain's second memo indicates that the decision was made in favor of oil platforms in the channel with little or no concern for the local consequences. He wrote, for example, that the platforms would stand at least five miles offshore, and that this "would certainly reduce the platforms' visibility from land to negligibility." The oil rigs, as Santa Barbara quickly learned, are about as high and approximately as invisible as twenty-story skyscrapers.

The attitude of the Interior Department bureaucracy was typified by one of its higher officials, Eugene W. Standley, who successfully opposed the request for a public hearing on the grounds that it would "stir up the natives." Standley, by a kind of poetic justice, was placed in charge of channel oil operations after the January 28 disaster.

One of the stirred-up natives was an artist named James Bottoms. He had first campaigned against the oil platforms because they spoiled the view. He went into high gear when the spill occurred, saying to his friend and boss, Marvin H. Stuart: "We've got to get oil out!"

Stuart, who is a public-relations expert, said: "That's it! GOO, for 'get oil out.' "

Bottoms and Stuart made plans for a mass organization named GOO. They enlisted former state senator Al Weingand, who assumed active leadership of GOO. At a public rally on the beach, Weingand attacked the government for selling out Santa Barbara. He reminded his hearers of a time, several years before, when he had flown over the channel with Secretary Udall and they had talked about creating a Channel Islands National Park. Udall promised to protect the channel against oil pollution. "No oil leases will be granted," he had said, "except under conditions that will protect your environment."

The hopes of the opposition got a lift on March 21 when President Nixon visited the city. Conceivably the President had read a letter sent to him by a serious-minded Santa Barbara boy, aged fourteen:

"Because of my age I am disqualified from voting for those public officials who could best represent my future needs: to wit: fresh air, a place to grow, sweet water to drink, and perhaps a consideration for progeny of my own . . . Santa Barbara, in fact any seaside city, must be considered as a place of the future for all of us, not none of us."

The President landed by helicopter on the specially cleaned beach and got his feet wet in the oily surf. Thousands of citizens, kept at a distance by stringent security measures, chanted: "Get Oil Out!" and displayed such signs as "Visit Santa Barbara's Dead Sea: A Project of Your Federal Government." Informed by Mayor Gerald Firestone that the city was opposed to all drilling in the channel, Mr. Nixon replied that he could understand that point of view, and later said publicly: "I shall, of course, consider this proposal."

The President is presumably still considering it. As the spill continued and the federal and state governments watched from a distance, this conservative community, which had voted solid majorities to both President Nixon and Governor Reagan, began to show signs of political restlessness. One source of discontent was the condition of Stearns Wharf, a city-owned structure that for nearly one hundred years had been a shipping base and a tourist center. The wharf had been leased by the city to a company headed by restaurant owner George V. Castagnola and it was being used as a service facility for the offshore oil wells. Night and day, its ancient timbers groaned and rattled under the wheels of company trucks.

On Easter Sunday a mass meeting of perhaps a thousand people, young and old, was held on the beach near the foot of Stearns Wharf. A number of citizens spoke. "Other Americans may not realize it but we are fighting their battles too" (conservationist W. H. Ferry). "To expel the invaders we must act now and vigorously, or our unique ecological syndrome will disappear, and Santa Barbara will become a second-rate town" (Dr. Thomas Bouchard, professor of psychology). "It is naked power which places man second in importance. This I believe is immoral" (Bishop C. Edward Crowther). "We need a new politics—the politics of ecology—based on reverence for the land and reverence for man" (Fred Eissler). "What we need is an environmental-rights movement along with a civil-rights movement. The chief obstacles to corrective action are apathy of citizens and the fantastic interwining of the oil industry with nearly all aspects of our society" (Dr. Norman K. Sanders, professor of geography and environmental science).

At the end of the meeting nearly half the crowd, spurred on by more militant speakers, marched out onto Stearns Wharf and took peaceful possession of the oil facilities. Among them were Macdonald, the co-author of this article, and his wife, carrying homemade signs: "Ban the Blob," "Let's Lose the Ooze." Exhilaration was tempered by the fear that violence could erupt. The fear was heightened when a large truck loaded with new oil casings rolled out onto the wharf behind us.

A number of young people led by a nationally known scholar sat down in front of the truck and forced it to stop. The driver climbed down from his cab and picked up a piece of iron for use as a weapon. Then he changed his mind and dropped it. The bloodless confrontation was kept that way by local policemen, who ordered the driver to back his truck off the wharf.

The symbolic victory was followed up by a group of seventy-four citizens, headed by a politically conservative painting contractor named John Schaaf, and including Macdonald and his wife, who picketed the wharf for fifteen days. We had only begun to nibble at the edges of the problem: the continuing spill in the channel and the continuing threat of the oil rigs there; the large investment behind them, roughly a billion dollars by now; the federal government guaranteeing the investment. But as late as the first day of June most of us still believed that the President's professions of concern for Santa Barbara would be made good.

With tax reform in the air, we believed, the Administration might move to reduce the 27½ percent oil-depletion allowance—one of the special subsidies to the oil industry which, according to Santa Barbara economist Walter J. Mead, made ultra-costly and essentially uneconomic operations, like those in the channel, profitable.

Mead, president of the Western Economics Association, is a recognized authority on the economics of the oil industry. He said emphatically that "under free market conditions there would be no oil drilling in the Santa Barbara Channel." Without the special benefits that they receive under our tax and import laws, the oil companies pumping Santa Barbara Channel oil could not compete with other sources.

We hoped that the oil companies themselves, having experienced the cost of enforced shutdowns (estimated at as much as $300,000 a day), and faced with further possible costs by Secretary Hickel's new requirement of "absolute liability" for pollution damage, might decide that the channel leases were a bad bargain. Anticipating this possibility, Representative Charles M. Teague had proposed a swap in which the channel oil leases could be traded for leases in the Elk Hills federal oil reserve in nearby Kern County.

But on the second day of June, the Administration squelched these hopes and prospects. A panel of scientists and engineers, appointed at the President's request by his science adviser, Lee DuBridge, recommended that the best way to stop the leakage, then in its 127th day, was to drill more wells and pump out the underlying oil. A panel spokesman said this would take ten to twenty years.

In Santa Barbara's view, these findings, already approved by DuBridge and the President, gave a green light to further exploitation of the channel and were evidently intended to do so. They arrayed the federal government squarely on the side of the oil industry and brought into the open the undeclared war between the government and its South Coast citizens, which now threatened to go on for our lifetime. Mayor Firestone, who is slow to anger, said: They (the drillers) "might be out there for a thousand years trying to take all the oil out."

Santa Barbarans were particularly disturbed by the fact that the DuBridge panel reached its decisions in secret. Only government and oil industry witnesses were invited to testify, and what they said was not revealed.

Opposition was never stronger than in the days following the government's new decision. Organized by GOO and brilliantly chaired by Al Weingand, a public rally was held on June 8 in La Playa Stadium; 1,500 people gathered in the stands overlooking the polluted harbor and listened to a series of fighting speeches.

Weingand and others called on the government to reveal the evidence on which the DuBridge panel had based its report—evidence that apparently came almost entirely from Union Oil and other industry sources and was, therefore, considered proprietary and secret. Other scientists, as Norman Sanders pointed out, could not even form an opinion without access to the factual basis of the panel's deliberations. Fred Eissler said, "Our geologists should have the opportunity of reviewing all of the data gathered and of cross-examining the geologists who appeared before the panel. The decision should be openly arrived at."

There were repeated demands that the government implement Representative Teague's idea and trade the leases in the channel for leases in the Elk Hills federal reserve. This is regarded by many Santa Barbarans as their best hope for relief. But some of their most thoughtful leaders, Supervisor Clyde among them, say that it may take another oil disaster in the channel to alert the government to the need for such action. By that time, they say, it may be too late for Santa Barbara, but not too late, perhaps, to save the rest of the southern California coast.

The most disturbing speech at the rally, and the most applauded, was delivered by Alan Cranston, the junior senator from

California, who had introduced a bill against further channel drilling. Cranston's bill had been stalled in the Senate, as Representative Teague's companion bill had been stalled in the House. The senator told his audience that before they could expect help from Washington they must get it from Sacramento. Until the state government banned drilling in the tidelands, which it controlled—i.e., within the three-mile limit—legislation banning it in federal waters would have no chance.

An extemporaneous local speaker who followed Senator Cranston brought the issues even closer to home: "When our city wharf is being used by the oil companies as a staging area for their offshore operations, how can we honestly ask either Sacramento or Washington for help?" Accepting the idea, the recently elected City Council voted to regain control of Stearns Wharf. It then killed a harbor expansion plan that would have vastly increased the *Lebensraum* for service operations to the oil industry.

The state government in Sacramento was showered with letters and telegrams and descended upon by a delegation headed by Lois Sidenberg of GOO, who had earlier delivered to the U.S. Senate anti-oil petitions carrying 100,000 signatures. A drilling ban was voted down by the industry-oriented finance committee of the State Senate. But a more independent body, the State Lands Commission, ruled decisively against further drilling in the state tidelands.

As Santa Barbara redoubled its grass-roots efforts, outside interest in the city and its survival was renewed. A man from the Ford Foundation studied our citizen movement. The Santa Barbara *News-Press* was joined in its editorial criticism of the DuBridge panel's recommendations by the Los Angeles *Times* and *The New York Times*.

But the Department of Interior, without adducing further evidence, authorized Union Oil to drill more wells in the area of the lease as a step toward reducing underlying pressure. Union proceeded to drill fifteen such wells and pump crude oil reportedly worth over $30,000 a day. Meanwhile, Secretary Hickel traveled about the country fulminating against polluted water.

Community resistance continued to mount. In the early months of the spill, a group of scientists and writers formed a committee intended to seek relief through public education and legal action. It was later incorporated as Santa Barbara Citizens for Environmental Defense.

SBCED was not alone in looking for legal relief. A leading local law firm had announced a private "class" suit seeking damages of $1.3 billion from Union Oil and its partners in the Platform A operation, Mobil Oil, Gulf Oil, and Texaco. Public suits are being brought by the state of California and the county of Santa Barbara. The county suit has been supported by SBCED both with money ($4,500 raised mostly by women of the Audubon Society) and in the difficult task of finding expert witnesses willing to stand up and testify against the oil companies.

Recently, SBCED and GOO cooperated in getting the legal services of the American Civil Liberties Union attorneys. On July 10, A. L. Wirin and Fred Okrand of the ACLU filed a suit in federal court on behalf of seventeen plaintiffs headed by Weingand and Norman Sanders, and including co-authors Macdonald and Easton. We claimed that our rights to a decent environment had been impaired by Secretary Hickel and his aides, and by the oil companies, and that this was done without due process of law.

The complaint in *Weingand v. Hickel* alleged that the government's decision to resume drilling in the channel had been reached in secret, without granting a hearing to the plaintiffs, and without due process had infringed their personal and property rights. A new concept of basic human rights was stated: "The personal right is the right to live in, and enjoy, an environment free from improvident destruction or pollution. The property right is the right to ownership, use and enjoyment of property, free from improvident invasion or impairment."

The plaintiffs asked for a temporary injunction against oil drilling in the federal waters while their case was being considered. On August 11 a federal district judge in Los Angeles denied their request. Wirin, a gray-bearded man of seventy with a vigorous, questioning mind, promptly appealed. He also obtained a hearing before a three-man federal court challenging the constitutionality of the Outer Continental Shelf Act under which oil development leases are granted without public hearings. The "natives" were finally getting their day in court.

At the same time the oil industry continued to protest that Secretary Hickel's new drilling regulations were too tough. The secretary proceeded to soften them and to modify the clause calling for "absolute liability" for polllution damage. Hickel gave some indication that the ACLU suit and other protests were having an effect by moving toward the Santa Barbara position. He "authorized" but did not require public hearings before new leases were granted. Despite oil-industry objections, he required the leasing agency, the Bureau of Land Management, to "evaluate the effect of the leasing program on the total environment, aquatic resources, esthetics and other resources."

The Santa Barbara Channel was placed in a special category, requiring special safeguards and leasing on a case-by-case basis. Although this seemed to be an admission of hazardous drilling conditions—ocean-floor leakage in the vicinity of Platform A, still flowing at the rate of hundreds of gallons a day, and smaller spills from other wells new and old—there was no apparent alteration in government-industry plans to convert the whole channel into a vast oil field.

On September 17 it was reported that the Department of Interior had authorized "massive" and "unrestricted" drilling in the channel. This was denied by William T. Pecora, head of the U.S. Geological Survey. But the truth of the report was attested by an affidavit filed in federal court by John R. Fraser, vice president of Union Oil, in connection with the suit of *Weingand v. Hickel*.

There is still hope that Congress or the courts will move to protect Santa Barbara and its channel. Sooner or later, the principle of the right to an environment unimpaired by improvident destruction will become part of our enforceable law. But it may come too late to save Santa Barbara. Then the best the city can do is to serve as an example of how something beautiful can be destroyed.

Our Arctic Will Never Be the Same: That Unstoppable Pipeline
BY THOMAS M. BROWN

Prudhoe Bay, Alaska. Summer flared abruptly as May became June on America's remote and wild northern rim. The thick ice on the rivers went out with a squealing roar audible for miles. The great herds of caribou funneled up through the precipitous passes of the spiny Brooks Range to the south, following the retreating snow to summer feeding and calving grounds on the North Slope. The unsetting summer sun soared and dipped in the crystal sky, often obscured by dank fogs from the Beaufort Sea and the thin cold rain. But slowly the sun burned through the ice of the countless lakes that riddle the flat, boggy land and the lakes bred billions of buzzing mosquitoes. Wild flowers bloomed, giving the dun tundra a flush of color. Soon the waterfowl returned, ducks and geese in small dark clouds against the sky and white swans in pairs. At the sea's edge the division between land and water, often imperceptible to the untrained eye in the white wilderness of winter, became clear: The pack ice withdrew sullenly from the shore, revealing the brooding black water

From *The New York Times Magazine,* October 14, 1973.
Copyright © 1973 by The New York Times Company.
Reprinted by permission.

below. But the ice was always there, just on the horizon, and even on the warmest days, when the thermometer nudged the sixties, the merest breeze was chill with winter.

Beneath it all, 6,000 to 10,000 feet down, lay the oil, the largest field ever found in North America—24 billion barrels of high-quality crude, 9.6 billion barrels of it recoverable, according to conservative industry estimates. The pressure mounted steadily to get it out. For if it was a summer much like any other on the North Slope, it wasn't in Washington.

There it was the first full summer of what the petroleum industry likes to call the energy crisis. Demand for gasoline, fuel oil, and natural gas outstripped supply. An open gas station at night or on Sunday was rare. Several hundred independent gas stations went broke. Motorists worried about whether they would be able to get home from vacations. Congressional mail heated up. Senator Henry M. Jackson, the Democrat from the state of Washington who heads the Senate Interior Committee, called the energy shortage the most serious problem, domestic or foreign, facing the nation.

After the Fourth of July recess, Congress debated the best way to get at the oil during a week of sweltering weather, which strained power supplies and led Senator John O. Pastore, Democrat of Rhode Island, to complain that something had to be done because "even now in the corridors we are dimming the lights so that the Capitol Building looks more like a nightclub than the Congress of the United States." Under intense pressure from the energy lobby, the Nixon Administration, and the state of Alaska, both houses passed bills authorizing oil industry construction of a 789-mile pipeline from Prudhoe Bay to the ice-free port of Valdez on Alaska's south-central coast at an estimated cost of $3.6 billion (a figure the industry said was growing $500,000 daily because of inflation). As this article went to press, the prospect was for early agreement on a compromise bill drawn in conference, a bill that is certain to be signed by President Nixon. And when summer comes again to the North Slope, work likely will be under way on one of the most controversial industrial projects in the nation's history.

Unfortunately, construction will begin without the nation's having confronted, much less answered, one of two critical questions about the project: Should a pipeline be built at all? Though the fate of much of the last major wilderness in the United States is at stake, that question was overwhelmed by the momentum of events—particularly industry's vast investment (now $2.5 billion) in the slope, committeed before the advisability of rapid development could be explored. J. H. Galloway of Exxon set it out prophetically in 1969, shortly after the pipeline was first proposed, at a time when conservationists still were mobilizing to question the implications of Arctic oil development.

"The Arctic world of nature as it has been evolving for millions of years doesn't need man, doesn't need you or me in order to get along," Galloway said. "But we need it. The world needs it and in the scheme of things as men and nations move, the oil is going to be extracted, and some of the country hitherto unmolested is going to be torn up in the process. Let's not fool ourselves; this activity is already far past the point of return."

The industry's determination to plunge ahead, coupled with the nation's deteriorating energy outlook, probably made it inevitable that development of the North Slope would proceed without adequate consideration of all environmental questions. The Senate Interior Committee noted in its report on pipeline legislation that during hearings "no witness seriously proposed that it would be in the national interest to postpone the development of Alaska Arctic oil and gas indefinitely. The relative lack of controversy over this issue is in contrast to previous hearings before this and other committees, and reflects rapidly changing public perceptions of the nation's energy needs."

So by the time Congress took up the pipeline question the environment was largely forgotten, and Congressional focus had shifted to the second major question: What is the best pipeline route to get the oil out?

Again there was controversy, but again the question was answered to industry's satisfaction, overwhelmed this time by the seeming urgency of the energy crisis. Thornton F. Bradshaw, president of Atlantic Richfield Company (ARCO), told the Senate Interior Committee that this summer's sporadic gasoline shortages "are just a tip of the iceberg and the iceberg itself is very massive indeed. The body of this iceberg will hit this nation in five years or within five years. This is where the Alaskan oil can help this nation if the pipeline is started now. If it is not started now, the enormous size of this iceberg bearing down on us may be too much for our children to handle." So Congress acted—though neither it nor the executive branch had ever seriously studied the proposed alternative route through Canada to the Midwest.

If the nation was much worried about the land and the animals, there was little evidence of it. And while Midwesterners in both houses pushed hard for at least a comprehensive examination of a pipeline through Canada, they were handily defeated by the trans-Alaska forces.

Environmental trouble on the North Slope began during World War II when modern man first invaded the far north in large numbers with tracked vehicles. The Navy dispatched crews to the enormous 26-million-acre Naval Petroleum Reserve No. 4 (commonly referred to as Pet 4) west of Prudhoe Bay to search for oil in the event of a prolonged war.

Thirty-seven test wells indicated promising geological structures and the Navy estimated that 15 billion barrels of recoverable oil ought to be there. The experience also taught a costly lesson about the Arctic tundra: When damaged, it heals slowly, if at all, because of the lack of sunshine.

The sun is the ultimate source of all energy for living things and the Arctic gets little of it, even in summer when its unsetting rays strike at a low angle, diluted by the earth's atmosphere. The relatively few species of plants—lichens, sedgers, dwarf shrubs, and flowers—which can endure the harsh climate typically take several years to reach maturity at a few inches of height. Animals get their energy second-hand from plants, so low plant productivity means there is relatively little energy available for plant-eating animals such as the caribou. In turn, there are relatively few plant-eaters for meat-eating predators, such as the wolf, to prey upon. Beneath the thin mat of insulating vegetation lies permafrost, a catchall term applied to any subsurface material constantly frozen for two or more years. Some permafrost is solid rock or well-drained gravel and poses no unusual construction problems. But much of it in Alaska is the "ice-rich" type—silt with a high frozen water content. When melted, it becomes an unstable soup.

The Navy crews wandered all over Pet 4 aboard bulldozers and smaller tracked vehicles, pulling their supplies behind on sleds, chewing up the tundra. The permafrost below melted and slumped, and bulldozer tracks grdually became water-filled ditches, eroding the land and changing its character over wide areas in ways still plainly visible today. The crews dumped garbage and broken equipment with abandon, and since deterioration is exceedingly slow in the Arctic, the litter is still there, too: oil drums and rusting machinery strewn in unsightly heaps across the tundra.

Many of the same mistakes were repeated in 1968–69 during the rush to explore the rest of the North Slope after ARCO made its historic strike at Prudhoe Bay. Seismic exploration crews roamed the slope from the coast to the Brooks Range foothills, chewing up the turf and leaving a trail of garbage, oil drums, powder boxes, and detonating wire. One bored driver for Geophysical Services, Inc., carved his company's initials indelibly into the tundra with his bulldozer blade in 200-foot letters—Arctic graffiti it may take nature centuries to erase. Drilling rigs were dragged across the tundra, gouging out ruts that have eroded further each summer. Temporary winter airstrips were carved into the land. Pits were bulldozed for sewage, and drilling mud, and garbage.

The result, according to the congressional testimony of Dr. Tom Cade, research director for Cornell University's ornithology laboratory, was that "except in some of the mountain fastnesses of the Brooks Range, I doubt that one can find a 100-square-mile plot of ground east of the Colville River—including the Arctic Wildlife Range—that does not show some irreparable sign of man's activities."

Under pressure from conservation groups, the oil companies quickly began to mend their ways, however. After disastrous experience with winter trails across the tundra, they began to build permanent roads of gravel 5 feet thick to insulate the tundra in summer and prevent the melting of the permafrost. Extensive experiments in revegetating damaged tundra were begun. Junk left on the tundra by seismic crews was collected. Countless thousands of oil drums, the most prevalent litter in the Arctic, were shipped out. Work camps and supply dumps were made spotless and kept that way. To keep drilling sites—and costs—down, development wells were drilled in neat rows through gravel pads, six wells to a pad, spaced 100 feet apart and angled down through the 2,000-foot-thick permafrost to the hot oil below in such a way that each pad served 3,800 acres. The result was impressive indeed, an industrial development that even environmentalist opponents readily conceded would have been difficult to improve upon.

But conservationists remain concerned because much damage was done in the initial exploratory rush, because even the best development practices leave their marks and because the pipeline will drive through the heart of one of the nation's last remaining wildernesses—the Brooks Range and the relatively small amount of land that remains untouched on the North Slope.

The Brooks Range is a closely packed jumble of imposing peaks of incredible variety, harboring scenery of unsurpassed splendor: tranquil sheltered valleys, brilliant green lakes, towering waterfalls with sheer drops of 1,000 feet, clear icy streams quick with white water and the silver shapes of char, grayling, and trout. Perhaps two hundred persons inhabit this vast wilderness, most of them concentrated at Anaktuvuk Pass, the last remaining inland Eskimo village in Northern Alaska.

From the peaks, the land rolls north until it reaches the Arctic coast, a distance that varies from 40 to 150 miles. Near the foothills, the land is rolling, hummocky, scored by rivers and streams, well-drained and dry in summer. Moving north, the hills dwindle and the rivers lose grade, looping and winding in serpentine coils through the lake-dotted coastal plain toward the sea, where they fan into wide deltas braided with gravel. The most plentiful large animal is the caribou, which numbers about 400,000 in two major herds, the Arctic and the Porcupine. The North Slope also supports lemmings, arctic foxes, wolves, wolverines, and a few barren-ground grizzlies, and provides breeding or molting areas for millions of migratory waterfowl. Some moose browse in protected valleys in the foothills, where the willow stands are tall enough to afford cover. Perhaps half the world's population of curly horned Dall sheep inhabit the crags of the Brooks Range. Polar bears prowl the offshore ice north of the slope.

The climate is brutal. Winter utterly dominates the land and its inhabitants. Spring and fall do not exist and the summers are brief, bright, and damp; it can snow in July. From late September into

May the land is blanketed with snow. For fifty-six days at Prudhoe Bay the sun never edges above the horizon; day is a pastel stain in the southern sky. Arctic storms can rage for days, and when the wind howls, "whiteouts" of blowing snow reduce visibility to a few feet. The temperature can drop to 65 below zero and sometimes does; almost always it is below zero from November through mid-April.

The list of potential disasters that oil development poses to this peculiarly vulnerable environment is lengthy and fearsome. Since North Slope oil will move through the pipeline at a temperature of 140 degrees, environmentalists fear the permafrost may be disrupted, threatening the structural stability of the pipeline, which could spill as much as 90,000 barrels of oil in a major break. Game specialists worry that the pipeline, which will be built aboveground over half its length in an attempt to minimize permafrost hazards, could form a barrier to caribou migrations with unforeseen, but probably harmful, consequences. Experiments seeking to determine the effect of the planned aboveground segments on the movements of the caribou so far have proved inconclusive.

The pipeline route crosses the Denali Fault, where some of Alaska's major earthquakes are born. From Valdez, the oil will have to travel 2,000 miles in tankers, posing the threat of spills at sea. And the state government insists that a gravel road, which will be built north from the Yukon River through the Brooks Range to the slope as a necessary adjunct to pipeline construction, conform to secondary highway standards. Governor William A. Egan says the road will be developed as an "Arctic wilderness parkway" whose users will be subject to "regulation for the protection of flora and fauna similar to that imposed on visitors to national parks." Nevertheless, it will be the first permanent road into a wilderness now accessible only by air (a trail plowed through the Brooks Range in 1968–69 by Governor Walter J. Hickel and in 1970–71 by Governor Keith H. Miller for winter use was an environmental and economic fiasco).

Unless the state does a much better job of regulation than its record makes likely, the road will open much easily scarred, slow-healing tundra land to abuse by four-wheel-drive and all-terrain vehicles. It will expose major game populations to vastly increased hunting pressure. It will be a scenic eyesore ("Eight hundred more miles of ditches for people to throw beer cans in," former State Senate President Jay Hammond once described it). And it will expose above-ground sections of the line to the threat of armor-piercing rifle bullets or other vandalism—no insubstantial threat in a state where most road signs have been riddled to near illegibility.

The oil industry has moved on a number of fronts to convince critics of the environmental soundness of the pipeline. As initially proposed, the Trans Alaska Pipeline System (which immediately became known by an unfortunate acronym, TAPS) was to have a capacity of 600,000 barrels per day and to cost an estimated $900 million. Construction time was to be three years, with oil flowing in 1972. As more became known about the size of the Prudhoe Bay reservoir, additional pumping stations were added to the design, raising its capacity to 2 million barrels per day and its cost to about $1.5 billion. Since then, the cost has climbed to the present estimate of $3.6 billion. Much of the increase is due to inflation, but a spokesman for Alyeska Pipeline Service Company, TAPS's successor, estimates that $500 million of the increase was directly attributable to design changes made in the interest of environmental safety.

Chief among the changes was the decision to construct about half the line aboveground (the original design had called for up to 95 percent of it to be buried) in order to lessen permafrost problems and to install many more valves to minimize oil spills in case of pipeline leaks or complete ruptures.

Industry-supported research indicates the pipeline route generally parallels the migration route of the Arctic herd of caribou, posing less of a problem than if the line crossed the caribou route repeatedly. Aboveground sections of the line will be equipped with underpassses and ramps for the animals, though whether they will use them remains problematic.

Alyeska says the line has been designed to withstand earthquakes up to 8.5 on the Richter scale with some structural damage—but without structural failure, which would cause major spills. They point out that a trans-Andes pipeline has survived numerous earthquakes, and that there were no serious pipeline breaks reported in the major quake in the Los Angeles area in 1971.

The tanker terminal at Valdez will be located on bedrock as a protection against earthquakes, and the tank farm, with its enormous storage capacity of 20 million barrels of crude, will be surrounded by 35-foot dikes to contain any spills. There will be a modern treatment facility to lower the oil-content in tanker ballast to no more than ten parts per million before the water is pumped into Valdez Arm, the 3-mile-wide inlet of Prince William Sound.

Since the Jones Act requires that American-built ships be used between American ports, tankers on the West Coast run will be modern vessels constructed in United States yards and subject to United States regulations, preventing the use of foreign vessels, which are responsible for many offshore oil spills. In addition, the Senate pipeline bill contained an amendment requiring that all new American tankers be built with double hulls as a further protection against spills; also, legislation is pending that would require tankers to be equipped with an ultramodern guidance system similar to that used by Apollo spacecraft.

Proponents of the trans-Alaska line are fond of calling it the most-studied, best-engineered project of its type in the nation's history. They also like to compare the effect of the pipeline on Alaska's vast area to that of a string across a golf course or a backyard—depending on the audience—a specious comparison, which environmentalists dismiss by saying it would be more "like cutting a knife wound through living flesh."

It is, of course, true that the pipeline itself will occupy only a tiny strip of Alaska's vast mass. But the real concern has never been limited strictly to the tactical question of construction and operation of a hollow tube of half-inch steel (though it alone poses serious environmental problems). Rather, fears have centered on the whole strategic happening: pipeline and road construction, the threat of oil pollution on both land and water, the possible interruption of game movements and the certainty of increased pressure on wilderness land and on animal species, both of which are particularly vulnerable. The question is not just whether the North Slope, much of which is already a mess, will be further damaged, but whether large areas of the mostly untouched Brooks Range will be needlessly scarred; not just whether the pipeline might crack in an earthquake, causing slight or major damage to the surrounding landscape depending on where it occurred, but whether the caribou will go the way of the buffalo.

These are hard questions and the answers to them are by no means certain. There is no doubt that the trans-Alaska pipeline design is much safer now than it was when first proposed in 1969. Nor is there any doubt now of the oil industry's goodwill in attempting to protect the environment. But whether serious environmental questions can be successfully disposed of by congressional passage of a bill declaring them settled remains to be seen.

Oil and natural gas fulfill about 75 percent of the nation's energy requirements. The United States used to produce all the oil and natural gas it could use, but that has changed drastically since the late 1960's—a result in large part of the use of ever more automobiles getting ever worse gasoline mileage. In addition, domestic crude oil production has begun a gradual decline as major fields have passed their peak productivity. Natural gas has grown scarce because of increased demand for clean-burning fuel to replace such previous energy sources as high-sulfur coal—and, the industry says, decreased exploration for new supplies because of artificially low gas prices imposed by the Federal Power Commission.

Crude oil consumption currently is about 17 million barrels a day, more than a third of them imported. By 1980, consumption is predicted to reach 24 million barrels a day, perhaps half of it coming from foreign sources. As much as 35 percent of consumption, according to State Department estimates, will come from the Middle East—if the Arabs are willing to supply it.

Whether they will be or not depends largely on King Faisal of Saudi Arabia, who controls an incredible 150 billion barrels of oil, four times as much as America's entire proven reserves, including Prudhoe Bay. Saudi Arabia could more than triple its production from the 6 million barrels per day by 1980. Politics rather than economics probably will determine whether Faisal will decide to do so, because his kingdom already receives more income from its oil than it can reasonably spend. Thus, the Saudis are hinting that further major increases in production may hinge on a substantial shift in Washington's policy toward Israel. "The United States stands behind Israel but gains nothing from the support of Israel, which is a burden," Faisal told two American newsmen in an interview last summer. "The real interest of the United States in this region is to cooperate with the Arabs."

Having to choose between chronic major petroleum shortages and a major change in policy toward an embattled ally with which the United States has such close ties would, if it came to that, be a nightmare for any national administration; hence the urgency to produce North Slope oil. The tapping of Prudhoe Bay, of course, will not reverse the trend toward increasing dependence on foreign oil; it would take a dozen such fields, very rapid development of other energy sources, or a major change in the America life-style to do that. Nonetheless, 2 million barrels per day will be a substantial addition to domestic production—enough to maintain the country's production level at the current 10 million to 11 million barrels per day, preventing import dependence from becoming worse as other American fields decline. The 26 trillion cubic feet of natural gas in the reservoir with the oil can provide the energy equivalent of about another million barrels of oil per day, helping to reduce demand for fuel oil by providing an alternative energy source.

After ARCO struck oil at Prudhoe Bay in February 1968 and confirmed the find with a second well drilled 7 miles away that spring, there were numerous proposals for getting the oil out, including railroads, giant aerial tankers, and nuclear-powered submarine tankers. Exxon spent $50 million converting the 115,000-ton tanker Manhattan into a giant icebreaker and sending it through the Northwest Passage for two summers, before concluding the project was financially unfeasible.

Gradually, the controversy settled down to which of two pipelines would be best—trans-Alaska or trans-Canada. Environmentalists contended a trans-Canada route would be superior environmentally, primarily because it would eliminate the tanker leg and because a gas pipeline to the Midwest could be built in the same corridor, minimizing environmental damage. The Interior Department's massive nine-volume environmental impact statement concluded that neither route was clearly superior from an environmental standpoint, as each had advantages and drawbacks. The main problem in making an environmental judgment was that not enough specific information was available about soil conditions and animal populations along the Canadian route. So as the energy pinch aroused increasing concern, the argument shifted to the economics of the two routes.

The basic economic issue was this: Should the oil go to the West Coast, where 25 percent of the population lives, which is more nearly self-sufficient in petroleum than any other part of the country, and which might have a crude oil surplus during the early years of pipeline operation? The West Coast also has the nation's major potential for new oil fields onshore, in parts of Alaska that are as yet unexplored, and offshore, in the Gulf of Alaska and California's Santa Barbara Channel.

Or should the oil go to the Midwest, where it would be available to the 75 percent of the population that lives east of the Rocky Mountains, an area of chronic petroleum shortages where prices are substantially higher than on the West Coast, and where prospects for major new petroleum finds are substantially less?

Though the trans-Canada route had a number of seemingly sound economic arguments to support it, it had one decisive drawback: delay. The Senate Interior Committee found that consideration "compelling," saying: "Regardless of whether the 1969 decision of the owner companies in favor of an all-Alaska route was the wisest or the most consistent with the national interest at that time, and regardless of whether the Administration's early commitment in favor of that route was made on the basis of adequate information and analysis, the committee determined that the trans-Alaska pipeline is now clearly preferable, because it could be on stream two to six years earlier than a comparable overland pipeline across Canada."

And indeed, the potential obstacles to a trans-Canada route were substantial, if not insurmountable. The business organization, financing, engineering design, and logistical preparations for the Alaska project are completed, while none of this work has been done for a trans-Canada route. A new environmental impact statement would have to be prepared for the Alaska leg of a trans-Canada pipeline because it would take a different route from that proposed by Alyeska. Canadian environmentalists have objected to a pipeline through their country. Indians and Eskimos in the Northwest Territories have begun court action seeking to prevent granting of a pipeline right-of-way until their aboriginal land claims are settled (a similar tactic effectively blocked construction of a trans-Alaska line until passage of the Alaska Native Claims Settlement Act of 1971).

And since Canada might eventually want access to the line for any oil found in its own Arctic areas, there would have to be some sort of agreement or treaty covering operation of the line. Also, Senator Jackson said during floor debate that one of the participants in the Alyeska consortium had promised a legal "battle to the end" if Congress attempted to force the line through Canada, raising the possibility of years of litigation.

Proponents of the trans-Alaska line contended that the delay was a critical consideration because by the time a trans-Canada line could be built, 3.4 billion barrels of North Slope oil could be moved to the West Coast through a trans-Alaska line, eliminating the need for that much foreign oil and stemming the nation's dollar outflow by $13 billion. In addition, they said, a trans-Alaska line would get North Slope natural gas to market years earlier, since for technical reasons the gas cannot be produced until oil production has been under way about two years.

The proponents also discounted one of the major arguments of environmentalists and Midwesterners—that substantial amounts of North Slope oil would be sold to Japan. Two recent studies, they said, showed the West Coast would be able to absorb all planned production from the North Slope; and, should a surplus exist, Alaska oil could be shipped to Japan in trade for Middle East oil contracted for by the Japanese. This bartered oil from the Middle East could be shipped from the Persian Gulf to the East Coast of the United States—a complicated arrangement, but one actually more financially attractive than shipping oil from the West Coast to the East Coast.

These arguments were persuasive to Congress. But there may have been another reason for the oil industry's intransigent opposition to a trans-Canada line, a reason that received relatively little attention during the pipeline debate: company profits. Dr. Arlon R. Tussing, an economist with broad experience in Alaska, put it this way in a staff memorandum for Senator Jackson's Senate Interior Committee: "A Canadian pipeline would entail changes in the pattern of ownership and a totally different regulatory and tax regime, which would sharply reduce the companies' flexibility with respect to pricing and accounting practices, with unforeseen but generally unfavorable effects on consolidated after-tax earnings."

The three giant, vertically integrated oil companies that hold the most productive North Slope leases have enormous profits at stake on the North Slope, and the trans-Alaska pipeline is a key link in their realization. The big three are a British Petroleum subsidiary acting in conjunction with the Standard Oil Company (Ohio), ARCO, and Exxon. In the mid-sixties, before any commercial oil discoveries had been made on the North Slope, they obtained, for a total of $12 million, state leases that eventually proved to cover about 90 percent of the Prudhoe Bay reservoir. BP-Sohio got about 55 percent of the bonanza, and ARCO-Exxon, in a joint venture, split about 35 percent. After ARCO found the reservoir, the state held another lease sale and collected $900 million for the unleased 10 percent of the reservoir plus a lot of unproductive land.

Thus, for a trifling sum—even including the estimated $20 million or so spent on wildcatting—three of the nation's largest oil companies acquired virtually complete control of the largest oil field discovered in North America. The reservoir's three pools cover about 670 square miles and, at the conservative 40 percent recovery rate quoted by the industry in estimating reserves, will produce at least 9.6 billion barrels of oil. That estimate almost certainly is far too low. ARCO already has publicly stated its intention of recovering 70 percent of its oil, a rate which, if applied to the entire field, would indicate recovery of 16.8 billion of the 24 billion barrels of oil now estimated to be there.

The market value of the oil and gas at Prudhoe Bay is astronomical: at least $64 billion, using the most conservative figures. Constantly rising oil prices, and ARCO's projected recovery rate, could make it worth three times that much over the twenty-year life of the field. During controversy in 1971 over landmark legislation (eventually passed largely intact) designed to protect state royalty and severance tax revenue against various possible marketing machinations by the companies, Governor Egan estimated that with production of 1.5 million barrels of oil per day, the oil companies would have combined pretax earnings of just under $1 billion a year. He was never convincingly refuted. Oil prices have risen since then and almost certainly will continue to do so, and Egan's calculations did not include the natural gas that will be available two years after oil production begins. It will be worth additional hundreds of millions annually.

The major oil companies will make astronomical profits from Prudhoe Bay as they have elsewhere because of the industry's corporate structure, which assures earnings at every level of the business—production, transportation, refining, and marketing. The companies' own production divisions will produce their oil from their own wells (on which the companies will get the federal government's 22½ percent depletion allowance). BP-Sohio, ARCO, and Exxon between them will own more than 80 percent of the trans-Alaska pipeline, through which they will ship their oil, charging themselves a tariff for doing so and making at least a 7 percent return on their investment in the line.

At Valdez they will load their oil aboard their own American-built tankers (much of the cost of which they will be able to retrieve through government subsidies for tankers built in the United States) and ship it to Washington State and California, where it will be refined in their own refineries. Then they will sell it in their own gas stations. Over the years they probably will make a minimum average of $2 per barrel—$30 billion before taxes if 15 billion barrels eventually are recovered.

In a letter to Senator Floyd Haskell, Democrat of Colorado, William J. Lamont, a lawyer now in private practice who worked on a pending antitrust investigation of Alyeska while with the Justice Department's enforcement division, said that the dominance of BP-Sohio, ARCO, and Exxon means "in substance, control over the pipeline and the related production agreements will give to three companies, operating virtually as one monopoly, control over the marketing of oil on the West Coast, and a greater share of total domestic oil production than would be permissible under any view of the antitrust laws."

The state of Alaska also has a tremendous stake in development of the North Slope, which helps explain why three state administrations have acted as cheerleaders for the trans-Alaska pipeline. The state owns the Prudhoe Bay land and will benefit directly from production royalties and severance taxes—in contrast to other oil states, where royalties generally go to private landowners lucky enough to have oil on their property. And Alaska needs the money. A sprawling land mass 20 percent the size of the rest of the United States, Alaska struggled through its first decade of statehood hampered by a tiny economy largely dependent upon the federal government, a widely dispersed population, high living and travel costs, a difficult climate and widespread poverty—a sort of frozen Appalachia. It is relying on oil to change that. Governor Egan has put it well:

"The issues of conservation of natural resources which face us today cannot be separated from the issue of conservation of human resources. We cannot lock up all the vast natural resources of the state of Alaska in every corner of the land, ignoring the cry of poverty, of human want, of human ignorance and disease which it is in our power to cure. We cannot ignore the economic loss which translates into increased unemployment, higher relief rolls, increased crime and human suffering which has already resulted from the uncertainty and delay on this project. Of the miseries of man, we in Alaska have more than our share. We have the ability to remedy these scourges if, and only if, human energy can be supported by natural resource development. We have the ability and the will to apply our means to these ends, while at the same time observing a standard of natural environmental quality control heretofore unknown in North America."

In addition to the $900 million collected in the 1969 North Slope lease sale, money which is being used to flesh out current state budgets, the state will receive royalties and severance taxes equal to about 20 percent of the wellhead price of North Slope oil (the prevailing price paid by refineries minus all transportation charges). At full production of 2 million barrels per day that should be at least $350 million per year (roughly the same as the budget for this fiscal year). Thus the state stands to make $5 billion to $8 billion over the life of the field at current tax rates and oil prices, both of which are likely to rise.

Businessmen, needless to say, plan on profiting from pipeline construction and have expanded their facilities in anticipation of the development. And the impact of construction on Alaska's small and isolated economy undoubtedly will be great. One study done last year for Alyeska predicted that construction of the line would create 18,000 new jobs—a 15 percent increase in the total number of Alaskan jobs—and add 40,000 persons to the present state population of 324,000. Robert R. Richards, vice president of the National Bank of Alaska and one of the state's respected economists, considers the Alyeska estimates far too conservative.

"All hell's going to break loose," he predicts. "Our projections show that within seven years of the start of construction of the pipeline, employment in Alaska will double and the population will increase by 60 percent. I'm of the opinion that the state will be in an entirely new economic era of sustainable economic growth," he says, contrasting that condition with the boom-and-bust mining cycles of the past.

Richards and other economists warn that a boom will have its costs—inflation substantially higher than the national rate and an acute housing shortage being among the most likely results. A majority of Alaskans seems to believe the boom will be worth the price, however. The old frontier ethic of "Get in, get it, and get out" still is very much alive. Every other auto, it seems, carries a pro-pipeline bumper sticker. They range from the routinely exhortatory ("Build the all-American pipeline") through anti-environmentalist ("Let the bastards freeze in the dark") to the offbeat political ("Watergate hell—let's pump our well"). Chambers of commerce throughout the state have been thumping the tub for instant construction of the pipeline since the project first was proposed. The Alaska press, with isolated exceptions, has uncritically accepted the oil industry's word on every major facet of Arctic oil development while relentlessly ridiculing the environmentalists—on the whole, a shabby performance by any standard of responsible professionalism.

This has left critical examination of the pipeline project to environmental groups—which, here as elsewhere, comprise a quite small fraction of the population—and to the Cordova District Fisheries Union, a group of about four hundred Prince William Sound fishermen who fear their livelihood will be threatened by water pollution. Their voices generally have been lost in the babble of boosterism.

After President Nixon has signed the compromise pipeline bill, the Wilderness Society, Friends of the Earth, and the Environmental Defense Fund, Inc. (which brought suit against the pipeline project more than three years ago and forced the Interior Department to devote an unprecedented amount of energy to preparation of an environmental impact statement), are expected to make one last-ditch attempt to halt the project. They are expected to contend that any congressional finding that the pipeline has met the requirements of the National Environmental Policy Act, and exempting the development from judicial review, is unconstitutional. The environmentalists so far have been much better at law than the oil companies, the Interior Department, and the state. Indeed, it was their success in having Alyeska's right-of-way request found in violation of a width restriction in the Mineral Leasing Act of 1920 that finally brought the project before Congress. But most legal observers consider a constitutional suit challenging Congress's authority an exceedingly slender legal reed if the final bill is at all like those passed by the Senate and House.

If it snaps, as expected, Alyeska will be ready to begin construction next spring.

We Are Killing the Sea Around Us
BY MICHAEL HARWOOD

A sunny morning at Matinicus Rock, off the mouth of Penobscot Bay in Maine. The swell rolling in from the Atlantic rises and crashes on the steep incline of the jutting granite; the waves suck back, pale green and foaming, and each ripple along their lines of force is clear and sharply defined. Wherever our boat passes, the water is speckled with the tiny young of marine organisms; they are no bigger than the point of a pin, and there are thousands of them in every cubic yard of sea. Dolphins slip by, in herds. Glistening whales rise, take in great drafts of air, and sink beneath the surface to feed on schools of shrimp. Birds are everywhere—terns, gulls, razor-billed auks, puffins, petrels, eider ducks, guillemots, shearwaters, phalaropes. The ocean here is rich with food and motion and life.

And yet this, like all the oceans of the world, may die under the stresses of pollution, just as Lake Erie has died. The size of the job has prevented us from killing the seas as fast as we killed Lake Erie: They cover 70 percent of the earth's surface. But we are killing them, nonetheless.

The process by which this is happening is varied and complicated. The outward and most visible signs, of course, are the white plastic bleach jugs, the plastic cups, the whisky bottles, the doll carcasses, which float forever, or at least until they wash up on our shores. Oil spills are highly visible, sometimes drifting onto beaches, ruining swimming and covering feet with tar. Sewage is often obvious, too—pieces of fecal matter and toilet paper floating by, even at beaches where the bacteria count is considered low enough for swimming. And in many harbors of the world one sees the water stained red or brown or yellow or green or white by the discharges of manufacturing plants. If you can't see it, you may be able to smell it—oil and sewage, for example.

The trouble is, the things that most of us see or smell and recognize as being harmful, and the news stories about a huge kill of fish here, a kill or a reproductive failure of seabirds there, the illness and death of human beings who have eaten food badly contaminated in the sea—all are treated as basically local and immediate phenomena. The real problem man faces involves widespread, daily, long-term pollution.

Scientists are agreed that the ocean can absorb a good deal of our wastes without danger to itself or us. But this requires considerable discrimination on our part and an awareness of how the ocean works. We know we don't have to do serious damage to all 140 million square miles of it—and the deeps beneath—before we suffer unacceptable consequences; we have only to cripple a good part of the 14 million square miles close to shore. For the sea is not a deep bowl, and the things we throw into it will not spread out and be diluted evenly, nor will they ultimately come to rest in the ocean's deepest parts, presumably farthest from shore.

The sea bottom declines out from the land rather gradually to the edge of the continental shelf. It is in this space, covered by about 10 percent of the seas' total surface area, that 90 percent of our food fish is spawned, raised, and caught, and it is here that most of our pollution takes place. The continental shelf is by no means regular in width or depth. It may extend out from dry land only a few miles or for hundreds of miles. It is cut by the troughs of river flows and of ocean currents. Beyond it, the deep-sea bottom is more markedly mountainous than the globe's land surface. The sea is stirred by internal rivers of its own—the Gulf Stream, the Humboldt Current, the West Wind Drift, and many more, underwater as well as on the surface.

In places, cold water wells up from the depths, bringing with it a rich burden of minerals, and in such areas of upwelling, the agitated surface is seething with life. The currents, passing each other or intersecting, toss up rough seas; circling, they create millponds in mid-ocean. The wind and tide pile water into hills, and down these sea slopes the surface water races. So the sea does not behave like a large pond or, more to the point, like a septic tank. Its patterns are complex and even now not well understood.

Rivers are the major sewer pipes contributing to the growing pollution of the ocean. Downstream flow the wastes of the kitchen, bathroom, laundry, hospital surgery; the pulp and metals and acids of factory discharges, the poisonous chemicals and fertilizers in runoff from farmland, the silt from deforested uplands, toxic oil products from filling stations and airports, the noxious liquors draining from garbage dumps.

In developed regions, that sort of outflow is considerable. I asked Dr. Jack B. Pearce, director of the Sandy Hook Sports Fisheries Marine Laboratory, if there was a map anywhere showing rivers that pollute the ocean. "You don't need a map," he said. "Any river that flows through an urban, industrial area is loaded with pollutants."

Some idea of the magnitude of the flow can be given by the amount of solids washed down. The relatively pristine Colorado River discharges only about 200 grams of solids in each ton of water, but the heavily industrialized Rhine feeds the ocean more than four times that much per ton of water, or some 60 million tons of solids a year.

The scouring action of rivers by itself would rinse a certain amount of minerals and metals from the continents, but a far greater volume than nature could produce actually reaches the ocean. Worldwide, the seas receive from the rivers each year an amount of iron estimated to be almost half as great as the amount of steel produced on the planet annually; most of that loss is the result of man's dumping. To take another marked example, phosphorus would be scrubbed from the land naturally at a rate of not quite 200,000 tons a year, but it actually reaches the sea at a rate of more than 6.5 million tons a year. Two and a half million tons of lead are washed down in rivers each year—thirteen times the amount that nature itself could provide.

Marine pollution, noted a report prepared for the Committee on Natural Resources of the United Nations Economic and Social Council early this year, "is essentially a river-management problem." Still, that's only one aspect of the situation. Harborside industries add their slugs of poison. Power plants there pour out heated water. Coastal cities generally pump their untreated or partly treated sewage directly into harbors or to outfalls a short distance offshore. Some communities barge sewage sludge and dredging spoils to dumping grounds several miles from the coast, and industries do the same with some of their wastes. Ships at sea contribute sewage and garbage and trash—and oil.

The world production of oil now approaches 2 billion tons a year, and 60 percent of it is carried, at some time or another, by ships. It is hardly a wonder that a million tons of oil are spilled accidentally into the ocean in the course of this traffic each year. More is added from drilling and pumping rigs offshore, more from onshore accidents, more from the deliberate dumping of oil residues at sea by oil transports whose tanks need washing out.

Canisters of wastes contaminated with low-level radiation are disposed of in the ocean; sooner or later they leak their contents. The world's military organizations still get rid of many chemical weapons by heaving them overboard, and so create time bombs for the future; it is an unpleasant—and sometimes lethal—surprise to fishermen, for instance, to haul up containers of mustard gas or explosives in their nets. Floating mines from past wars still present serious hazards in some parts of the world, and so do the unexploded shells of naval and air bombardment practice at sea.

A good deal of pollution enters the ocean on wind and rain—an estimated 200,000 tons of lead and a million tons of oil from engine exhaust each year, and perhaps as much as 5,000 tons of mercury, which is found in fuel and is also used in papermaking and released into the atmosphere when the paper is burned. Half the pesticides in the ocean, by one estimate, have come out of the sky. Pesticides travel long distances by air; the summer monsoon winds pick them up in Africa, for example, and lay them down in the Bay of Bengal on the far side of India, while at other times of year the trade winds carry them the other way, across the Atlantic into the Caribbean.

All of these factors have an effect upon the intricate relationships within the marine environment, which have developed in a process that took millions of years. Minerals in the water feed plants, which combine the food with sunlight, in photosynthesis, to produce carbohydrates and oxygen. The smallest of these plants, phytoplankton, are microscopic. Tiny marine animals, called zooplankton, along with the larvae of larger organisms, browse on the pastures of phytoplankton, and are themselves eaten by larger carnivores—the start of a chain of events that eventually reaches the largest marine carnivores, and man. Vegetable-eating organisms feed on the larger plants, too, and join the food web. The waste products of all this activity settle to the bottom, where they help nourish and hide bottom-dwelling animals, which are consumed by bottom-feeding carnivores, which are food for creatures higher up the chain, and so on.

The species of marine life to be found in a particular area vary according to a number of features, including the saltiness of the water, the temperature, the richness or lack of minerals and other elements, the clarity of the water, the character of the bottom, the depth, the season, and the presence of other organisms.

There is a good deal of flexibility built into the system, since the natural environment constantly changes by itself and sometimes suffers natural disasters. It can take care of certain amounts of oil, of metals, of bacteria, of silt, of chemicals. But in an instant of geologic time, mostly in this century, man has suddenly presented the ocean with chemical compounds it never knew and volumes of waste it simply isn't equipped to cope with.

Human sewage, for example. Given enough time, salt is lethal to the bacteria in these wastes. But when the bacteria enter the water with a great deal of sewage and fresh water—which dilutes the salt—events may take quite another course. At least some of the bacteria survive long enough to be taken up by shellfish, which feed by straining water through their systems. Once the bacteria are inside the shellfish, they've found a home, like the boll weevil.

Infectious hepatitis germs collect there in numbers sufficient to make the shellfish a hazard for man to eat, and shellfish have been found to collect polio virus to a concentration sixty times that of the surrounding water.

Meanwhile, the nutrients that entered the water with the bacteria stimulate the bacteria's growth. If the load of sewage is considerable and prolonged, these nutrients encourage the growth of certain marine animals and plants. The system may eventually go haywire and be strangled. The growth becomes too rapid; in the accelerated cycle of life and death, oxygen is literally sucked out of the water, leaving alive only those bacteria that don't require oxygen. This process goes even faster if the sewage—as it almost always does—contains more than human wastes. Some chemicals kill marine organisms outright, increasing the load of decomposing matter that eats up oxygen; others stimulate the surviving plants and animals, adding to the oxygen demand; and still other chemicals and oil products by themselves demand oxygen from the water.

Many harbors and bays and estuaries around the world are being affected in this manner by domestic sewage and by industrial effluents. Even some areas off coasts are receiving too many barge loads of sewage sludge and other wastes. New York City's "dead sea" dumping ground, nine miles outside the harbor, is a notable example.

The water may not die completely; it will go through various stages—back and forth, perhaps, depending on such factors as the sewage load and the water temperature and the swiftness of currents and accidents of weather. Still, some rather disagreeable things may happen. Ten to 15 million menhaden, a commercial fish processed for bait and fertilizer and oil, were killed in Florida's Escambia Bay at Pensacola in a single day last summer. The bay receives industrial pollution, and the fish kill was just one of a series there over the last decade; the blame has been laid to the low level of oxygen in the water. The fish smothered. And the lobsters and crabs and fish that survive for long periods in water heavily polluted by sewage suffer from cancerlike growths and lesions and other diseases.

We have lived with some of the effects for years. Swimming is forbidden at beaches. Often, shellfishing is ruined; two members of the Fisheries Research Board of Canada reported last May that fully a quarter of the shellfish beds along Canada's Atlantic coast have been closed because of bacterial contamination. And, though fishing villages there would benefit from being able to set up fish-processing plants, they are prevented from doing so because their harbors, potential inexpensive sources of water for processing, are not clean enough to be used that way.

That's a fair picture, though a very limited one, of the sorts of burdens we are placing on the sea. And sewage is only one of the harmful effluents. Toxic metals, such as copper, mercury, lead, and zinc, are absorbed and concentrated in huge amounts by marine organisms, which are not able to break the metals down or wash them through their systems except over long periods of time. Concentrations of copper occur naturally in seawater at the rate of about three parts per billion, and that is harmless. A solution containing one-tenth of a part per million is toxic to marine life, and concentrations of one part per million have been shown to kill soft clams in less than two weeks and in nine days to slow down by 70 percent the ability of kelp to produce food and oxygen.

A Japanese researcher reported last year on a phenomenon seen in and around several bays in Japan: "green oyster." Outflows containing high concentrations of copper turn the flesh of oysters green. The river-borne waste of the copper refineries in Hitachi, on the northeast coast, are lethal to oysters within more than half a mile of the river mouth, and for up to three miles from the river mouth green oysters can be found, the green diminishing in color as the distance increases.

The Japanese, of course, are very alert to the potential danger of toxic metals in seawater, having seen close at hand the lethal effects of one metallic compound concentrated in fish. In 1953, in and around Minamata, people began falling ill with a strange neurological disease: They lost control of their limbs; some went dumb, some went mad. In the next several years, at least one hundred sixteen people were affected—including nineteen babies born defective—by what came to be known as "Minamata disease." Of those, forty-three died.

Then, in 1965, Minamata disease appeared again, in Niigata

prefecture. Thirty people became ill and five of them died. The cause of this illness, it was discovered, was methyl mercury, eaten in fish taken from water contaminated by it. The source of the mercury was manufacturing plants that used mercury catalysts. The concentration of all forms of mercury in Minamata Bay was relatively low, yet the amounts of methyl mercury found in fish were as high as fifty parts per million, which meant to the scientists that the fish had accumulated the compound in their systems to concentrations perhaps as much as 500,000 times as great as that in the water.

This ability of marine organisms to concentrate such poisons to sometimes incredible levels is of particular concern to biologists and public-health officials. DDT and its many cousins among the halogenated hydrocarbons also accumulate in greater and greater doses in their way up the food chain, slowing reproduction, injuring and causing chemical changes in marine creatures; one of the end results of this concentration has been the failure of a variety of fish-eating birds, such as ospreys, bald eagles, and pelicans, to breed as they should.

These poisons seem to attack the reproductive system of birds, perhaps upsetting the hormone balance, which leads to sterile eggs for many of the birds and the thinness, or even absence, of eggshells to protect the embryos. The "it's only birds" attitude toward this phenomenon may be very misleading. Before people were struck down by Minamata disease, fish-eating domestic cats in the neighborhood exhibited the same symptoms that later showed up in human beings; some of the cats went crazy and threw themselves off docks and drowned.

At the head of Wild Harbor River in West Falmouth, Massachusetts, two scientists from the Woods Hole Oceanographic Institute slog out onto a mud flat, sometimes sinking up to the cuffs of their shorts in the ooze. Near the middle of the exposed tidal riverbed, they take core sample, pressing an old coffee can open-end-down into the mud and dumping the mud into plastic bags. One man scrapes a sample from the surface of the flat using a large metal spatula, and empties it into a glass jar. They push back toward the bank and move to another sampling station downriver.

They are doing a study of the aftereffects of an oil spill that occurred nearly two years ago at a spot some two miles by water from here. This late afternoon, small slicks spread on the water in their footprints after they have climbed the bank; a scientist bends over, grabs a handful of mud, sniffs it, nods: "Oil." In places in the marsh it is not necessary to go to such trouble, for the smell is obvious.

The spill they are studying has demonstrated some important facts about oil in the marine environment: An oil spill may break up and sink beneath the surface, and the beaches may be cleaned, giving the appearance that the sea has safely taken care of the accident, while its effects actually persist and even grow. This spill seemed quite small at first. A barge on its way to refuel a power plant on the Cape Cod Canal ran aground off West Falmouth. No more than 700 tons of fuel oil ran off into Buzzards Bay. A team of scientists went to the area of the spill and began taking samples. The kill of fish, crabs, lobsters, shellfish, and other marine animals had been massive, but this was not unexpected; many fractions, or compounds, of oil are extremely toxic to sea life—as, indeed, they are to man. And among other things, oil contains elements that cause cancer in experimental animals. In one dredge haul 93 percent of the organisms brought up from the bottom near the spill were dead or dying, and the tide was leaving windrows of dead fish on the beaches.

To give themselves some base lines against which to judge the effects of the spill and the pace of the area's recovery, the scientists located one of their sampling stations outside of the area that they expected the oil to spread. Three weeks later, the oil had reached that station, and dead organisms appeared with the oil in the samples there. Chemical analysis identified the oil as part of the spill. The control station was moved farther out; in three months, that area, too, was contaminated. The researchers didn't know quite how it was happening, but after eight months, the oil had spread several miles to the north and west and affected at least 5,500 acres of bay and marsh. Moreover, the zones of worst damage seemed to be moving outward, too.

The effects of the oil in the polluted zone remained the same for months afterward; populations did not quickly restore themselves. Toxic fractions of oil were absorbed into the flesh of oysters, clams, scallops, and other shellfish, and stayed there; the scientists believe that the polluted shellfish will never wash themselves clean of this burden. Finally, this year the outer limits of the oiled area began to recede, and populations of marine invertebrates showed some first signs of recovery.

At the head of Wild Harbor River, where an estimated four tons of the oil had been enough virtually to ruin twenty-two acres of marsh, the green Spartina grass, a resilient plant, is moving back into flats and onto banks where it had been wiped out. Still, the oil has seeped down at least a foot and a half into the mud there. Wherever it has drifted in its spread from the point of the spill, it will prevent any rapid comeback, and its effects may well be evident for many years.

Most oil-tanker traffic passes near coasts—the western shore of Europe, the Mediterranean, the Persian Gulf, the East Coast of the United States—and a great deal of the accidental spilling takes place quite close to shore. Tanker routes are insufficiently regulated, which leads to accidents. Added to that coastal pollution is the oil from offshore wells and the many millions of tons of oil and oil products that flow in from rivers. Satisfactory methods that could be applied everywhere to remove oil or render it harmless before it damages the sea have not yet been worked out. There are bacteria in seawater that eat oil and break it down, but the most toxic of the oil compounds are also the hardest for the bacteria to work on. Probably not all oil spills have as disastrous or long-lasting effects as the West Falmouth accident did. But the implications of the Woods Hole study are not comforting.

Oil, toxic metals, DDT, and sewage all have one thing in common: not only do they present some threat directly to man's health when accumulations are great enough in the marine environment; more important, at far lower levels they disrupt the environment—throw it off kilter, speed up its machinery or slow it down. DDT and mercury are among a number of elements known to inhibit the growth and reproduction of phytoplankton—the base of the food chain. A serious break in the chain at any point would have its effects on the supply of fish, but the crucial point is at the beginning. There is considerable debate, to be sure, about the potential of the sea to provide sufficient food for the billions of additional people the demographers expect by the end of the century, but however that may be, it would be a poor idea to cut off a part of the earth's food supply.

The amounts of pollutants in the water can be minute in terms of the volume of water, but three things tend to increase the poisons where they count—in the food chain. The first is the concentration factor, the capacity of marine organisms to store pollutants. The second is the location of the pollution; most of it occurs where most of the fish are born, bred, and fed. And the third is the longevity of much of the pollution. Experimenters have had some success in adding chemicals to DDT to shorten its life, but at present it is estimated to keep half its strength for anywhere from ten to fifty years; such persistent elements build up in the environment.

Furthermore, we don't yet know very much about the effects of a great many "familiar" effluents, and almost nothing about the thousands of new compounds (the plastic bleach jugs are a gross example of the type) we are pouring out daily, which the sea has never seen before and may often not have ways of working on. It is possible for marine scientists to take at least some of the pollutants and test them in the lab, to see how each affects the chemistry of seawater and how it reacts on various representative marine species over the short and the long run. To some extent, this is now being done. But to keep up with all the components of our waste appears to be out of the question.

Biologists are concerned even more about the synergistic effects of these wastes on the environment. A simple example is nickel and copper; nickel is relatively nontoxic, but put it into water with copper effluent, and you multiply the toxicity of the copper by ten. Now take constantly varying amounts of iron and zinc and sewage and arsenic and oil and detergent and turpentine and fertilizer and a hundred chemical compounds whose structures don't even appear in the scientific literature, and you have a mix, reacting to itself as well as to the sea's chemistry, whose specific effects you can't guess at in advance, except to suggest they might not be very good. Then heat the water a few degrees with water that has been used to cool a power plant, and you may get a different result; put the mix into Arctic waters and it will probably react differently; dredge or mine in the area, and you will add a load of silt, which will screen sunlight in the water and change the composition of the bottom, and the result may change again. Dredging and mining may also uncover a variety of poisons that were buried long ago in the mud. Return those to the food web, and you have still another factor to worry about.

Even when the pollutants are diluted to supposedly harmless concentrations in the water, their combined persistence in the environment is thought to present a danger to the marine food chain. But here the scientists are on the edge of uncharted waters again. They have some evidence that such low-level combinations of pollutants weaken certain key links in the chain—inhibiting growth and reproduction, changing fish-migration routes, and increasing the vulnerability of marine organisms to disease as well as to pollutants. They suspect that such pollution mixes are the cause of certain genetic changes in fish observed recently in coastal waters. There are a number of unexplained phenomena, particularly some mysterious population explosions in the sea and kills of fish and plants and sea mammals and ocean birds, which may be associated with long-term, low-level pollution. But no one knows for sure.

"We are profoundly ignorant of much that goes on in the marine environment," wrote Oscar Schachter, director of research for the United Nations Institute for Training and Research, and Daniel Serwer, an assistant research fellow in UNITAR, in a paper published early this year. "The oceans are, along with extraterrestrial space and the interior of the atomic nucleus, one of the frontiers of scientific and technological research. The present ignorance is not limited to isolated details like the number of fish in the sea, though that too is a question that cannot now be answered satisfactorily. We lack knowledge of fundamental aspects of the physical, chemical, and biological working of the oceans."

Dr. R. B. Clark, a British scientist and editor of the monthly *Marine Pollution Bulletin,* has commented: "Most knowledge of the biological consequences of marine pollution is derived from studies in temperate waters. Information about these environments is woefully inadequate, but it is encyclopedic compared with what we know about even the basic ecology of Arctic and tropical waters, let alone the consequences of effluent disposal and accidental pollution in them."

That is one reason the problem is so ominous. At the same

time, we can see that we're already having some serious effects on the edges of the ocean. Coastal marshes—crucial spawning, nursery, and feeding areas—are being gobbled up by developers, dredgers, and dumpers. Just between 1954 and 1968, for instance, the eastern seaboard of the United States lost more than 5 percent of its coastal wetlands and 4 percent of its shallow-water habitat. Many estuaries, harbors, and bays are no better than sumps, and more are on their way to achieving that status. The Mediterranean and the Baltic, both seas that suffer from severe pollution and have water-circulation patterns that hamper recovery, are in serious trouble.

Since so much of industry and so many communities depend on the ocean to catch their refuse, the difficulties—economic, political, and administrative—of regulating this pollution are enormous. The rapid growth of the world's population and the industrialization of the developing nations are multiplying the problem; just to keep the ocean as clean as it is today, we would have to set increasingly strict codes and enforce them. The demand for oil, for one thing, is growing at a fantastic rate, and increased offshore drilling, the transport of oil in bigger and bigger tankers, and the addition of new tanker routes can only make the threat to the ocean from that source more serious. Nuclear power will undoubtedly be utilized at a rising rate, presenting a double problem of radioactive contamination and thermal pollution by reactor cooling systems.

It's a complicated business, and the response of governments and individuals has been understandably slow and not well coordinated. Scientists might be expected to try to generate action, and some do, but in general they prefer to keep working in their specialties and avoid the hurly-burly of political activism. There are drawbacks to this. As one scientist told me, "You can shout loud, so that no one will hear you." But once they get publicly involved, on a large scale, they have no time left to do science, and most of them feel that plugging along with their work is the better choice. Furthermore, they have found that they do not convey their knowledge, via the popular media, as well as they would like. "In presenting to the public the conclusions drawn from complex data," wrote a pollution ecologist in Wales last year, "the scientist often finds that he has been misquoted or that his views have been translated into emotive prose by journalists." Scientists are concerned that the public reaction to the problem will deflect governments from supporting the kind of research that needs to be done. Dr. Clark noted recently: "In a period of contracting research funds, there is a danger that all programs will be crash programs and the very necessary long-term investigations will be swept aside."

And within the scientific community itself, there is a communications problem. Not the least factor is a diversity of basic approach that hampers the discussion of regional and international situations. When scientists from Denmark, Finland, Poland, the Soviet Union, Sweden, and the two Germanys began to investigate together the pollution of the Baltic, they had difficulty even deciding on a standard measure by which to express amounts of pollution.

National governments have legislated on water-quality standards, but until recently not much attention was paid to marine pollution. Not only does this legislation, when it exists, vary from country to country; as in the United States, administrative responsibilities within each country are often fragmented among agencies—which, naturally, compete with one another. There are regional conventions, mostly European, dealing with the disposal of radioactive waste, detergents, and oil. The World Health Organization has set standards for permissible mercury levels in food; the International Atomic Energy Agency has standards for radioactive-waste dumping—but no nation is forced to meet those standards. Some do; some don't. The International Convention for the Prevention of Pollution of the Sea by Oil prohibits the deliberate dumping of oil—as in tank-cleaning—in certain parts of the sea, and will shortly limit tank size and tank locations aboard oil transports, but the regulations are not wide-ranging. Various other international agreements deal with oil spills, particularly cleaning them up and compensating nations for damage, and with safety regulations in shipping radioactive material and dangerous chemicals. Others set standards for civil liability for nuclear accidents. An international agreement bans weapons on the seabeds beyond territorial waters.

The approach, in short, has been piecemeal, and there's no reason to expect it to be much changed in the future. Between nations there's a good deal of "after you, my dear Alphonse" on questions of stopping pollution, and a certain natural tendency to think of the other fellow as a worse polluter than you. And each nation must bear in mind, when it considers regulation, the consequences of putting its industries and its economy at a competitive disadvantage, should other nations not follow suit.

One solution would seem to lie in action by the United Nations and its various special agencies. At present, a host of U.N. connected groups are working on different aspects of the problem. They are helping spur scientific study, offering training in pollution research, setting standards, advising governments, organizing conferences, creating clearinghouses for information and initiating international agreements. Responsibilities are fragmented here, too, and the U.N. system is not devoid of bureaucratic infighting. But some progress has been made, and more is clearly on the way.

In the second and third weeks of June next year, in Stockholm, the U.N. will hold its important Conference on the Human Environment. Intensive preparations have been going on for more than a year and a half. Ocean pollution is on the agenda, and one looked-for product of the conference is a treaty to regulate the dumping of wastes from ships and barges.

The Inter-Governmental Maritime Consultative Organization, which among other things administers several of the international oil-pollution conventions, will meet in 1973 to consider augmenting those conventions—possibly to include all ocean pollution. It will probably also try to improve the regulation of oil dumping.

Such things move very slowly. Furthermore, the U.N. cannot provide all the answers. It lacks the clout. "At best," says Dr. Clark, "the United Nations can hope for international regulation of activities outside territorial waters and exhortation to nations to behave reasonably inside their territorial waters." More regional compacts would help, but they, too, could provide only another part of the solution. Paradoxically, though the world as a whole is the ultimate victim of marine pollution, its cure now depends at the roots on individual governments and the people they serve.

One consideration that might motivate governments and industries to stop polluting is economics. No one can put a price tag on pollution, but one might do a little extrapolating from what is known. The Council on Environmental Quality, for example, estimates that nearly a fourth of the United States' shellfish crop could not be harvested in 1969; the polluted shellfish had a value of at least $63 million. That's along the coasts of part of one continent. Harvests of shrimp and crabs must be similarly affected, at considerable cost. Add in the loss of finfish catches—both through massive kills and by more subtle damage. Then figure the expense of cleaning water and beaches and the losses to tourist industries after oil spills; it cost more than $5 million just to clean up the Santa Barbara spill in 1969. Consider the social cost of temporarily ruining public beaches with oil and of ruining them more or less permanently with sewage. Now add on the cost of the materials wasted. The lead that runs as effluent into the ocean via rivers each year has a value: on the current London market that much lead is worth nearly $600 million. The copper we wash away, if sold as wire bars, would be worth about $5 billion a year. There is simply no way to tot up all the immediate expense of our wastefullness—not to mention the long-range costs—but one could guess that we are throwing away hundreds of billions of dollars a year by throwing stuff into the ocean.

The sea can be cleaned up. As a matter of fact, it will do most of the job without our help, if we just let it alone; that's what is happening at West Falmouth now. To encourage restoration, some industries are cutting back, in various ways, their contributions to pollution. Work is being done to produce wastes that will not harm the sea. Public opinion is aroused, and governments are certainly making a start at regulation and enforcement.

Perhaps we have already begun to turn around. But it was less than twenty years ago that a savvy observer, author Peter Matthiessen, commented that "man has as yet been unable to damage the chemistry of the sea"—which gives some idea of how quickly the damage has become widely evident. Such a rate of acceleration is going to be difficult to deal with if we go about it as we are now—everybody moving cautiously and keeping a suspicious eye on his neighbor. If we don't act purposefully, with much more research and with worldwide regulation, our pollution will (who knows how soon?) exceed the ocean's ability to clean itself. Once that happens, deterioration is likely to be rapid and recovery very difficult.

"Lake Erie may or may not be restored within fifty years," Dr.

Max Blumer of Woods Hole wrote last December, "but a polluted ocean will remain irreversibly damaged for many generations." And who would care to argue that a dead ocean would not mean a dead planet?

What to Do With Waste?
Use It Over and Over and Over Again
BY LAMONT C. COLE

Nature's way of dealing with wastes is to recycle them—use them over and over again. All earthly life, for example, is based on proteins, which are nitrogen compounds. But early in the history of the earth the atmosphere contained no more than traces of free nitrogen (and oxygen). The earliest organisms obtained the nitrogen they needed from ammonia, a compound of nitrogen and hydrogen. Then organisms evolved that took in nitrogen in excess of their needs and released molecules of nitrogen gas into the atmosphere as a waste. Today this ability to release unused nitrogen is mostly confined to certain bacteria and some very primitive algae, but they do the job on such a huge scale that nitrogen, which is essential for all life, including our own, is constantly recycled into and out of the atmosphere and with oxygen now accounts for 99 percent of the atmosphere's bulk.

The story is the same with oxygen. Green plants evolved fairly early in the history of life. They had the knack of obtaining energy for their life activities from sunlight, and in so doing they produced large quantities of oxygen as a waste by-product. They disposed of this by dumping it into the atmosphere. Then additional types of organisms evolved, including animals, which could make profitable use of that waste oxygen, in the process converting it to a waste product, carbon dioxide, which was a valuable raw material for green plants.

The story is much the same for the other chemical elements of biological importance. In principle, almost all of the commodities used by living things can be recycled. (The only noteworthy exceptions are the radioactive elements, which change irrevocably into other elements, and energy. But we have a large source of the latter in sunlight, which promises to go on supporting life for a very long time.)

Man, an upstart on earth, does not yet adequately appreciate the cyclic nature of the commodities he uses. He perhaps understands that water evaporates and returns to earth as precipitation, but when he stumbles across a new concentrated deposit of a useful mineral, his immediate inclination is to mine the deposit and disperse its contents. Our present economics and even laws, such as our "depletion allowances," encourage this. So the great Mesabi iron deposits of Minnesota are largely to be found today in automobile graveyards, in rusting cans in dumps, along highways, and in lakes, and in weapons around the world.

It is only where nature has concentrated minerals that modern man, guided by modern economics, finds it worthwhile to mine them. The amount of gold in the earth's seawater is beyond the dreams of any Midas, but it is not economically feasible to extract it. Unfortunately, the trend of our modern style of life is to mine nature's concentrations of useful commodities and to disperse them throughout the environment as gold is dispersed in the seas.

Phosphorus is an element essential to all life and we are throwing it away, letting it wash into the oceans to be deposited in sediments. We tolerate great damage to the environment in mining phosphate rock and converting it to fertilizer because our modern agriculture couldn't do without it. But then we throw it away, in human and animal wastes, in detergents and pesticides, so that it has become a serious water pollutant in the United States. If our cost accounting included the environmental damage from producing phosphate and looked to the future when it will be in short supply, we should surely conclude that the only rational thing to do is to remove the phosphate from sewage and reclaim it as fertilizer.

During the Johnson regime in the White House we heard lots of talk about automobile graveyards but saw little positive action. The steel in auto bodies can, of course, be reused, yet the economics of our present way of life is such that in the United States we merely abandon one million old automobiles each year. In New York State it is estimated that private business can make a profit from "mining" a pile containing as few as two hundred old cars. The economic problem is how to bring the abandoned cars together into piles of two hundred. Should the state foot the bill or should the purchaser pay a deposit to be refunded when the hulk is turned in to a disposal center? It would help if mining depletion allowances were reduced enough to make it at least as expensive to mine and refine new ore as to reclaim used metal.

A little preplanning in Detroit would also help. One reason steel companies don't like to melt down old automobile hulks is that the car contains a certain amount of copper wiring—estimated to average about four pounds per car—which is so inaccessible that it is not economical to pay a man to remove it. When the hulk is melted, the copper forms an alloy with the steel, reducing its value for future use. It has been suggested that if aluminum were used in place of copper, it would form a slag instead of an alloy and could easily be skimmed off the molten metal.

An alternative approach has recently been announced by the U.S. Bureau of Mines. If the parts containing copper are dipped and slightly agitated in a bath of molten calcium chloride salt—itself a voluminous and troublesome waste from some industrial process—about 99 percent of the copper can be "sweated out" of even such relatively enclosed structures as generators and electric motors. The copper collects as a pool at the bottom of the tank of calcium chloride and is recovered. Some companies have long wondered what to do with their mountains of waste calcium chloride, and now it may at last become useful. It would appear to be worth exploring the possibility of using several successive baths of this material at different temperatures to separate various metals from a mixture. Tin might be sweated off steel cans, and aluminum, which melts at a lower temperature than copper, might be separated from automobile hulks or parts ahead of the bath that removes the copper.

Another salvageable item is the virtually indestructible aluminum beverage can, a controversial object among environmentalists. It can easily be melted and the metal used over, and at least one metals company will buy back its old cans—but at so low a price that only a small fraction is reclaimed. Again, some sort of high, mandatory deposit—say 25 cents per can—might correct the situation.

In any case, the aluminum industry is a prodigious consumer of electricity, which is something to be considered in these days of threatened power shortages. It takes about ten kilowatt hours of electricity to separate a pound of aluminum from its ore but only about one-fifth as much to melt a pound of used aluminum. Perhaps we should revise our economic system to ensure that virtually all aluminum is recycled. Or perhaps we should decide to do entirely without such things as aluminum beverage cans, which are certainly not one of life's necessities. The old steel cans coated with tin at least eventually rust and disappear. And even these had salvage value during the tin shortage of World War II.

Even better were the old refillable glass bottles, which made an average of twenty round trips between store and customer before they cracked or broke and became solid waste to be disposed of in landfill areas—areas which are today in critically short supply. Even if for some reason we decide not to refill bottles, glass is easy to melt and use over. Again the problem is economic—how to gather the glass and sort it by color. Here I detect what I hope are early stirrings of a public conscience. Markets are putting out collection bins for used glass, and one campus I visited recently had separate bins for glass of various colors.

The solid wastes produced in urban areas of this country each year now include about 60 million tons of paper and paper products. This too could be largely recycled with an annual saving of millions of oxygen-producing trees (about seventeen trees per ton of recycled paper). I am now on the mailing lists of several organizations that print their literature on recycled paper. Usually the paper is treated to remove ink before reuse, but I recently received a publication where this step had been omitted, and the paper had an interesting and not unattractive blue-gray tinge. At present we recycle an estimated 20 percent of our paper; this percentage could probably be at least tripled. Each time paper is ground up for recycling the cellulose fibers become shorter and the paper correspondingly weaker, so it is desirable to add some fresh fiber each time. We could, nevertheless, save a great deal of timber by recycling as much as possible.

Paper, along with garbage and other municipal refuse, can also be burned as a source of energy. There are incinerators in West Germany, and a few experimental ones in this country, that burn municipal refuse with virtually no air pollution and generate electricity in the process. The remaining ash is used in making concrete blocks for building. Some plants are so successful that they solicit garbage from surrounding areas.

Incinerators that do not release pollutants like sulfur dioxide, however, require a high capital investment. There is also a major problem in the polyvinyl-chloride plastics, which damage incinerators because they yield hydrochloric acid when burned. This raises questions of economics again: Why can't a product be kept off the market until a satisfactory method for its ultimate disposal is discovered? And shouldn't the price of a product reflect the cost to society of its ultimate disposal?

The U.S. Bureau of Mines has recently announced another approach. Its scientists have treated garbage, waste paper, and animal manure with carbon monoxide and steam to produce crude oil of low sulfur content. They estimate that with this process our current annual production of such refuse could be made to yield 2 billion barrels of oil.

Natural gas, which is usually nearly pure methane, is a very clean fuel. The federal government has adapted some of its fleets of vehicles on the West Coast to burn natural gas with a great reduction in pollution. It is also estimated that the engine life of these vehicles will be doubled. We are told that it is not practicable to burn natural gas in our cars because we don't have enough of it. But we can make methane from garbage. The English gentleman who was written up in the papers for running his car on chicken manure evidently attracted a lot of attention, judging from the number of inquiries I have received.

In this country a number of sewage-treatment plants do use the methane they generate to run their lights and machinery, but if we adopted a general public policy of making methane from our garbage we might find out that we have enough for a variety of purposes. This may imply that every home connected to a sewer should be equipped with a garbage grinder and our sewage-treatment plants modified to make the generation and collection of methane one of their primary functions.

Pollution has been described as "resources out of place." Thus the sulfur dioxide that pours from our stacks to create a health problem and to corrode stone and metal is a potential source of either sulfur itself or sulfuric acid—two valuable industrial chemicals. The way we now mine sulfur in the Gulf states damages the environment, but one business-oriented magazine petulantly announced last year that if we removed the sulfur from stack gases "it might upset the economics of sulfur."

We might consider even more imaginative approaches. Not long ago a new process was announced for burning coal without releasing sulfur dioxide by partly oxidizing the coal in a bath of molten iron. This presumably produces iron-sulfur compounds that could be taken to a sewage-treatment plant and used to remove phosphates. Advanced sewage-treatment plants, such as the one at Lake Tahoe in California, which produces a potable effluent, use activated carbon to remove some of the wastes.

Activated carbon, in turn, is one of the end products now yielded by pyrolysis, or destructive distillation, a process in which nearly all kinds of organic debris are destroyed by heating them to high temperatures in containers from which oxygen is excluded. Even discarded tires can be subjected to pyrolysis to produce combustible gas, liquid oil, and carbon.

As a biologist I am perhaps prejudiced toward the biological treatment of wastes. Algae will soak up phosphates like sponges as well as take up twenty or so other elements, including the nitrate-nitrogen which, along with phosphates, is a principal cause of the algal blooms now causing our bodies of water to deteriorate. I would like to see us investigate the use of algae to remove the plant nutrients from sewage, then harvesting the algae for fertilizer or animal food. Sanitary engineers with whom I have discussed this all seem to know instinctively that it would not be economical, and so far I have been unable to verify a report about one U.S. company that is said to be growing algae commercially as animal food. In Japan, however, several species of algae are grown commercially as food for man.

In any case, if we could put a dollars-and-cents value on environmental quality, we would conclude that it is economical to remove the nitrogen and phosphorus from sewage by whatever means are necessary. As it is, I expect someone to complain that it might upset the economics of the fertilizer industry.

Fertilizer, of course, is related to our environmental difficulties in a number of ways. In most of the world, farmers still spread the manure from their animals on their fields for fertilizer, as farmers formerly did in this country. Even human body wastes are used in this way in Asia and elsewhere. But in the United States we now crowd our cattle into feed lots for fattening and buy artificial fertilizers for the fields. This creates a monstrous problem of pollution and/or disposal of animal body wastes—around 2 billion tons a year.

Any intelligent American who has watched his environment for several years must be aware that pollution is growing worse. He should also know that we are using up nonrenewable resources at a rate that is increasing constantly and that we have added 24 million people to our population in the last ten years—enough to populate one of those much publicized "new cities" of 100,000 inhabitants roughly every two weeks. He may also know that at least one quarter of our public water supplies now fail to meet U.S. Public Health Service standards and that we have scarcely any sewage-treatment plants that are adequate to protect the waters into which their effluents flow.

Clearly, instead of throwing away resources, we must learn to recycle all we can. I don't think the answer lies in "self-destruct" bottles that disintegrate when empty or in a series of "Mount Trashmores," the name given to a mountain of trash providing ski and toboggan runs south of Chicago. The wastes we discard have value if we can just adjust our economics to make their recycling profitable. Factories and power plants don't have to release fly ash from their stacks into the atmosphere—some samples of fly ash have actually been found to contain enough gold and silver to yield assays comparable to some ores that are mined in the West.

When confronted with facts such as I have presented here, some persons inevitably respond by blaming our ills on our free-enterprise system and the profit motive. I want to emphasize that I consider this a misinterpretation of the situation.

In the first place, our federal government is one of the very worst offenders when it comes to wasting resources and damaging the environment. Second, Russia has the same environmental problems we do, and for the same reasons. Both countries are at present committed to ever-continuing "growth and development."

President Nixon, no doubt with the counsel of his economic advisers, has concluded that the gross national product, or total of all goods and services produced in the nation, should be made to grow at slightly more than 4 percent per year. Anything that grows at this rate will double in size about every seventeen years.

I am a scientist, not an economist or politician, and I wouldn't presume to tell our policy-makers just what they must do. But I'm absolutely certain of the direction in which we must move. I have more confidence in our basic rationality than did another author who entitled an essay "Is Survival Economically Feasible?"

Babies vs. the GNP | Concern over the quality of life in America has blossomed so swiftly and so pervasively in the last few years that it is hard to imagine a time when air and water pollution, congestion, and, indeed, the environment in general were not active social and political issues. As might be expected of any new mass movement, the environmentalists have been quick to acquire an orthodoxy and a litany all their economic own. Of all the analysis cries that have arisen, perhaps none is quite so superficially appealing, or so profound in its long-range social and economic implications, as zero population growth—"ZPG" in the slogans of the day.

Better Life Is Goal

Herman P. Miller, the distinguished demographer who heads the population division of the United States Census Bureau, noted long ago that "the anti-natalists are touting population control not as a way to avoid domestic famine and pestilence, but as a way to achieve a better way of life—to reduce pollution, crime, crowding, traffic jams, and so forth."

There is little debate, as Dr. Miller noted in a brief but very thoughtful analysis appearing in the May issue of the *Record,* the monthly publication of the National Industrial Conference Board, that for the world as a whole, overpopulation "presents a serious survival problem."

But Dr. Miller raises a number of questions as to whether this is the case for the United States at the present time. "At some point," he said, "the population of the United States will undoubtedly have to stop growing. The only real question is when—should we be greatly concerned about that problem now?"

One of the great contributions of modern technology to society in recent years has been development of systems analysis—the ability, often with aid of a computer, to look at a total organization, to see how its parts interact and how a change in one will affect the behavior of the others.

So perhaps it is ironic that the proponents of zero population growth seem to have given so little thought to its consequences—not only in relieving the growing pressure on the limited resources of air, water, and land, but also in affecting the ability of the economy to generate the resources required to deal with the massive problems of the environment.

Hendrick S. Houthakker, who is now a member of the President's Council of Economic Advisers, noted in an address not long ago that "it may seem old-fashioned, indeed reactionary, to emphasize the growth of output as the first objective of economic policy.

"It is now fashionable," Dr. Houthakker said, "to stress the deleterious effects of growth, especially on the environment, and some wits have gone so far as to say that GNP means gross national pollution. The notion of further growth conjures up visions of more cars, more highways, more pesticides, and more of many other things that are not as popular as they used to be."

As Dr. Miller conceded that an eventual end to population growth in this country will be essential, Dr. Houthakker stated frankly that there is "much justification" for the concern about the environment.

"Nevertheless, we should be very wary," he argues, "of the currently widespread belief that deterioration of the environment is the necessary consequence of economic growth, and that consequently the only thing we can do for the environment is to stop growth itself."

"Provided we plan our affairs rationally," he continued, "there is no reason at all why growth of output should go at the expense of the environment. In fact, it would be more correct to say the opposite: that economic growth itself is necessary to bring about an improvement in our physical and social surroundings."

Dr. Miller warned that "before embracing the concept of a stationary population too warmly, we had better face up to the fact that such a population would be much older than the present one. It would have an equal number of people under fifteen and over sixty, and the average age would be thirty-seven as compared with twenty-eight at present.

"An affluent society with a stationary population," he went on to say, "would probably be more resistant to change than our present society, because wealth and conservation tend to increase with age. If the present establishment seems intolerable to the youth of America," he asserted, "imagine how it might be under a stationary population where rich old men would be even more likely to be running things."

Link Between Ills
There is some connection between pollution, high crime rates, transportation problems, and other social ills and the rate of population growth, Dr. Miller stated.

But the connection is only partial. "Pollution, traffic jams, delinquency, and crime are no worse in France, England, and Holland than in the United States," Dr. Miller said, "despite the fact that population density in these countries is between five times and thirty times as great as in the United States."

Trying to deal with the social problems we now have by persuading women not to have babies, he continued, "is like trying to treat cancer with a sedative. It might relieve the pain, but it won't make the problem go away."

What we need, he said, is a national commitment to use our

growing affluence to attack our domestic problems. "Perhaps there was a time," he said, "when each of us could maximize his satisfaction by spending his hard-earned money as he saw fit without taking others into account. If there ever were such a time, it no longer exists.

"Each of us can only maximize his own satisfaction today," Dr. Miller concluded, "by taking the needs of others into account."

Specialists Split on Role of Population in Pollution and Crime | Chicago, December 27—Four specialists divided today on the role of overpopulation in corruption of the environment, the rise in crime, and the increase in per capita cost of government.

Some argued that overpopulation was to blame, yet counterarguments were presented holding that the fault rested chiefly with how things were done, not with how many people were doing them.

The discussion was a highlight of the annual meeting of the American Association for the Advancement of Science.

Dr. Paul Ehrlich, professor of biology at Stanford University, cited experiments there showing, he said, that under increased crowding, men become more aggressive, although women do not. Thus crime and disorder can be expected to increase as the population increases, he said.

Dr. Barry Commoner, director of the Center for the Biology of Natural Systems at Washington University in St. Louis, argued that with a properly designed technology the country could support a considerably larger population without damage to the environment.

The trouble, he said, is not that, for example, there are more people wearing more clothes than before, but that clothes are now made of synthetic fibers. Manufacture of those fibers under processes now in use is far more polluting to the environment than raising cotton or sheep, he added.

Dr. Ansley Coale, director of the Office of Population Research at Princeton University, agreed with Dr. Commoner that the heart of the problem was not in population growth. It lies in the fact that modern economics reward the man who produces what the people want at the lowest possible cost, he said.

The American who does that "gets rich on profits," he said. The Soviet plant manager who does so "gets promoted."

Although a plant may drench those living downwind with noxious fumes, this does not show up on the company's books, he said. He proposed that economic incentives and penalties, including jail terms, be used to correct the situation.

Dr. Garrett Hardin, professor of human ecology at the University of California at Santa Barbara, argued that per capita services become costlier—not cheaper, as many believe—with greater concentrations of population. Thus, he said, telephone service costs more in a large city than in a small one because far more switching systems are required.

When the number of people increases fourfold, the number of possible links between them multiplies sixteen times. Thus, in a large city, there cannot be direct links between all subscribers.

Instead, there are telephone exchanges through which such traffic is routed and in an emergency that impels more than a small percentage of subscribers to place calls at the same time, such a "hierarchical" system can serve as a bottleneck, bringing communications to a standstill.

The same kind of hierarchical apparatus, Dr. Hardin said, comes between the citizen and those making decisions "at the top." The greater the population, he argued, the more remote does the citizen become from those decisions, and democracy becomes increasingly meaningless.

Furthermore, he said, it can be expected that by the year 2005, when the United States population is expected to have doubled, the crime rate will be four times greater than it is today.

Also, as production demands for a growing population escalate, the cost of keeping pollution down to acceptable levels will become rapidly greater. "The bigger we are, the worse off we are," he said. "The bigger the poorer."

Dr. Ehrlich, author of the book *The Population Bomb* and one of the more articulate advocates of an immediate halt in population growth, told a news conference before the session about tests at Stanford on crowding effects. He withheld details until the results were published but said that groups of men and women were asked to perform various tasks in varying degrees of crowding.

In some cases, a crime was described, and they were asked to assign an appropriate punishment. In other instances they were asked to play games in which they could either "go all out" for total victory or play a more cautious game.

The men responded to crowding by assigning more severe punishments and playing more aggressively, whereas the women showed no significant effect, Dr. Ehrlich said.

Dr. Coale challenged statements by Dr. Hardin that increased crime and higher per capita government costs in California could be attributed to population growth. Crime rates, he said, are also up in those states that have lost population.

He then cited the experience of San Diego. As the population of that community grew toward the million mark, its pollution filled the harbor with sludge, rendered its beaches unfit for swimmers, and drove fish from the bay. But now, with the population exceeding a million, the water is cleaner, the beaches are usable again, and the fish are coming back.

The reason, he explained, is that a large sewerage plant has reduced the discharge of wastes into the bay. Thus, he said, there seems to be economy in size because large communities can build disposal facilities that result in less per capita pollution than in small towns and villages.

Only Dr. Commoner, however, argued that all efforts should be focused on technological improvements. The population problem, he said, is beyond the reach of scientists and in any case will take care of itself.

Pollution Linked to Rise in Wealth | Washington, February 18—Dramatic gains in American affluence in the next thirty years will pose a far greater threat to the quality of life than increased population, the Census Bureau's leading authority on income said today.

Herman P. Miller, chief of census population studies, said the average family income, measured in constant purchasing power, would jump from $9,800 in 1968 to $21,000 in the year 2000. This increase is likely to be paralleled by what he calls an increase in "pollutant power."

About two-thirds of the potential increase in pollution and pressure on resources "would take place even if our population stopped growing tomorrow but continued to increase its income and to spend its money in the same old way," he said.

Mr. Miller presented his analysis in a lecture at the University of Indiana. The text was made available here.

Mr. Miller adopted a more conciliatory tone toward the population control movement than have other census officials. Like them, he asserted that slower population growth would not make a major difference.

Some Difference Seen

But, he said, it could make some difference, accounting for perhaps a third of the increased pressure on the environment.

"There is no clearly good reason why our population should continue to grow," he said. "A slower rate of growth would make it easier to cope with many of our domestic problems."

At the same time, Mr. Miller said, "the detrimental impact of affluence on the environment has not received sufficient attention," which prompted his analysis of this relationship.

The experience of the last thirty years, as measured, for example, by energy consumption or car registrations, shows far faster increases than population, he said.

"Because of our rising income per capita, more people can afford to take vacations, send their children to college, buy automobiles, more expensive houses, electrical appliances. Each of these activities creates pressure on the resources—overcrowded colleges, parks, beaches, and highways," he said.

In the next thirty years, Mr. Miller said, these income gains— and accompanying environmental pressures—will accelerate.

His projection of an average family income of $21,000 in the year 2000 assumes that the population will increase by about 75 million to 280 million, that the workweek will decrease somewhat, that women workers will increase about 10 percent, and that productivity will nearly triple.

The pressure created by such affluence, he said, is likely to be compounded by a continued concentration of the population in urban areas.

This will occur for two reasons, Mr. Miller said. One is that the

ENVIRONMENTAL POLLUTION

continued loss of the more affluent population by central cities is already making it "extremely difficult to provide adequate services for those who continue to live there."

The second is that suburban areas keep gaining people, "thereby placing a further strain on the resources in those places."

The answer to these problems, he said, must go far beyond population control efforts.

PART 4
ECOLOGY AND THE FUTURE

The complex problems of today's world lead one inevitably toward an ecological point of view. That is, an understanding of the problems requires an appreciation of the extensive ramifications of interrelationships among all species of life and between organisms and inorganic substances. The basic linkages among the many components of nature are the cycles of energy-producing matter, such as the oxygen, carbon, and nitrogen cycles. In the first article in this final section Dr. LaMont C. Cole, the distinguished biologist, describes the cycling process and indicates some of the factors affecting it. Man's activities, he points out, have accelerated the flows of chemicals in the cycling process and thereby increased the rate of energy losses from the system.

In his article on "Continuous Growth or No Growth?" Bertram G. Murray, Jr., presents a biologist's view of economics. The analogy he poses between ecosystems and economic systems is intriguing, though how far it can be carried remains to be determined. The ecological problem at the human level is vastly more complex than at the biological level; it subsumes all that the biologist has to contend with and more. Its complexity is such that few knowledgeable people would be willing to trust "an international team of planners" with the management of the world economic system, as Murray suggests. But the author is correct in his contention that radical changes in policies affecting the environment are urgently needed.

This point is subjected to a searching analysis by Peter Passell and Leonard Ross in their article "Don't Knock the $2 Trillion Economy." The easy generalizations about the evils of growth prove, on careful inspection, to rest upon faulty assumptions and incomplete awareness of all that is involved in economic growth. One of the great needs in discussions of public issues is a recognition that the problems concerned are the products of the interactions of many forces. That, of course, is what debate, if properly conducted, is calculated to reveal.

In the fourth paper Roger Revelle draws a close parallel between ecology and ethics. An awareness of the ethical issues involved in our environmental exploitation should lead us to a wiser and more thoughtful approach to our use of resources and our treatment of space. Social costs must be counted with economic costs in any calculation of benefits from technological efficiency. The manifest need is for greater emphasis upon ecological education if man is ever to succeed in dealing with the complex problems created by his interactions with the world around him.

Finally, the ethical interpretation of the ecological problem is further translated into a religious concern by Edward B. Fiske. If a "theology . . . of man's relationship to his environment" will contribute to a sane and responsible use of resources, it should be encouraged. But if it obscures or becomes a substitute for the "theology" of man's relation to man, it will defeat its purpose.

In closing these introductory remarks something should be said about the dangers of ecological enthusiasm. Current ecological issues are so infected with the public interest that the scientific expert finds it difficult to confine himself to his field of competence. His impatience with the slow pace at which corrective and protective measures are developed leads him to speak out on behalf of the policies he thinks are indicated. To put himself forward, however, as an arbiter of moral and aesthetic standards is to presume upon his knowledge and to mislead the uninformed. And if, in presenting himself as an authority on such matters, he reveals an unexplained conservatism and an ethnocentric view of political and social life, he risks losing his scientific credibility.

Can the World Be Saved?
BY LAMONT C. COLE

My title here is not my first choice. A year or so ago, a physicist discussing some of the same subjects beat me to the use of the title I would have preferred: "Is There Intelligent Life on Earth?" There is evidence that the answer to both questions is in the negative.

In recent years, we have heard much discussion of distinct and nearly independent cultures within our society that fail to communicate with each other—natural scientists and social scientists, for example. The particular failure of communication I am concerned with here is that between ecologists on the one hand and, on the other, those who consider that continuous growth is desirable—growth of population, industry, trade, and agriculture. Put another way, it is the dichotomy between the thinkers and the doers—those who insist that man should try to know the consequences of his actions before he takes them versus those who want to get on with the building of dams and canals, the straightening of river channels, the firing of nuclear explosives, and the industrialization of backward countries.

From *The New York Times Magazine,* March 3, 1968.
Copyright © 1968 by The New York Times Company.
Reprinted by permission.

The message that the ecologists—the thinkers, if you will—seek to impart could hardly be more urgent or important. It is that man, in the process of seeking a "better way of life," is destroying the natural environment that is essential to any kind of human life at all; that, during his time on earth, man has made giant strides in the direction of ruining the arable land upon which his food supply depends, fouling the air he must breathe and the water he must drink, and upsetting the delicate chemical and climatic balances upon which his very existence depends. And there is all too little indication that man has any intention of mending his ways.

The aspect of this threat to human life that has received the least public attention, but which is, I believe, the most serious is the manner in which we are altering the biological, geological, and chemical cycles upon which life depends.

When the world was young, it did not have the gaseous atmosphere that now surrounds our planet. The water that fills the oceans and furnishes our precipitation, and the nitrogen that makes up most of our atmosphere, were contained in the rocks formed in the earth's creation. They escaped by various degassing processes, the most dramatic of which was volcanic action.

The amount of oxygen in the atmosphere was negligible before the origin of living organisms that could carry on photosynthesis of the type characterizing green plants, which during daylight hours take in carbon dioxide and give off oxygen. At first, there was virtually no accumulation of oxygen in the atmosphere. The oxygen produced by marine organisms was used by a combination of natural biogeochemical processes that are still operative today—the liberation of incompletely oxidized iron salts in the weathering of silicate rocks and the decomposition of organic matter. But very gradually, some dead organisms began to pass out of circulation by being deposited in sedimentary rocks where some of them became the raw material for the creation of coal and oil. The oxygen that these well-buried organisms would have used up, had they remained on the surface and been subject to decomposition, was allowed to remain in the atmosphere. And eventually, perhaps not until 400 million years ago, this unused oxygen brought the level of oxygen in the atmosphere to slightly over 20 percent.

This is the same percentage of oxygen in the atmosphere

today. Apparently, the combination of green plants and oxygen-using organisms, including animals, became very efficient at taking oxygen from the atmosphere and returning it at equal rates. And this is true in spite of the fact that photosynthesis stops during the hours of darkness and practically stops during winter on land areas in high latitudes. It does continue, however, in low latitudes (although often greatly reduced by seasonal drought) and in the ocean (where marine micro-organisms suspended in water near the surface produce 70 percent or more of the world's photosynthetic oxygen). And we have been fortunate that atmospheric circulation patterns move the air about the globe in such a way that we have not had to be concerned that man would run out of oxygen to breathe at night or in winter. As we shall see, man is today pushing his luck.

Another chemical element essential to life is carbon. Plants use carbon dioxide to build their organic compounds, and animals combine the organic compounds with oxygen to obtain the energy for their activities. And all this is possible only because, millions of years ago, the deposition of organic matter in sedimentary rocks led to the creation of a reservoir of oxygen in the atmosphere.

The carbon-oxygen relationship is essential to photosynthesis and thus to the maintenance of all life. But should this relationship be altered, should the balance between the two be upset, life as we know it would be impossible. Man's actions today are bringing the imbalance upon us.

The carbon dioxide in the atmosphere is created in large measure by combustion. Before the time of man, the combustion in the earth's forests was spontaneous. Early man set forest fires to drive game and burned timber for warmth. He went on to find other uses for combustion and to find new combustible materials. First it was coal for heat and power, then oil and natural gas. The exploitation of these so-called fossil fuels made it possible for more people to exist on earth simultaneously than has ever been possible before. It also brought about our present dilemma: The oceans are the world's great reservoir of carbon, taking carbon dioxide from the atmosphere and precipitating it as limestone; we are now adding carbon dioxide to the atmosphere more rapidly than the oceans can assimilate it.

Industrial facilities, automobiles, and private homes are the big consumers of fossil fuels but to appreciate the magnitude of the problem, consider very briefly a still minor source of atmospheric pollution, the airplane, which may have disproportionate importance because much of the carbon dioxide and water vapor produced by the combustion in its engines are released at high altitudes where they are only slowly removed from the atmosphere.

When you burn a ton of petroleum hydrocarbon, you obtain as by-products about one and a third tons of water and about twice this amount of carbon dioxide. A Boeing 707 in flight accomplishes this feat about every ten minutes. I read in the papers that ten thousand airplanes per week land in New York City alone, not including military aircraft. If we assume very crudely that the 707 is typical of these airplanes, and that its average flight takes four hours, this amounts to an annual release into the atmosphere of about 36 million tons of carbon dioxide. And not all flights have a terminus in New York.

Thus the amount of carbon dioxide put into the atmosphere is rising at an ever-rising rate. At the same time, we are removing vast tracts of land from the cycle of photosynthetic production—in this country alone, nearly a million acres of green plants are paved under each year. The loss of these plants is drastically reducing the rate at which oxygen enters the atmosphere. And we do not even know to what extent we are inhibiting photosynthesis through pollution of freshwater and marine environments.

The carbon-oxygen balance is tipping. When, and if, we reach the point at which the rate of combustion exceeds the rate of photosynthesis, we shall start running out of oxygen. If this occurred gradually, its effect would be approximately the same as moving everyone to a mountaintop—a change that might help to alleviate the population crisis by raising death rates. However, the late Lloyd Berkner, director of the Graduate Research Center of the Southwest, thought that atmospheric depletion might occur suddenly.

The increase in the proportion of carbon dioxide in the atmosphere will have other effects. Carbon dioxide and water vapor are more transparent to shortwave solar radiation than to the longwave heat radiation from the earth to space. Thus the increased proportion of these substances in the atmosphere tends to bring about a rise in the earth's surface temperature, the so-called greenhouse effect, altering climates in ways that are still highly controversial in the scientific community but that everyone agrees are undesirable.

One school holds that the increase in temperature will melt the ice caps of Greenland and the Antarctic, raising the sea level by as much as 300 feet and thereby obliterating most of the major cities of the world. Another school believes that higher temperatures will bring about an increase in evaporation and with it a sharp rise in precipitation, the additional snow falling upon the ice caps will start the glaciers moving again, and another Ice Age will be upon us.

And these represent only the lesser-known effects of combustion on the world. They do not include the direct hazards from air pollution—on man's lungs, for example, or on vegetation near some kinds of industrial plants. Nor do they include the possibility, suggested by some scientists, that we will put enough smoke particles into the air to block solar radiation, causing a dangerous decrease in the earth's temperature. Just to indicate the complexity and uncertainty of what we are doing to the earth's climates, I should mention that the smoke-caused decrease in temperatures would most likely be offset by the carbon-dioxide-caused greenhouse effect.

In any case, if we don't destroy ourselves first, we are eventually going to run out of fossil fuels—a prospect surely not many generations away. Then, presumably, we shall turn to atomic energy (although, like the fossil fuels, it represents a nonrenewable resource; one would think that its present custodians could find better things to do with it than create explosions). And then we will face a different breed of environmental pollution.

I am aware that reactors to produce electricity are already in use or under development, but I am apprehensive of what I know of the present generation of reactors and those proposed for the future.

The uranium fuel used in present reactors has to be reprocessed periodically to keep the chain reaction going. The reprocessing yields long-lived and biologically hazardous isotopes such as strontium 90 and cesium 137 that should be stored where they cannot contaminate the environment for at least one thousand years; yet a goodly number of the storage tanks employed for this purpose are already leaking. At least these products of reprocessing can be chemically trapped and stored; another product, krypton 85, cannot be so trapped—it is sent into the atmosphere to add to the radiation exposure of the earth's biota, including man, and I don't think that anyone knows a practicable way to prevent this.

To soothe our concern about the pollution of the environment involved in fission reactors, we are glibly offered the prospect of "clean" fusion bombs and reactors. They do not require reprocessing and thus would not produce the strontium, cesium, and krypton isotopes. But to the best of my knowledge, no one knows how this new generation of reactors is to be built. And even if development is successful, fusion reactors will produce new contaminants. One such is tritium (hydrogen 3), which would become a constituent of water—and that water with its long-lived radioactivity would contaminate all environments and living things. The danger of tritium was underlined in an official publication of the Atomic Energy Commission in which it was suggested that for certain mining operations it might be better to use fission (i.e., "dirty") devices rather than fusion (i.e., "clean") devices "to avoid ground water contamination."

A prime example of what irresponsible use of atomic power could bring about is provided by the proposal to use nuclear explosives to dig a sea-level canal across Central America. The argument in its favor is that it is evidently the most economical way to accomplish the task. Yet consider the effects upon our environment. If 170 megatons of nuclear charges will do the job, as has been estimated by the Corps of Engineers, which apparently wants to do it, and if the fission explosions take place in average materials of the earth's crust, enough cesium 137 would be produced to give every person on earth a radioactive dosage 26.5 times the permissible exposure level. Cesium behaves as a gas in such a cratering explosion, and prevailing winds in the region are from east to west, so the Pacific area would presumably be contaminated first. And cesium moves right up through biological food chains, so we could anticipate its rapid dissemination among living things.

The sea-level canal proposal also poses other dangers, whether or not atomic explosives are used. In that latitude, the Pacific Ocean stands higher than the Atlantic by a disputed amount I believe to average six feet. The tides are out of phase on the two sides of the Isthmus of Panama, so the maximum difference in level can be as great as eighteen feet, and the Pacific has much colder water than the Atlantic.

Just what would happen to climates or to seafood industries in the Caribbean if a new canal moved a mass of cold Pacific water in there is uncertain, but I have heard suggestions that it might create a new hurricane center or even bring about diversion of the Gulf Stream with a drastic effect on the climates of all regions bordering the North Atlantic. We know that the sea-level Suez Canal permitted the exchange of many marine species between the Red Sea and the Mediterranean. We know that the Welland Canal let sea lampreys and alewives enter the upper Great Lakes with disastrous effects on fisheries and, more recently, on bathing beaches. We just don't know what disruptions of this sort a sea-level canal in the Isthmus might cause.

So much of the danger to man is summed up in that simple phrase "We don't know." For example, consider the nitrogen cycle, which provides that element all organisms require for the building of proteins. Nitrogen is released into the atmosphere, along with ammonia, as a gas when plants and animals decay; live plants use both elements to build their proteins, but they cannot use nitrogen in gaseous form—that task is accomplished by certain bacteria and primitive algae in the soil and the roots of some plants. Animals build their proteins from the constituents of plant proteins. As in the case of oxygen, the rates of use and return of nitrogen have reached a balance so that the percentage of nitrogen in the atmosphere remains constant.

If any one of these numerous steps in the nitrogen cycle were to be disrupted, disaster would ensue for life on earth. Depending upon which step broke down, the nitrogen in the atmosphere might disappear, it might be replaced by poisonous ammonia, or it might remain unused in the atmosphere because the plants could not absorb it in gaseous form.

Are any of these possibilities at hand? Has man's interference with natural processes begun to have a serious effect on the nitrogen cycle? The point is, we don't know—and we should, before we do too much more interfering.

We are dumping vast quantities of pollutants into the oceans. According to one estimate by the United States Food and Drug Administration, these include a half-million substances, many of which are of recent origin, including biologically active materials such as pesticides, radioisotopes, and detergents to which the ocean's living forms have never before had to try to adapt. No more than a minute fraction of these substances or the combinations of them have been tested for toxicity to life—to the diatoms, the microscopic marine plants that produce most of the earth's oxygen, or to the bacteria and microorganisms involved in the nitrogen cycle.

If the tanker Torrey Canyon had been carrying a concentrated herbicide instead of petroleum, could photosynthesis in the North Sea have been stopped? Again, we don't know, but Berkner is said to have believed that a very few instances of herbicide pollution, occurring in certain areas of the ocean that are high in photosynthetic activity, might cause the ultimate disaster.

Man has developed ingenious products and devices to bring about short-range benefits. He is constantly devising grandiose schemes to achieve immediate ends—the UNESCO plan of twenty years' ago, for example, to "develop" the Amazon basin, which I am happy to say has since been judged impracticable. Surely man's influence on this earth is now so predominant, so all-pervasive, that he must stop trusting to luck that his products and schemes will not upset any of the indispensable biogeochemical cycles.

The interference with these delicately balanced cycles is not, however, the only instance of man's misuse of his natural heritage. He has also succeeded in rendering useless huge tracts of the earth's arable land.

We hear a lot today about "underdeveloped" and "developing" nations, but many of them might more accurately be called "overdeveloped." The valleys of the Tigris and Euphrates rivers, for example, were supporting the Sumerian civilization in 3500 B.C. By the year 2000 B.C., a great irrigation complex based on these rivers had turned the area into the granary of the great Babylonian Empire (Pliny says that the Babylonians harvested two crops of grain each year and grazed sheep on the land between crops). But today less than 20 percent of the land in Iraq is cultivated; more than half of the nation's income is from oil. The landscape is dotted with mounds, the remains of forgotten towns; the ancient irrigation works are filled with silt, the end product of soil erosion; and the ancient seaport of Ur is now one hundred and fifty miles from the sea, its buildings buried under as much as thirty-five feet of silt.

The valley of the Nile was another cradle of civilization. Every year the river overflowed its banks at a predictable time, bringing water to the land and depositing a layer of soil rich in mineral nutrients for plants. Crops could be grown for seven months of the year.

Extensive irrigation systems were established in the valley before 2000 B.C. The land was the granary of the Roman Empire and continued to flourish for another two thousand years. But in modern times, economic considerations have inspired governments to divert the land from food to cash crops such as cotton in spite of the desperate need for more foodstuffs to feed a growing population. In 1902 a dam was built at Aswan to prevent the spring flood and to make possible year-round irrigation, and since then the soils have deteriorated through salinization, and productivity in the valley has decreased.

Salinization is a typical phenomenon of arid regions where evaporation is greater than precipitation. Rainwater soaks into the earth, dissolving salts as it goes; when the sun appears, evaporation at the earth's surface draws this salty water upward by capillary action, and when this water in turn evaporates, it leaves a deposit of salts on the surface. The essential condition for salinization to take place is a net upward movement of water.

Irrigation in arid areas, though it may have short-range benefits, can also be fraught with long-range dangers. The large quantities of water used in irrigation are added to the water table, raising it to the level of the irrigation ditch bottom—that is to say, the ground below that point is saturated with water. Otherwise, of course, the water in the ditches would soak right down into the earth immediately below, rather than spreading outward to nourish land on either side. But this results in a sideward and then upward movement of the irrigation water toward the surface. And when the salt-laden water reaches the surface and evaporates, salinization occurs. Unless great care is taken, irrigation can thus eventually ruin land—and it has often done so. The new Aswan High Dam is designed to bring another million acres of land under irrigation, and it may well prove to be the ultimate disaster for Egypt.

Such sorry stories could be told for country after country. The glories of ancient Mali and Ghana in West Africa were legends in medieval Europe. Ancient Greece had forested hills, ample water, and productive soil. In the land that once exported the cedars of Lebanon to Egypt, the erosion-proof old Roman roads now stand several feet above a rock desert. In China and India ancient irrigation systems stand abandoned and filled with silt.

When the British assumed the rule of India two centuries ago, the population was about 60 million. Today it is about 500 million, and most of the nation's land problems have been created in the past century by deforestation and plowing and the resulting erosion and siltation, all stemming from efforts to support this fantastic population growth.

Overdevelopment is not confined to the Old World. Archaeologists have long wondered how the Mayas managed to support what was obviously a high civilization on the now unproductive soils of Guatemala and Yucatán. Evidently they exploited their land as intensively as possible until its fertility was exhausted and their civilization collapsed.

As recently as the present decade, aerial reconnaissance has revealed ancient ridged fields on floodplains, the remnants of a specialized system of agriculture that is believed to have transformed much of South America. This same system of constructing ridges on seasonal swamps—to raise some of the land above the flood level for planting and to capture some of the floodwater—has been observed in Tanzania in Africa. The South American ridges occur in areas now considered unfit for agriculture, and though any cause and effect relationship between ridges and land ruin has not been established for those areas, it has been demonstrated in Africa where the practice is known to accelerate erosion.

Even our own young country has not been immune to deterioration. We have lost many thousands of acres to erosion and gullying and many thousands more to strip mining. It has been estimated that the agricultural value of Iowa farmland, which is about as good land as we have, is declining by 1 percent per year. In

ECOLOGY AND THE FUTURE

our irrigated lands of the West there is the constant danger of salinization.

We have other kinds of water problems as well. We are pumping water from wells so much faster than it can be replaced that we have drastically lowered water tables; in some coastal regions the water table has dipped below sea level, with the result that salt water is seeping into the water-bearing strata. Meanwhile, an estimated two thousand irrigation dams in the United States have become useless impoundments of silt, sand, and gravel.

So this is the heritage of man's past—an impoverished land, a threat to the biogeochemical cycles. And what are we doing about it?

I don't want to comment on the advertising executive who asserts that billboards are "the art gallery of the public" or on the industry spokesman who says that "the ability of a river to absorb sewage is one of our great natural resources and should be utilized to the utmost." In the face of such self-serving statements, the efforts of those who try to promote conservation on aesthetic grounds seem inevitably doomed. It makes one wonder, are we selecting for genotypes who can satisfy all their aesthetic needs in our congested cities? Are the Davy Crocketts and Kit Carsons who are born today destined for asylums, jail, or suicide?

There have been suggestions made for new ways to supplement the world's food production. We hear talk of farming the ocean bottoms, for example. And there are efforts to use bacteria, fungi, or yeasts to convert petroleum directly into food for man. This is superficially attractive because it appears to be more efficient than first feeding the petroleum to a refinery and then the gasoline to tractors and other machines which eventually deliver food to us. But it is a melancholy fact that the metabolism of bacteria, fungi, and yeasts does not generate oxygen—as do the old-fashioned green plants.

What alarms me most is that only infrequently, and usually in obscure places, does one come across articles by authors who recognize that no matter what we do, it is impossible to provide enough food for a world population that increases at a compound interest rate of 1.7 percent a year. Thus, there appears to be no way for us to escape our dependence on green plants; and even with them, there is no way for us to survive except to halt population growth completely or even to undergo a period of population decrease if, as I anticipate, definitive studies show our population to be already beyond what the earth can support on a continuous basis. Just as we must control our interference with the chemical cycles that provide the atmosphere with its oxygen, carbon, and nitrogen, so must we control our birth rate.

In order to accomplish this end, natural scientists, social scientists, and political leaders will have to learn to overcome that failure of communication which I referred to earlier. And all three will have to learn to communicate with the general public. This is a large order, but I have found in recent years that intercommunication is possible between ecologists and social scientists who are concerned with population problems.

For example, as a natural scientist, it would not occur to me that in many cultures it is important to save face and prove virility by producing a child as soon after marriage as possible. In these cultures, population planners must evidently aim at delaying the age of marriage or spreading the production of children after the first. And after it has been pointed out to me, I can easily see that a tradition to produce many children would develop under social conditions where few children survive to reach maturity and families wish to assure that they will have descendants.

In a Moslem country like Pakistan, where women will not allow themselves to be examined by a male physician, birth control by such measures as the intrauterine device (IUD) is impracticable, and it is difficult to convey a monthly schedule of pill-taking to the poorly educated. However, just as the reproductive cycles of cattle can be synchronized by hormone treatments so that many cows can undergo simultaneous artificial insemination, so the menstrual cycles of populations of women can be synchronized. Then the instructions for contraception can take such a simple form as: "Take a pill every night the moon shines." But in a country like Puerto Rico the efforts of an aroused clergy to instill guilt feelings about the decision a woman must make each day can render the pill ineffective. Here, the IUD, which only requires one decision, provides an answer.

In any case, there is ample evidence that people the world over want fertility control. Voluntary sterilization is popular in India, Japan, and Latin America. In Japan and in Western European countries that have made legal abortion available upon request the birth rates have fallen dramatically. With such recent techniques as the pill and the IUD, and the impending availability of antimeoitic drugs, which inhibit sperm productivity in the male, and anti-implantation drugs, which can prevent pregnancy when taken as long as three days after exposure, practicable fertility control is at last available.

Kingsley Davis, a population expert at the University of California at Berkeley, has recently expressed skepticism about schemes for family planning on the grounds that they do not actually represent population policy but merely permit couples to determine their family size voluntarily. This is certainly true, but the evidence is overwhelming that a great many of the children born into the world today are unwanted. I think we must start by preventing these unwanted births and then take stock of what additional measures, such as negative dependency allowances, may be called for.

Japan has already shown that a determined people can in one generation bring the problem of excessive population growth under control. The Soviet Union seems finally to have abandoned the dogma that overpopulation problems are by-products of capitalism and couldn't exist in a socialistic country. So a beginning has been made. It now becomes more urgent that social and natural scientists get together and try to decide what an optimum size for the human population of the earth would be.

I shall try to end on a note of optimism. We have seen the start of efforts at meaningful birth control. A five-year study, known as the International Biological Program, is investigating the effects that man is having on the environment. If the world's best minds can at last come to grips with the population problem and effect its control, and if this can be achieved before some miscalculation, or noncalculation, sends the earth environment into an irreversible decline, then there indeed may be some hope that the world can be saved.

Continuous Growth or No Growth?
What the Ecologists Can Teach the Economists
BY BERTRAM G. MURRAY, JR.

The intensifying debate between the "pessimists" and the "optimists" reached a peak recently with the publication of "The Limits to Growth," a report prepared by an M.I.T. team headed by systems analyst Dennis L. Meadows for the Club of Rome's "Project on the Predicament of Mankind." The authors, using an admittedly simplified world model, fed data into a computer and concluded "with some confidence that, under the assumption of no major change in the present system, population and industrial growth will certainly stop within the next century, at the latest." In taking exception to this conclusion, those who are optimistic about future economic and population growth point out what Meadows's team had already admitted: the lack of hard data, the difficulty of modeling the effects of technological innovation, and the impossibility of modeling changes in human value systems. In addition, some pro-growth adherents emphasize the potentially disastrous economic consequences of a no-growth policy; for instance, Peter Passell and

Leonard Ross, writing in this magazine last March 5, conclude: "Quite simply, growth is the only way in which America will ever reduce poverty."

There can be no doubt that Americans are being offered a choice—no, they are being told they must make a choice—between a continuous-growth economic system and a no-growth economic system. What's more, Americans will make a choice, even unwittingly, because acceptance of current economic policies is one alternative. But how are Americans to decide who is right, the optimists or the pessimists? Is the argument entirely esoteric or academic? What evidence is there to support one side or the other?

First, Americans must come to understand the nature of forecasting the future. All forecasts are derived from models of the real world. Simplified assumptions are always made, whether one is predicting the consequences of economic growth or the need to build nuclear power plants now to satisfy the energy demand in 1992. Scientific models are evaluated on how well they predict and describe. But models are evaluated by human beings, and therefore models are often accepted or rejected on emotional grounds, whether they describe economic, biological, or physical relationships. Even Albert Einstein could ignore the later developments of quantum theory because their statistical nature conflicted with his belief that "God does not play dice with the world."

In the social sciences, models are also evaluated according to the goals and values of the system. Capitalism or socialism, democracy or fascism are neither good nor bad except as they conform to the goals and values of the societies that practice them or to those of neighboring societies.

Both ecologists and economists have developed models that describe the cause and effect relationships within their respective systems. It seems incredible that ecologists and economists have not shared their ideas before now because both study the same phenomena, albeit in different populations. Ecologists study competition between individuals and between populations for resources, the growth of populations, and the movement of materials (e.g., water and minerals) in ecological systems (ecosystems). Economists study competition between producers for markets, the growth of production, and the movement of goods and resources within economic systems. In each of these areas, ecologists and economists have models which have entirely different consequences. A comparison of these models may enable us to understand better the choice we are going to make between continuous-growth and no-growth economic systems.

Biological growth of all kinds has a characteristic pattern with respect to time. Regardless of the nature of the population —whether birds, or bees, or protozoans, or the cells of human beings—its numbers grow slowly at first, then increase rapidly before slowing and leveling off at some equilibrium level at which the cells of the tissue or organism, or the animals in a population, are dying at the same rate that new ones are being formed or born. This is the so-called steady state.

The economic model of American businessmen, economists, and politicians demands continuously increasing growth, as reflected by the goal of increasing the gross national product. Undeniably, economic growth has brought Americans the highest standard of living anywhere in the world. By contrast, a no-growth, or steady-state, economic system has such consequences as declining material wealth and increasing unemployment as population increases. Given such a choice most reasonable persons would select the continued growth of the American economy. But can a 4 percent annual increase in the GNP, which requires doubling the production of goods and services in seventeen years and quadrupling them in thirty-four, be sustained?

Such continuous-growth curves are not unknown in biological and physical systems. When cells continue multiplying in animal tissues, we call them cancer cells. Their growth is not indefinite. Indeed, they eventually kill the host organism. Populations of animals that are increasing have a similar fate, a decisive population crash. A classic case is that of the deer population inhabiting the Kaibab Plateau on the northern rim of the Grand Canyon. In 1907, game managers began removing the deer's natural predators, the mountain lions, wolves, and coyotes. The deer population increased rapidly from 4,000 to an estimated 100,000 in 1924. This growing population seriously depleted the resources of its environment, and it finally crashed. Sixty thousand deer died of starvation and disease in the winters of 1925 and 1926. The population continued declining, finally leveling off at around 10,000. (The implication of this and similar cases with respect to the world's rapidly increasing human population should be clear, but this is not the point at issue here.)

In physical systems, an example of such exponential growth is the chain reaction of fissioning uranium-235 nuclei. A single neutron splits a uranium nucleus, giving off two or three more neutrons (average, 2.5), which in turn split two or more uranium nuclei, giving off increasingly large numbers of neutrons that split increasingly large numbers of uranium nuclei, resulting in a nuclear explosion that generates vast amounts of energy for a short period of time.

Thus, in biological and physical systems, continuous growth can lead to disasters—death from cancer, a sharp increase in death rate leading to population decline, inefficient use of energy in nuclear explosions. Conditions are evidently optimal for increasing growth for a time. If a cancer cell, a deer, or a neutron could think and talk, it might say, "My, things couldn't be better, for we seem to be thriving." But we human beings can think, and we know by observation that these conditions are short-lived. In nature most populations are in equilibrium. By some means or another, an increase in numbers is followed by a decrease. After accumulating uranium-235 atoms in a bomb or power plant, we humans are careful in regulating the production of neutrons.

In biological and physical systems, then, the consequences of increasing growth are precisely those forecast in "The Limits to Growth" for human population and industrial growth. Although this forecast could be considered "theoretical," there is ample observational evidence from analogous systems to increase the probability of its correctness. Because of numerous modifying factors, the accuracy of the forecast with respect to the timing of the collapse is more difficult to evaluate. Thus, we can be fairly certain that collapse will occur but less certain as to when.

A second area of interest to ecologists is the biogeochemical cycles. These describe the movement within ecosystems of minerals, water, oxygen, carbon dioxide, and other nutrients essential for life. For example, carbon dioxide in the air is incorporated into organic molecules (carbohydrates, etc.) by photosynthesis in plants. The plants are eaten by animals, which in turn may be eaten by other animals. Carbon dioxide is returned to the air through the chemical breakdown of organic molecules through metabolism and decomposition. Once back in the air, the carbon dioxide can be incorporated again into new organic molecules. In other words, carbon dioxide follows a cycle between the atmosphere and living organisms. The other nutrients also recycle through an ecosystem but often in more complex ways. An ecosystem such as a pond, a field, or a forest is maintained because of this recycling of essential nutrients, which results because one species' waste is some other species' food. But recycling is not 100 percent efficient. In the course of time there is a net change in the chemical make-up of the ecosystem. This results in a continuously changing environment, a process called succession. The ecological status quo cannot be maintained without perfect cycling.

In a simplified man-made ecosystem, we can better observe the consequences of interfering with nutrient recycling. The minerals removed from the soil by a corn crop, for example, find their way to market either directly as corn or indirectly via corn-fed pigs rather than back into the soil. Several consecutive crops seriously deplete the fertility of the soil, at least for corn plants. Smart farmers rotate their crops, each crop replacing those minerals the previous crop removed. One crop's waste (what it puts in the soil) is another's nutrient.

Man's complex technological society demands from its environment not only food but also large amounts of raw materials for building houses, factories, cars, television sets, and so on. The recycling of these materials is virtually zero. Iron, for example, is mined where it is concentrated in the earth, processed into steel, and formed into cars, which after a few years' use are allowed to rust away in some field. The iron in this dispersed state is no longer mineable. A technological ecosystem that does not recycle materials is no more likely to be sustained indefinitely than a cornfield.

Recycling is increasing in the United States (as with soda bottles and newspapers), but it is not yet a way of life. Just look at our overflowing dumps.

Ecologists and economists have strikingly different views on the effects of competition in ecosystems and economic systems, respectively. A cornerstone of ecological theory is the competitive exclusion principle. Simply, this principle states that competing species cannot coexist indefinitely. If two species are utilizing a resource that is in short supply, one of them will be eliminated as a competitior, either by being forced out of the ecosystem or by being forced to use some other resource. As a result, in communities of animals, ecologists normally find that each species differs from the others in its utilization of the resources in the environment.

The competitive exclusion principle is consistent not only with observations in natural situations but also with laboratory experiments. In the 1930's, G. F. Gause, the Russian ecologist, demonstrated the "struggle for existence" between species of yeast cells and between species of protozoans. Later Thomas Park and his colleagues at the University of Chicago undertook an elegant series of experiments with flour beetles. In each case only one species could survive. Again and again, the evidence seems to indicate that competition reduces the number of competitors.

The economists' model of competition is notably different. Competition is supposed to maintain diversity and stability in economic systems; it is assumed that with numerous producers competing for the market, no single producer could control the industry and therefore fix prices and limit the entrance of new producers into the business. In competing for markets, producers would increase efficiency and reduce prices or increase quality at the same price. Either way, the consumer benefits. Or so say the optimistic economists, businessmen, and politicians.

To the contrary, the evidence suggests that competition in economic systems has the same effect as competition in ecosystems. It reduces the number of competitors. The more efficient or larger producers force the less efficient or smaller out of business or buy them out, resulting in monopoly. This was recognized, practically if not theoretically, in the nineteenth century, and Congress passed the Sherman Antitrust Act of 1890, which unfortunately does not eliminate industry dominance by one or a few corporations. The number of competitors continues to become smaller, prices and profits increase, and the huge corporations and conglomerates are more difficult if not impossible to manage efficiently. The railroads and Lockheed are examples.

Americans must face several unpleasant facts squarely. First, they must understand that the American economic model—one that values increasing growth, waste (nonrecycling of essential materials), and competition—is inherently unstable. This model violates, either actually or theoretically, ecological principles that have been established by observations: Competition results in elimination of competitors; continually growing populations eventually collapse; and ecosystems whose essential materials are not recycled cannot be sustained. There is no reason to believe that economic systems based on principles that bring collapse to ecological systems are immune to a similar fate. Indeed, some economists implicitly agree. Leonard Silk reported in the *Times* last spring that at a Bryn Mawr College symposium on "Limits to Growth," economists suggested that businessmen might manage to hang on for several decades longer than write capitalism off already as a lost cause. There is no question that collapse is inevitable. The question seems to be how much longer businessmen can continue making profits at the expense of future generations. For nonbusinessmen a reasonable course of action would be to take steps now that will prevent or at least ameliorate the effects of the crash.

A second unpleasant fact that we Americans are going to have to face is the necessity of reducing our current standard of living. The current disparity between the conditions of living in the developing countries and those in the developed countries, especially in the United States, will not be tolerated. Inasmuch as the American standard of living depends upon imports of raw materials from the developing countries, the decision to reduce our level of affluence may not be ours to make but will be forced upon us as the developing countries increase their demands on the earth's resources for their own consumption. There is great danger here. Without international regulation of economic systems, the countries will be competing with one another for resources, a condition that often leads to war. With today's weapons, such competition, unlike biological competition, does not guarantee a survivor.

Compounding this situation is the necessity to permit increasing economic growth and a rising standard of living in the developing countries while the developed countries are scaling down their own standard of living. The United States may still remain Number 1, but Numbers 2 and 10 and 100 will not be so far behind as they are now.

Like it or not Americans must now decide between two alternatives: (1) the status quo—an economic system that offers short-term profits to a few and disaster within generations, if not decades (for some it has already arrived) and (2) an economic system that provides for the long-term survival of humankind at a decent standard of living. Whatever is decided in the immediate future in the United States will have long-term global effects.

It probably should be mentioned that neither socialism nor communism is an acceptable economic system for providing for man's long-term economic survival. It turns out that all of man's economic systems are pro-growth and wasteful, and therefore unstable. The alternative economic system has yet to be formulated. In broadest outline, this economic system will have to be consistent with ecological theory. First, it will have to be, over-all, a no-growth system. Some growth will occur in individual enterprises as they develop new technologies, but other enterprises will have to be curtailed. Such a no-growth economic system will have to be tied in with a no-growth population policy. Second, the new system must demand the recycling of as much as possible of those materials we now call waste. For instance, old autos must be made into new autos. And, when raw materials cannot be extracted from worn-out finished products, these products must be converted into other products. And human and animal wastes must be converted into useful fertilizer. And so on. Third, the effects of competition must be recognized and controlled. Competing businesses must be ecologically responsible in their consumption of raw materials, production of pollution, and reuse of materials.

Such an economic system would have to be highly regulated, and because both modern economies and environmental problems cross international boundaries, a worldwide, environmentally responsible economic system would have to be managed by an international team of planners, most reasonably organized by the United Nations.

Government legislation affecting business practices is not a new idea. Capitalism has been evolving for more than a century. At one time, the entrepreneur's sole responsibility was to make a profit. Without restriction, the quest for profit led to extensive abuses of labor, which became sufficiently widespread and evident by the late 1800's to move governments to pass laws that forced socially responsible management policies on business. The conflict between management and labor continues, but no one now suggests that child labor, fourteen-hour days, and ten-cents-a-day wages should be reinstituted. The quest for profit also led to extensive abuses of our environment, which are only now becoming sufficiently evident to lead to the notion that government should pass laws that force environmentally responsible policies on business. The time to begin planning and instituting changes is now, if we are going to avert the disaster inevitable under our present economic policies.

I am pessimistic about the future—not because the problems we face are technically or economically insurmountable but because they seem humanly insurmountable.

The generation in political power grew up during the period of man's greatest "progress." More people are living better now than ever before. This increase in living standards undeniably resulted from economic growth and competition, sufficient reason for understanding why those persons who lived through that stage in man's history should be reluctant to give up their faith in economic growth and competition.

At the same time technological innovation, in agriculture, medicine, and industry, for example, has bordered on the miraculous, culminating in putting a man on the moon. These successes have engendered a faith that in technology lies the solutions to today's problems. But the technology of the past made use of nature's laws rather than denied them, and it must do so in the future as well. Technologists will not be able to use physical laws to get around ecological laws. Still, the myth of technological innovation remains.

A second hurdle in the way of rational decision making is the misunderstanding that Americans have regarding the relationship of economic systems to governing systems. There is a widespread notion that capitalism and democracy are synonymous. But economics deals with the production and flow of goods, whereas government deals with the means by which people establish policies to live by. A government-regulated economy is not inconsistent with a democratic form of government. If the American people evaluate the advantages and disadvantages of a no-growth economy against those of a continuous-growth economy and decide that environmentally responsible legislation is necessary for our long-term survival, such legislation could be determined democratically by the people through their representatives. Indeed, the issue is not whether or not government should interfere with economic policy but what that economic policy should be. Should the government encourage economic growth, as it has in the past, or should it favor ecologically sound economic policies?

Finally, increasing the public's understanding of the alternatives being considered is proceeding too slowly. Many people refuse to listen to any suggestion that conflicts with the long-cherished American ideals of production, profit, competition, and growth. Perhaps the outstanding example of the conservationists' failure to educate even those with a direct economic interest is the whaling industry. Despite the extermination of local populations of whales from the eastern Atlantic, the northern Atlantic, and then the northern Pacific oceans during the preceding three centuries, the whaling fleets of seventeen nations continued the intensifying hunt into the southern oceans following the end of World War II. One after another species approached extinction, and one after another whaling fleet ceased operations until now only Japan and Russia maintain active fleets: If it proved impossible to convince the whaling companies that conservation of whales through regulating the kill was in their own long-term interest, what chance is there to convince the city dweller of the need to conserve wilderness, or the suburban and rural resident of the need to improve living conditions in the cities, or industrialists, businessmen, and people in general of the need to reduce production and consumption?

The future is not entirely black. At least the problems of overpopulation, overconsumption, and pollution are being discussed by a diverse group of persons. But whether the ultimate causes of our problems ever become understood, whether the solutions become clear, and whether those solutions are ever carried out remain to be seen.

Don't Knock the $2 Trillion Economy
BY PETER PASSELL AND LEONARD ROSS

Wealth," wrote John Kenneth Galbraith in *The Affluent Society,* "is not without its advantages and the case to the contrary, although it has been made, has never proved widely persuasive." But times have changed since 1958. We have become a richer nation but not, by common agreement, a happier one. The gross national product has gone up 64 percent; but what of the gross national pleasure?

To many, there is an undeniable connection between consuming more and enjoying things less. A new generation of economists, environmentalists, and law professors gifted with advanced consciousness has pronounced its curse upon economic growth. "You could very comfortably have stopped growing after the First World War," the British economist Ezra J. Mishan recently said in this magazine. "There was enough technology to make life quite pleasant. Cities weren't overgrown. People weren't too avaricious. You hadn't really ruined the environment as you have now, and built up entrenched industries so you can't go back."

From *The New York Times Magazine,* March 5, 1972.

That, in a nutshell, is the case against growth: more is less. More automobiles, cassette recorders, and cook-in-a-pouch vegetables. Less satisfaction in the quality of the common life.

The case sounds simple, but it is really a sheaf of complaints misleadingly wrapped as one. Anti-materialism tells us that we have so much now that more can't really make us happier, while elitism confides that mushrooming incomes for the masses can only dilute the pleasures of those on top. Ecological conservatism says that the process of growth ruins our environment and may even risk the extinction of life. Anti-materialism warns that prosperity in the rich nations is hewn from the hides of other countries' poor.

Actually the sharp contrast in living standards between the United States and the rest of the industrialized world suggests the obvious virtues of the trillion-dollar economy. The average factory worker in Britain, earning half the wage of his Yankee counterpart, may in many respects lead an adequate existence. But he does it living with his wife and children in a three-room apartment, often without a refrigerator. The chances are good that his family shares a bathroom at the end of the hall. There is plenty of food on his dinner table, but too much of it is starch. To save money, his annual vacation is spent at a cheap seashore hotel a hundred miles from home. His kids cannot afford to go to college or, often, even to finish school.

Of course, none of this really proves that Englishmen are less happy than Americans. England may enjoy a less materialist culture than ours, and its poorly paid factory workers may be less prone to base their self-esteem on making money. To critics of growth, this cultural difference is far from accidental. Growth itself, they say, speeds up the treadmill of industrial life, creating the acquisitive values necessary to sustain it. As Mishan preaches, "The more affluent a society, the more covetous it needs to be. Keep a man covetous—'achievement-motivated' is the approved term—and he may be kept running hard to the last day of his life."

Growth does indeed require some sacrifice, since today's consumption needs to be channeled into building tomorrow's greater economc capacity. The societies which have achieved rapid growth—nineteenth-century Britain, the United States, Germany, Russia, China, Japan—have often stressed the will to delay gratification. Mishan writes: "Our eyes are ever on the clock and our calendars marked for weeks and months ahead. . . . This greed for the rewards of the future . . . hastens us through our brief lives . . . and cheats us of all the spaciousness of time."

A fashionable new critic of modern life, Charles Reich, links the materialist urge to Consciousness II, the submergence of the individual to the needs of the corporate state. Materialism disciplines the factory worker or lawyer to endless boredom on the production line or in the office and numbs him to the pain of traffic jams and half-hour lunch breaks. In the process, "economic progress destroys nature, adventure, traditions, and the local community."

Growth, indeed, has historically been associated with a tolerance for regimentation and sacrifice in the name of false gods. As recently as 1961, advocates of growth praised its virtues not in terms of added trips to the beach, senior citizens' housing, or more generous pensions, but in the shabby clichés of national purpose: beating the Russians to ICBM's, the moon, and the hearts of the Third World.

Growth, then, often reflects some unappetizing values. But for the most part it does not create those values. American materialism and German regimentation could survive decades of economic stagnation. The low-growth Eisenhower years did not wean Americans from their dependence on tangible signs of success nor soften them up for an eventual change of consciousness. If, as Reich believes, Consciousness II contains the seeds of its own destruction, the agent of transformation is not growthlessness but affluence.

Even if America could remake her culture by reducing her growth rate, it is not clear that the trade would be worth making. English values, for example, are not unambiguously preferable to our own; if our treadmill is competition, theirs is the class system. Which stereotype of the British are we to believe: the content industrial laborer, protected against disaster by social insurance and nourished in his self-regard by a sense of tradition, or the disgruntled mill worker trapped by the endless monotony of near poverty in a sooty North Country metropolis?

Luckily, the question need not be answered. For better or worse, most Americans unambiguously cherish middle-class comforts. And the process of slowing growth is more likely to cause unnecessary ulcers than it is to alter our materialistic values. Thanks to the enormous capacity of the U.S. economy, Americans have since World War II lived better than the English live today. But the average workingman is still far from achieving affluence. His take-home pay, after taxes, is about $110 a week. That suffices to keep the wolf from the door (especially if his wife also works) but buys few real luxuries. Our typical wage-earner knows quite well what to do with extra cash. He could use money for roomier housing to make the presence of his children less harassing; money for movies and restaurants and baby sitters as an alternative to Saturday night in front of the television set; money to support aging parents under a different roof.

The only way he has to get those things is through growth. The economic pie just is not big enough to go around, no matter how we choose to slice it. A reasonable growth rate, however, could easily double the average American's income in the next twenty-five years.

The *dolce vita* image of overabundance does not fit the facts—only 10 percent of all families make $15,000 after taxes. And the durability of the myth is puzzling. Perhaps it can be explained as a creation of the people who better fit the stereotype, the relatively few Americans with lots of money to spend and little experience at spending it. America is very good to the few million assorted professionals, successful businessmen, and intermediate-rank executives who earn $20,000 or more a year. They are largely responsible for the explosive demand for foreign travel, wine, and gourmet food, expensive stereos, ski, boat, and hobby equipment, second homes and third cars, etc.

The media, from magazines to television, cater to upper-middle-income interests and world view simply because it is good business. "Typical" well-dressed matrons sell convenience foods from gleaming stainless-steel and Formica kitchens that belong to $100,000 homes. Young moderns discuss the merits of color TV's in impossibly well-furnished dens from the same establishments. Those who can't afford all the trappings are still urged to buy as many of them as possible.

The importance of the prosperous minority has become the

representation of American success and their failings the target of pop sociologists. Unsurprisingly, the critics of prosperity are members of the privileged classes generalizing from the waste and ennui of wealthy suburbs to the whole nation.

Of course it is true that every American city has neighborhoods of sprawling homes filled with tasteless furniture, gin-sotted housewives, and spoiled teen-agers. But most Americans buy tasteless furniture because it's cheap and drink more to relieve fatigue than ennui. The obvious fact that a three-car garage and ski weekends in Switzerland don't guarantee happiness is a less than convincing reason for denying aspirants a chance at bourgeois living.

A less charitable interpretation of upper-middle-class criticism of growth is that the elite understands it has more to lose than gain from the diffusion of the bourgeois standard throughout the United States. Wealth in America provides membership privileges in a rather exclusive club. And like most clubs, the tangible and intangible benefits of membership decline as the club expands.

Nature lovers grieve for their loss of privacy in national parks as more people can afford to make the trip. Skiers must endure endless lift lines and reckless adolescents on busy slopes where they once schussed in peace. Hit plays sell out months in advance; opera tickets are unpurchasable; grand cru Burgundy prices are bid up by nouveaux wine enthusiasts; vacationers must wait for hours to pick up mail at the London American Express.

Prosperity means that nobody wants to clean other people's homes, take care of other people's children, or grease other people's cars. Increasingly, service industries are manned by the resentful poor instead of the cheerful daughters of the working classes waiting to get married.

Intangible status losses accompany these very real losses in comfort and serenity. One of the virtues of a winter vacation in the Caribbean used to be the uniqueness of sporting a tan in January. Now this sign of affluence is shared with a half-million secretaries who can afford a week at the Montego Bay Holiday Inn. What is the purpose of shopping at Tiffany's or Neiman-Marcus if everybody else does too?

Such are the rules of a democratic society that this loss of privilege is only rarely marshaled as an argument against growth. The point is transformed into generalized *Angst* about materialist values, concern for the environment, and enthusiasm for population control. Automobiles are cast as the villains of a physically and spiritually depleted society with no recognition of the mobility they symbolize for most Americans. Conservation addicts ignore the pleasure of hoi polloi, whose campfires reduce the clarity of the air and whose conversations break the awesome silence.

It would be unfair to tar all the opponents of growth as elitists securing their room at the top. Economic growth has real costs, which must be weighed against the benefits. Few of us are immune from the irritation of pollution linked to prosperity. River water used as a coolant by thousands of factories is dumped back, warmed and reeking with chemicals. Insecticides washed off millions of farms into the national water supply threaten to make fish toxic to man. Electric power plants, garbage incinerators, and automobiles defile the air with gases, slicing years off the lives of city dwellers.

It is even plausible, though not very convincing, that these side effects of prosperity have completely canceled out the benefits of further material accumulation. By this reasoning, a proper accounting would show that a billion-dollar increase in output creates more than a billion dollars' worth of damage from extra pollution. Put another way, the argument implies that growth is an illusion. Each new kilowatt of electricity has less value than the house paint and human lungs destroyed by the accompanying smoke. At least one industrial economy, Japan, is taking the ecological argument to heart. After decades of 10 percent to 15 percent growth and the worst urban pollution in the world, the Japanese have decided to slow down. Resources will be diverted from heavy industry to environmental amenities such as breathable air and swimmable water.

Economists have little quarrel with the need to weigh the costs of prosperity against the benefits, but they don't believe that the solution requires a slackening of growth. Pollution, they say, doesn't come from growth but from our perverse system of incentives to industry. Today firms aren't charged for using the biosphere as a dumping ground, so they poison the air and foul the water. Any resource for which no charge is made would likewise be over-used by business. If precious metals were free, every steam shovel would be made of platinum. Since nobody is charged for using the environment, its value is ignored. The answer is not to stop aiming for growth but to start charging for pollution.

If Con Ed were forced to pay for its abuse of the air, the management would learn how to clean up its own mess. If autos were taxed according to the content of their emissions, General Motors would find it worthwhile to build sweet-smelling engines. Halting growth would do far less to scrub the environment than a simple policy of making business put its money where its exhaust is.

A corollary to the environmental arguments against growth is the notion that fuel for the economic machine is finite; the more rapidly we grow, the more we hasten the day when the earth will be stripped of all usable raw materials. This natural-limit theory of growth is at the core of the elaborate computer simulation of the world created by engineer Jay Forrester of the Massachusetts Institute of Technology, which predicts economic collapse within a few generations. As a disciple, Anthony Lewis of the *Times,* writes: "Growth is self-defeating . . . the planet cannot long sustain it. . . . To ignore that tendency, to predict that growth can go on forever, is like arguing that the earth is flat. Only the consequences are more serious."

The fallacy in this reasoning is the assumption that raw materials will always be used in the future as they are today: when the last drop of oil is burned, the last truck will sputter to a halt. But the history of technology gives us every reason to believe that long before we run out of Arabian oil we will begin extracting petroleum from the vast reserves of oil-shale rocks and tar sands. And long before we run out of those reserves, cars will be powered with other sources of energy.

Appeals to faith in technical change are more than a cheap debating technique to counter the Forrester school. The technology of substituting plentiful materials for scarce ones grows every day. Silicates made from sand replace copper and silver radio circuitry; European cattle feeds are enriched with nutrients made of natural gas converted by bacteria; mattresses are filled with polyurethane which never was closer to a Liberian rubber tree than Bayonne, New Jersey. Among long-range prospects is the controlled-fusion reaction. This capture of the power of the hydrogen bomb could provide all the energy we would need for several billion years. Technology, of course, is neither entirely benign nor entirely predictable. But it would be foolish to act on the assumption that science has nothing more to offer.

Critics have used similar arguments about raw materials to link growth with our drive for economic and political domination of the Third World. Expansion at home, they say, requires the exploitation of natural resources abroad, and simultaneously provides the wherewithal for American military adventurism. On the one hand, U.S. factories consume the irreplaceable mineral treasures of foreign lands—oil, copper, silver, phosphates, uranium, rich agricultural soils—thereby creating an economic rationale for imperialism; on the other, growth itself gives the United States the capacity to build the military machinery of imperialism without domestic sacrifice. Vietnam proved that the U.S. economy can pay for guns and still wallow in butter.

This assault on growth raises two quite separate questions: Is American growth dependent on foreign raw materials? If so, does our consumption of these resources hurt the nations in which they are found?

The ties between growth and imports are as tenuous as the idea that resource scarcity places a severe limit on growth. The American economy does use an increasing amount of the world's minerals. But that does not mean that we are becoming more dependent on them. Today, raw materials brought in from abroad constitute less than 1 percent of the U.S. gross national product, and with few exceptions these materials can be found in North America (though at somewhat higher cost).

If we were cut off from foreign supplies we would simply start mining or synthesizing our own. The increase in cost would represent a very modest fraction of the gross national product, for in a giant economy such as ours, the technology of growth creates the option of self-sufficiency as rapidly as it generates a demand for raw materials: Gasoline could be extracted from Colorado's deposits of shale rock instead of the Libyan Desert; nuclear-power reactors could breed most of their own fuel instead of depleting African uranium.

Of course, in the process of the expansion of world trade, American companies like Anaconda, Alcoa, and Gulf have developed private stakes in the control of foreign resources. Corporate interests can more than occasionally be translated into American foreign policy; at its bleaker moments, the U.S. State Department has been the drone of Wall Street. But growth itself is not the villain and actually serves to weaken the rationale for imperialism. Gunboat-diplomacy makes even less sense now for the United States than it did in 1906.

Nor is it true that American economic growth is necessarily injurious to the Third World. Underdeveloped countries need dollars to buy industrial products more than they need their own raw materials. Chile has more use for turbines and tractor parts than for mountains of copper ore. The only way it can buy these goods is through trade. A slowdown in American growth would simply mean reduced American demand for most of the products of the world's poorer nations.

Although growth implies trade, it does not necessarily imply increasing subjugation of foreign industries to American corporations. Indeed, as foreign economies themselves grow through increasing trade with the United States, their governments become more likely to reject the paternalistic relationships of yesteryear. It is the most impoverished lands, with the lowest trading volume, that are most thoroughly company nations. Liberia was until recently run by Firestone Tire and Rubber; but Brazil, its neofascist military government notwithstanding, plays off American against Japanese capitalists and kowtows to neither Esso nor Mitsubishi. American growth, reflected in rising imports, breeds complex economies abroad which can more readily withstand the pressures of foreign capital.

So far we have spoken only of the arguments against growth— the fruits of progress, it seems to us, need not be electric can openers, sulfurous rivers, and castrated banana republics. But rapid growth as a national policy has a *raison d'être* more pressing than the extension of the good life beyond Scarsdale. Quite simply, growth is the only way in which America will ever reduce poverty.

On the face of it, there should be an easy solution to poverty in the United States. A redistribution of only 5 percent of the national income could bring every family up to a minimum $5,000 income. But as of this writing, even President Nixon's welfare reform proposal—for a $2,400 minimum income for a family of four—remains mired in Congress. Explicit redistribution of income is still political anathema.

Liberals like to believe that growth in public programs with broad constituencies—such as health insurance, aid to colleges and universities, federal housing programs and public works—can accomplish indirectly the redistribution that would never be voted directly. But, for the most part, these and other government programs simply funnel money to the middle class.

Federal transportation subsidies overwhelmingly aid the automobile, not the subway; farm programs sustain the squire, not the serf; urban renewal calms the middle classes and dispossesses the poor. National health-insurance proposals would multiply the burden of the payroll tax, heavily concentrated on the working poor.

The attraction of growth is that nobody gets to vote on the slice of its benefits saved for the poor. While the relative share of income that poor people get seems to be frozen, their incomes do keep pace with the economy. It's more lucrative to wash cars or wait on tables today than twenty years ago. Even allowing for inflation, the average income of the bottom tenth of the population has increased about 55 percent since 1950. Twenty more years of growth could do for the poor what the Congress won't do.

Growth is not a romantic goal, nor is it a military or strategic imperative. It offers at most a partial substitute for the measures which America should take to create a humane society. We do not argue for growth as an obsession or an object of heroic sacrifice, but simply as a sober undertaking for a nation in which scarcity is not for many a thing of the past.

Human Ecology and Ethics Are Inseparable
BY ROGER REVELLE

The twenty-first century may witness a world of half-starved, depressed human masses, gasping for air, short of sweet water, struggling to avoid the constant presence of one another, living at a degraded, subsistence level with all those fellow creatures that now share our planet either exterminated or domesticated and bred out of any resemblance to what they once were.

Alternatively, the world of the twenty-first century could be a happier one in which most human beings would be better fed than at present and would have more hope for the future. Our wonderful green and blue planet would still be an abundant and smiling home, not only for men but also for other living things.

Which of these alternative futures comes true depends primarily on what we do today and during the next twenty to thirty years. We are indeed in a race with time, and time is not on our side.

We can hope that in times to come the concept of the earth as a spaceship, with fixed and finite resources that must be shared by all its human passengers, will become ever more apparent as population, agriculture, and industry grow.

A growing sense of responsibility of all men for each other cannot be expected to flow from the unlikely well of altruism, but from the desperately practical fact that our very survival as men depends on working together and helping each other.

Our affluence and our technology have been largely responsible for the deterioration of the environment that has become so evident in recent years, though our growing population and our increasingly dirty habits have also played a part. New science and new technology can help us make things better.

Science can help in building the structure of concepts and natural laws that will enable man to understand his place in nature. Such understanding must be one basis of the moral values that should guide each human generation in exercising its stewardship over the earth.

For this purpose, ecology—the science of interactions among living things and their environment—is central. Human societies and their total environment form the highest and most complex level of ecological integration.

Advances in the still rudimentary science of human ecology depend in part on mutual understanding and cooperation among social and natural scientists and humanists, and in part on the development of new methods for studying interacting processes in complex systems.

These systems are, in fact, so complex that they cannot be thought through in the unaided human brain. The development of large, high-speed computers may have come just in time to extend our intellectual capacities so that such systems can be at least partially understood.

Environmental problems usually involve conflicts of interest among individuals or groups and complex combinations of gains and losses.

One role of the economist is to introduce as much rationality as possible into striking a balance between these gains and losses. His difficulty is that the invention of tools for economic measurement of human sensory or emotional delight and deprivation is at an early stage.

Some pollution effects can be priced—for example, the costs of soot removal and sandblasting of buildings, extra laundry and dry cleaning bills in a smoky city, or the accelerated deterioration of rubber tires and nylon stockings caused by sulfur oxides where high-sulfur coal is the principal fuel.

But how much is it worth to have a beautiful view of the city from a high building? What value can be placed on the priceless California redwoods? The intrinsic worth of clean outside air to society is obvious. But no one can buy or sell any part of it, and hence no market can emerge and no values, in the economic sense, can be established.

It is easy to see that the economists' rational analysis must be supplemented by political action; yet there are numerous difficulties here. These include uncertainty among many about what they really want, political passions, inability of many people to perceive their environment, the complexities of most environmental questions, and the difficulties of formulating the issues in such a way that they can be put to a yes or no vote.

Clearly, there is a role for education in dealing with the maintenance and improvement of environmental quality.

In this respect, the functions of education are threefold: production of the many kinds of specialists who will be required to deal professionally with the problems, formulation and inculcation of the moral and intellectual values on which environmental improvement must rest, and creation of a heightened sensitivity among young people to the world around them—the ability to use their senses and to respond to what they perceive.

To preserve and improve our environment, many things must be done, much money must be spent, and many hard choices made. Fundamental to all else are new ethical attitudes toward our own land and the limitation of our own human numbers.

Historically, generations of white, Anglo-Saxon Americans have had no doubt that it was their duty to increase and multiply so that they might take dominion over the continent. Our dominion has been a harsh one for our fellow creatures.

While our own numbers have risen from 4 million in 1790 to more than 200 million today, many other species have been extinguished or drastically reduced.

The wood bison and woodland caribou are gone; American elk and gray wolves roam no more through the eastern forests, nor do the giant herds of bison graze on the prairies; Guadalupe petrels, masked bobwhites, heath hens, passenger pigeons, and sand-shoal ducks have all followed the great auks to extinction.

Swallowtail kites, whooping cranes, prairie chickens, California condors—even our national symbol, the bald eagle—are struggling to survive, as are moose and red wolves, lynx, bobcats, cougars, and more than a hundred other species.

A sad and cautionary tale, but perhaps an inevitable part of a unique event in history—the creation within a scant three hundred years by a nation of egalitarian Puritans of a continent-spanning, world-bestriding colossus of a country.

To create a new land ethic, we need to return to the sense of awe and kinship for the natural world that characterized both primitive man and our intellectual ancestors, the Greeks. Our aim should be not to control nature, but to live in harmony with it.

We need especially to conserve for the greatest public good such limited resources as the coastal shoreline, estuaries, and wetlands. Above all, we need to preserve diversity.

The public good should be paramount in the use of land, but private rights must be respected. A new land ethic must be accompanied by practical devices to compensate property owners for the constraints imposed on their free use of their own land.

In thinking about the future population size of the United States, two basic premises are clear: quality is inescapably related to quantity, and we must balance our numbers against our ability to provide human services and a human environment for all our citizens.

No one can say today what the optimum size of the United States population should be, but we know that we already have human resources in excess of our present ability to use them fully as human beings.

The growth of our numbers exacerbates every environmental problem: the dull ugliness of our cities, the deterioration of natural areas, the increase of ecological imbalances, the depletion of natural resources, the growth of urban pathology, and the proliferation of noxious wastes.

Though man is the most adaptable of animals, we need to remember that our physiological character, sensory capacities, and behavior patterns evolved in a sparsely populated world. Our continually growing numbers demand an ever-increasing complexity of interactions and produce a multiplication of stimuli that could overwhelm our inherited capacities.

At least until we learn more about ourselves and can use our knowledge to ensure lives of happiness and fulfillment for all our fellow citizens, control of population growth must be a high-priority national goal, fostered by government policies and programs.

Before adopting a particular policy to reduce fertility, government leaders need to ask themselves several kinds of questions, including whether the policy is politically acceptable to most people and how effective it will be.

But the most fundamental questions are ethical ones: Will the policy enhance the freedom of human beings as individuals, and will it advance justice for all human beings as members of society? These two ethical ideals of individual freedom and distributive justice often are, or seem to be, more or less incompatible.

The task of law-givers throughout history, however, has been to strike a workable balance between them, so it must be with the establishment of population policy.

Family planning programs, designed to give full freedom to individual couples to determine the number of their children and the spacing between births, are matters of free choice. Repeal of laws restricting abortion and free availability of medically safe abortions would further enhance the freedom of individual women and of married couples.

But the freedom of husbands and wives to make reproductive decisions must be tempered by concern for the rights and interest of others. The first and most obvious interest to be protected is that of the children already born within the family. The birth of additional children may affect them adversely in a variety of ways.

Next come all other members of society whose economic welfare and social well-being are lessened by rapid population growth, and the younger and subsequent generations, whose opportunities will be diminished by the economic stagnation and loss of amenities caused by this growth.

Finally, the interests of other nations and societies must be taken into the account because all nations ultimately make demands on the same pool of resources.

Governments have an obligation to protect the interests of all these groups. One of the most difficult of population questions is to think through and justify policies and procedures to accomplish this end.

The Link Between Faith and Ecology
BY EDWARD B. FISKE

Over the centuries the growth of Western science and technology has been closely tied to Judeo-Christian religious values. Isaac Newton and other early scientific giants explained their activities and findings in religious terms. The fundamental teaching of Genesis that man is created in God's image and intended to have "dominion" over the rest of creation gave ultimate significance to the scientific method.

As men become increasingly concerned with polluted streams, foul air, and other evidence that technological advances do not necessarily constitute progress, it is not surprising that some of these fundamental religious assumptions are also coming to be questioned. The result is what may prove to be the most far-reaching new religious issue of the 1970's—the theology of ecology or man's relationship to his environment.

This fall the National Council of Churches established an Environmental Stewardship Action Team that hopes to put theologians, scientists, and others to work on the problem. Several conferences

From *The New York Times,* January 4, 1970, p. 5.

have already been held by an association of seventy-five religious thinkers known as the Faith-Man-Nature Group. Another is scheduled this month at St. Xavier College in Chicago.

Religious Remedy

The fundamental assumption of these groups—one that is shared by ecologists outside the church—is that the current environmental crisis is not simply scientific and political in nature. "Since the roots of our trouble are so largely religious," wrote Lynn White, Jr., a historian, in *Science* magazine, "the remedy must also be essentially religious, whether we call it that or not."

For support of his view he cited the teachings of St. Francis of Assisi, who, he said, tried—unsuccessfully—to "substitute the idea of the equality of all creatures, including man, for the idea of man's limitless rule of creation." Mr. White proposed that the thirteenth-century saint—"the greatest spiritual revolutionary in western history"—become the patron saint of ecologists.

Most work in the field begins with the recognition that despite the fundamental biblical affirmation of the goodness of creation, Christian thought has entertained ideas that have, as Julian Hartt, a Yale theologian, put it last week, "legitimized man's total exploitation of his environment."

One such emphasis has been an excessive other-worldliness— a tendency to see God as totally transcendent, or outside the world, and the consequent assumption that Christianity is essentially concerned with man's fate in the next world rather than in this one.

Individualist

Another is the rampant individualism that has characterized much of post-Reformation theology. For many Christians, salvation is simply a matter between the individual and God and has no necessary connection to his relationship either to other persons or to the world in which he finds himself.

Such thinking may be regarded as the equivalent in the ecological area of assertions by sociologist Max Weber and others that aspects of Calvinistic piety contributed to economic exploitation during the development of capitalism.

While some might argue that it might have been better for the natural order if Baal and other nature gods had triumphed over Jehovah when the Israelites moved into Canaan, theologians of ecology argue that these tendencies of individualism and other-worldliness are essentially distortions of the Christian faith.

The Christian God, they say, is transcendent, but the "incarnation" of Christ is a sign that God is also involved in history and the natural process. The salvation of an individual, they continue, cannot be dissociated from that of all men and indeed—as St. Paul wrote in Romans 8—from that of nature itself.

They emphasize that man's "dominion" over creation is tempered by responsibility and an ethic of love and that the raping of natural resources for personal gain is essentially sinful. "We are basically dealing with the problem of greed," said Daniel Day Williams, a Union Seminary theologian.

Joseph Sittler, a Lutheran theologian active in the field, declared, "Reason says that destroying clean air is impractical. Faith ought to say it is blasphemous." Others have suggested that evils resulting from the destruction of the ecological balance must be understood as a form of divine judgment.

Largely Academic

Thus far the new interest in ecology has been largely academic, but church leaders hope that local congregations—like elements of the new left on college campuses—will soon make issues such as air pollution part of their social action programs.

This may not be as uncontroversial as it sounds. Ecologists now recognize that fighting for clean air and water is not like supporting motherhood but involves fundamental shifts in national values and priorities.

"If we're serious about increasing the quality of life for all men," said the Reverend Norden C. Murphy of the NCC, for instance, "we may have to declare a moratorium on how much we consume. We may have to reject the assumption that a gross national product that goes up each year is a good thing."

Suggested Readings

Bahr, Howard M., Bruce A. Chadwick and Durwin L. Thomas. *Population Resources and the Future: Non-Malthusian Perspectives* (Provo, Utah: Brigham Young University Press, 1972).

The Biosphere. A Scientific American Book (San Francisco: W. H. Freeman, 1970).

Brown, Harrison. *The Challenge of Man's Future* (New York: Viking Press, 1954).

Brown, Harrison, and Edward Hutchings, Jr. *Are Our Descendants Doomed?* (New York: Viking Press, 1970).

Burch, William R., Jr. *Daydreams and Nightmares: A Sociological Essay on the American Environment* (New York: Harper & Row, 1971).

Freedman, Ronald (ed.). *Population: The Vital Revolution* (Chicago: Aldine Publishing Co., 1964).

The Fitness of Man's Environment. Smithsonian Annual II (New York: Harper Colophon Books, 1968).

Hawley, Amos H. *Human Ecology* (New York: Ronald Press, 1950).

Hutchinson, Sir Joseph (ed.). *Population and Food Supply: Essays on Human Needs and Agricultural Prospects* (Cambridge: Cambridge University Press, 1969).

McKaye, Benton. *The New Exploration: A Philosophy of Regional Planning* (New York: Harcourt Brace, 1928).

Malthus, Thomas Robert. *Population: The First Essay* (Ann Arbor, Mich.: University of Michigan Press, 1959).

Michelson, William. *Man and His Urban Environment: A Sociological Approach* (Reading, Mass.: Addison-Wesley, 1970).

Rapid Population Growth: Consequences and Policy Implications. National Academy of Sciences (Baltimore: Johns Hopkins Press, 1971).

Resources and Man. Committee on Resources and Man, National Academy of Sciences (San Francisco: W. H. Freeman, 1969).

Revelle, Roger, Ashok Khosla, and Maris Vinaorskis (eds.). *The Survival Equation* (Boston: Houghton Mifflin, 1971).

Revelle, Roger and Hans H. Landsberg (eds.). *America's Changing Environment* (Boston: Beacon Press, 1970).

Storer, John H. *The Web of Life* (New York: Signet Books, 1956).

Thomas, William L., Jr. (ed.). *Man's Role in Changing the Face of the Earth* (Chicago: University of Chicago Press, 1956).

Wrigley, E. A. *Population and History* (New York: McGraw-Hill, 1969).

INDEX

Abortion, 56–57, 212
Abraham, Joyce, 80, 81
Adair, Red, 133, 134
Adaptation, 13–14
Aerojet-General, 119
Affluent Society, The, 223
Africa(ns), 4, 32, 72, 102ff., 108, 112
Age, 191
Agency for International Development, 74
Agriculture, 8–9, 207–10. *See also* Food; Green revolution; Plants
Aid, foreign, 64–65, 104–5ff.
Aid to Dependent Children (ADC), 41
Air, 40, 122, 124–29; atmospheric gases, 201–4, 216 (*see also* specific gases)
Aircraft (airplanes), 127–28, 203

Alaska, 122, 148–63
Alaska Native Claims Settlement Act, 158
Algae, 72, 181, 186–87, 206
Allen, Alan A., 133
Alston, Walter, 82
Aluminum, 113, 183, 184
Alyeska Pipeline Service Company, 153, 158, 162, 163
Amaru (Indian poet), 88
Amazon Basin, 207
America. *See* United States
American Association for the Advancement of Science, 111, 192
American Civil Liberties Union (ACLU), 144, 145
Ammonia, 181, 206
Anaktuvuk Pass, Alaska, 151
Andes, 153
Animals, 71, 72, 182, 187, 202,

Animals (cont.)
  206, 220, 236; Alaskan, 149,
  151ff.
Arabs, 32, 155–56
ARCO, 150, 156, 159, 160
Argentina, 72
Aristotle, 22
Arsenical compounds, 125
Asia, 4, 9, 21, 32, 71, 72, 102, 108,
  112. See also specific places
Aswan, 208, 209
Atlantic Ocean, 205–6
Atmosphere. See Air
Atomic energy. See Nuclear
  energy
Audubon Society, 144
Aurangabad, India, 76ff.
Australia, 132–33
Automobiles (cars), 40, 94, 125,
  185, 217; recycling, 183–84
Avco Manufacturing, 119

Babylonian Empire, 207
Bacteria, 168–69, 181, 206, 207
Bai, Saroo, 79
Baltic Sea, 176, 177
Baltimore, Md., 53–55, 58
Bartz, Robert V., 116
Beaufort Sea, 146
Beckman Instruments, 119
Bees, clover and, 13–14
Beetles, flour, 218
Begadjah, Indonesia, 89–101
Belgium, 34
Bendix Aviation, 120
Berkner, Lloyd, 203, 207
Beryllium, 125
Best, Winfield, 56

Bicycles, 93–94
Birds, 67, 171, 236
Birth control, 20, 31, 34–35, 42ff.,
  46–61, 100–1, 211–12, 237
Birth rate, 3, 7–8, 29–30, 33,
  43–44, 46ff., 66ff., 100–1,
  211–12. See also Birth con-
  trol; Population
Blacks, 58
Blackwelder, Justin, 58
Blumer, Max, 180
Bonner, James, 64, 71, 72, 116
Borgstrom, Georg, 70
Borlaug, Norman F., 64, 73–75
Bottles, 93, 184, 187
Bottoms, James, 138–39
Bouchard, Thomas, 140
Bradshaw, Thornton F., 148–49
Brain power, 115ff., 118–20
Brazil, 31
Britain and the British, 23–25, 68,
  124, 126, 127–28, 191, 224ff.
  (see also specific places);
  clover and bees in, 13–14;
  immigrants, 32; and India,
  209
British Petroleum (BP), 159, 160
Brooks Range, 146, 151, 152, 154
Brough, John, 88n
Brown, Harrison S., 116–18
Brown, Thomas M., 122, 148–63
Bryn Mawr College, 219
Bryson, Reid, 87
Byron Jackson, 119

Cade, Tom, 150
Cain, Stanley A., 138
Calcium chloride, 183

Calcium fluoride, 125
California, 40, 136, 137, 144, 160, 194. *See also* specific cities
California, University of, 135
California Institute of Technology, 116, 117, 119
Calories, 71–72
Canada, 33, 39–40, 170; and Alaska pipeline, 149, 157–58
Canal, sea-level, 205–6
Cancer, 172, 215
Cans, beverage, 184
Capitalism, 219ff.
Carbon, 186, 198
Carbon dioxide, 182, 201ff., 216–17
Carbon monoxide, 125, 185
Caribbean, 32, 206
Caribou, 151ff.
Castagnola, George V., 140
Cats, 171; bees, clover, and, 13–14
Cattle (cows), 93, 187
Census-taking, 2–3
Central America, 21, 72, 205–6
Cesium 137, 204–5
Chicago, 187, 240
Children. *See* Education; Population
Chile, 231
China, 21, 29, 30–31, 34, 209, 224
Chlorine, 125
Chowka, India, 79–80
Christianity, 239–41
Cigarettes, 93
Clams, 172
Clark, R. B., 175, 177, 178
Climate, 204; Indian, 76–88

Clothes, 192
Clover, bees and, 13–14
Club of Rome, 213
Clyde, George, 137, 142
Coal, 117, 118, 124, 125, 186, 201, 202
Coale, Ansley, 192–93, 194
Cobalt, 112, 113
Cole, LaMont, 123, 181–88, 198, 200–12
Colorado River, 166
Columbia-Presbyterian Medical Center, 42
Commoner, Barry, 192, 194
Communism (Communists), 20, 24, 28–29ff., 96, 104, 220
Competitive exclusion principle, 218
Conant, James B., 39
Condorcet, Marquis de, 23
Conference on the Human Environment, 178
Congolese, 103
Consciousness II, 225
Consolidated Edison, 229
Continental Oil, 120
Contraception. *See* Birth control
Convair, 119
Copper, 112, 170, 174, 179, 183, 184
Cordova District Fisheries Union, 162
Corn, 217
Cornwall, England, 130
Council on Environmental Quality, 178–79
Cows. *See* Cattle
Crabs, 169, 172, 179

Cranston, Alan, 142–43
Crime, 59, 192–94
Crowther, C. Edward, 140
Curry, Robert R., 132, 134–35
Cushing, Richard Cardinal, 49
Cycles, cycling process, 198,
    201–12, 216–17

Dall sheep, 151
Darwin, Charles, 5, 22
Darwin, Sir Charles, 64, 66–68
Davis, Kingsley, 20, 26–35, 59,
    212
DDT, 171, 173, 174
Death rate, 3, 4, 29–30, 33, 34,
    43–44, 203; infant mortality
    in Begadjah, Indonesia, 100
Deer, 215–16
Democracy, 221
Demographic transition, 3–4ff.
Dempsey, David, 20, 46–61
Denali Fault, Alaska, 152
Destructive distillation, 186
Detergents, 177, 207
Developing countries, 64–65,
    102–10, 219–20. See also
    Birth control; Food; Third
    World; specific countries
Diatoms, 207
Dickens, Charles, 24
Disraeli, Benjamin, 24
Djalak, Kjai, 96
Djojodikuromo (hamlet chief,
    Indonesia), 90–91, 95, 96, 99
Douglas Aircraft, 119
Dow Chemical, 120
DuBridge, Lee, panel, 141ff.
Du Pont de Nemours, E. I., 119

Dutch. See Holland and the
    Dutch

Earthquakes, 135, 152, 153–54
Easton, Robert, 130–45
Ecology, 12–17, 197–241
Economics, 198, 213–22, 223–32
Education, 38–39, 115, 119, 235;
    in Indonesia, 100
Edward I (king of England), 124
Egan, William A., 152, 159ff.
Egypt, 72; Nile region, Aswan,
    208, 209
Ehrlich, Paul, 59–60, 192, 193–94
Einstein, Albert, 214
Eisenhower years, 225
Eissler, Fred, 138, 140, 142
Electricity, 40–41, 184
Elgin National Watch, 120
Elk Hills, Calif., 141, 142
Engineering and Science, 66
England. See Britain and the
    British
Environmental Defense Fund,
    Inc., 163
Eskimos, 151, 157–58
Ethics, 198–99, 233–38
Europe, 4, 28, 29, 60, 71, 72. See
    also specific countries
Evelyn, John, 124
Exxon, 156, 159, 160

Faisal, king of Saudi Arabia,
    155–56
Faith-Man-Nature Group, 240
Federal Power Commission, 155
Ferry, W. H., 140
Fertilizer, 187

Firestone, Gerald, 139, 142
Firestone Tire and Rubber, 231
Fish, 169ff.
Fiske, Edward B., 199, 239–41
Florida, 169
Fly ash, 187–88
Focus, 112
Food, 8–9, 33, 64, 66–101, 118, 173ff., 187 (*see also* Plants); Malthusian theory and, 23, 24; symposium on resources, 66–75
Food and Agriculture Organization, 9
Food and Drug Administration, 207
Ford Foundation, 42, 74, 143
Ford Motor Company, 120
Forrester, Jay, 229
France, 60, 191
Francis of Assisi, St., 240
Franklin, Benjamin, 22
Fraser, John R., 145
Fremont-Smith, Eliot, 20, 21–25
Friends of the Earth, 163
Fuels, 112, 117, 118, 202ff. *See also* specific fuels
Fungi, 210

Galbraith, John Kenneth, 38, 223
Galloway, J. H., 148
Garbage. *See* Recycling
Gas, 13, 147, 148, 155ff., 185, 186, 202. *See also* specific types
Gasoline, 127–28, 136, 147, 148
Gause, G. F., 218
General Motors, 229
Geophysical Services, Inc., 150

Germany, 126, 185, 224, 225
Ghana, 106, 209
Gianini, G. M., 119
Gilfillan Brothers, 119
Glass, 184
Godwin, William, 23, 24
Gold, 182, 188
GOO, 139, 142ff.
Government, 38. *See also* specific agencies, programs
Granite, 117
Gray, Naomi, 56
Great Britain. *See* Britain and the British
Great Lakes, 206
Great Lakes Carbon, 120
Greece, 209
Greenhouse effect, 204
Green revolution, 9, 64, 73–75, 89ff.
Greep, Roy O., 59
Guatemala, 209
Gulf Oil, 119, 144
Gulf Stream, 206
Guttmacher, Alan F., 20, 46–61
Guttmacher, Dorothy, 53
Guttmacher, Leonore Faith Giddings, 53
Guttmacher, Manfred, 53–54, 55

Hammond, Jay, 153
Hardin, Garrett, 193, 194
Hartt, Julian, 240
Hartzog, George B., Jr., 136
Harvard, 42
Harvard Alumni Bulletin, 59
Harwood, Michael, 164–80
Haskell, Floyd, 160

Hazlitt, William, 24
Health, Education and Welfare, Department of, 58
Hellman, Louis, 50, 52, 55
Hepatitis, 169
Hercules Powder, 119
Hickel, Walter J., 133, 141, 143ff., 152
Holland, Jerome H., 58
Holland and the Dutch, 94–95, 191
Houthakker, Hendrick S., 190–91
Hoyle, Fred, 64, 66–68
Hughes Aircraft, 119
Hume, David, 22
Hycon Manufacturing, 119
Hydrochloric acid, 126, 185
Hydrofluoric acid, 125
Hydrogen, 3, 125, 181, 205

Income, 194–96, 226, 231–32. See also Poverty
India(ns), 32, 34, 47, 58, 73, 103, 209, 212; and monsoons, 64, 76–88
Indian Desert, 87
Indians, American, 157–58
Individualism, 240–41
Indonesia, 64, 89–101
Ingles, Nelson, 78, 80
Inter-American Development Bank, 74
Interior, Department of the, 131, 135, 138, 143, 156, 163
International Atomic Energy Agency, 177

International Biological Program, 212
International Business Machines, 119
International Convention for the Prevention of Pollution of the Sea by Oil, 177
International Maize and Wheat Improvement Center, 74
Intrauterine devices (IUD's), 50, 51, 211
Iowa, 209
Iraq, 207–8
Iron, 112, 113, 166, 182, 201, 217
Israel, 155–56
Italy, 60

Jackson, Henry M., 147
Jaffe, Fred, 56
Jakarta, 93
Japan(ese), 34, 71, 95, 158, 170, 187, 212, 222, 224, 228, 231
Johnson administration, 183
Jones Act, 154
Josopanitro (village chief, Indonesia), 91, 94ff., 98
Judeo-Christianity, 239–41

Kaibab Plateau, 215–16
Kelp, 170
Kennedy, John F., 108
Kimble, George H. T., 122, 124–29
King, Kerryn, 131
Korea, 60
Krypton 85, 205

Lake Erie, 164, 179
Lake Tahoe, 186

Lamont, William J., 160
Land, 16–17, 71, 207–10, 236
Land Management, Bureau of, 145
Latin America, 4, 9, 29, 30, 35, 48, 58, 60, 212. *See also* Central America; South America; specific countries
Lenin, Nikolai, 107
Lewis, Anthony, 229
Liberia, 231
Lilienthal, David, 20, 35–45
Lippes, Jack, and Lippes Loop, 50
Literacy, 11
Lincoln Parish, La., 58
Lindsay, George N., 57
Life in the Making, 55–56
Lobsters, 169, 172
Lockheed Aircraft, 119
London, 124ff., 179
Los Angeles, 125, 126ff., 144, 153
Los Angeles *Times,* 143

MacDonald, Ross, 130–45
McNamara, Robert, 64, 68–69, 70
Maine, 164
Mali, 209
Malthus, Thomas, 4–6, 20, 21–25
Marx, Karl, 24
Massachusetts, 171–73
Massachusetts Institute of Technology (M.I.T.), 213
Matthiessen, Peter, 179
Mauritius, 34
Mayas (Ancient), 209
Mead, Walter J., 141

Meadows, Dennis L., 213
Mediterranean, 176, 206
Mencken, August, 55
Mencken, Henry L., 54–55
Menhaden, 169
Mercury, 112, 113, 167, 170–71, 173, 177
Mesabi Range, Minn., 182
Metals, 112–13, 125, 166, 170, 173. *See also* specific metals
Methane, 185, 186
Mexico, 9, 29–30, 64, 73–75; Yucatán, 209
Mice, bees, and clover, 13–14
Middle America, 32. *See also* Central America; Mexico
Middle East, 124, 155–56, 158. *See also* specific places
Migration, 32–33
Miller, Herman P., 189–92, 194–96
Miller, Keith H., 152
"Minamata disease," 170–71
Mineral Leasing Act, 163
Minerals, 9–10, 112–13, 117, 166ff., 182–84, 217. *See also* specific kinds
Mines, Bureau of, 183, 185
Mines (weapons), floating, 167
Mines and mining, 205. *See also* Minerals; specific ores
Mishan, Ezra J., 223ff.
Mobil Oil, 144
Monopoly, 218
Monsoons, 64, 76–88
Moon, 113–14
Moose, 151

More, J. Cordell, 138

Moslems, 211. *See also* specific
    countries

"Mount Trashmore," 187

Murphy, Norden C., 241

Murray, Bertram G., Jr., 198,
    213–22

Music, Indian, 87

Nakshatra Wadi, India, 77, 78–79,
    85–86

Nash, Roderick, 135

National Academy of Sciences,
    41–42

National Conference on Air Pol-
    lution, 127

National Council of Churches,
    239

National Environmental Policy
    Act, 163

Navy, U.S., 149–50

Newton, Isaac, 239

New York City, 40, 41, 56, 125,
    169, 203

New York State, 57, 183

New York Times, The, 143

New Zealand, 125

Nickel, 174

Nigeria, 106

Nile River, 208

Nitrogen, 181, 187, 198, 201, 206

Nitrogen oxide, 125

Nixon, President Richard M.
    (administration), 139, 141,
    147, 162, 188, 231

Nkrumah, Kwame, 106

Nobel Peace Prize, 73

North America, 72. *See also*

Canada; United States

North American Aviation, 119

North Slope, Alaska, 146, 149ff.,
    158

Nuclear energy (atomic energy;
    fusion), 40, 113, 117, 118,
    176, 204–5, 216, 229–30. *See
    also* Radioactivity, radiation

Oceania, 72

Oceans, 122, 164–80, 202, 205–6,
    207

Oil (petroleum), 117, 167, 171–73,
    176ff., 185, 186, 201ff., 229;
    Alaska pipeline, 148–63;
    food from petroleum, 210;
    Iraqi, 208; Santa Barbara
    and, 122, 130–45

Okrand, Fred, 144

Outer Continental Shelf Act, 144

Oxygen, 169, 170, 181–82, 184,
    186, 198, 201ff., 210

Oysters, 170, 172

Pacific Ocean, 205–6

Pakistan, 9, 32, 47, 74, 78, 103,
    211

Palodkar, Manek Rao, 81–82

Panama, Isthmus of, 206

Paper, 93, 184–85

Park, Charles F., Jr., 65, 112–14

Park, Thomas, 218

Passell, Peter, 198, 213–14,
    223–32

Pastore, John O., 147

Paul, St., 241

Pearce, Jack B., 166

Pecora, William T., 145

Penobscot Bay, 164
Pensacola, Fla., 169
Pesticides, 167–68, 207
Petroleum. *See* Oil
Philippines, 9, 64
Phosphate, 166–67, 183
Phosphorus, 182–83, 187
Photosynthesis, 72, 201ff., 217
Phytoplankton, 168, 173
Pigs, 98, 217
Pill, the, 52, 211
Pitt, William, 23–24
Pittsburgh, 127
Pius XII, Pope, 32
Plank, Stephen J., 43
Planned Parenthood–World
    Population, 20, 46ff.
Plants, 71ff., 168, 181–82, 186,
    201ff., 217 (*see also* Food;
    Green revolution; specific
    plants); Alaskan, 149
Plastics, 185
Plato, 22
Pliny, 207
Plumb, Robert K., 65, 115–20
Poems from the Sanskrit, 88n
Polar bears, 151
Polio, 169
Pollution, 11–12, 121–96, 228–29,
    235. *See also* specific pollu-
    tants
Population, 2–8, 19–61, 66–73,
    116–18, 123, 189–96, 211–12,
    215–16, 235–38. *See also*
    Food
Population Bulletin, 69–70
Population Council, 42, 48, 50
Population Crisis Committee, 58

Population Policy Panel, 59
Poverty (the poor), 20, 23–24, 30,
    41–43, 54ff., 231–32. *See also*
    Developing countries
Progestin, 60
Proteins, 181, 206
Protozoans, 218
Prudhoe Bay, Alaska, 146ff., 156,
    159ff.
Puerto Rico, 34, 211
Puget Sound, 126
Pyrolysis, 186

Race (color), 31–32; black mili-
    tants and birth control, 58
Radioactivity, radiation, 167, 182
    (*see also* Nuclear energy);
    radioisotopes in ocean, 207
Radios, 94
Ram, Sita, 78–79, 85–86
Ramo-Wooldridge, 119
Rand Corporation, 119
Reagan, Ronald, 139
Record, 190
Recycling, 123, 181–88. *See also*
    Cycles, cycling process
Red Sea, 206
Reich, Charles, 225
Religion, 199, 239–41
Resources (raw materials),
    64–65, 111–20, 229. *See also*
    Economics; specific materi-
    als
Revelle, Roger, 38, 198, 233–38
Rhine River, 166
Rice, 9, 64, 89ff.
Richards, Robert R., 162
Richfield Oil, 119

Rivers, 166–67
Rock, John, 58–59
Rockefeller, Nelson, 56–57
Rockefeller Foundation, 73, 74
Rocks, 117, 118
Role of Psychiatry in Law, The, 55
Ross, Leonard, 198, 214, 223–32
Rousseau, Jean Jacques, 22, 23
Ruby, Jack, 55
Ruhr valley, 126
Russia (Soviet Union), 29ff., 34,
     70ff., 104–5, 106, 188, 212,
     224; whaling, 222

Sacramento, Calif., 143
St. Louis, Mo., 127
St. Xavier College, 240
Sakharov, Andrei D., 68, 70
Salinization, 208–9, 210
Salt, 168. *See also* Salinization
Sanders, Norman K., 140, 142,
     144
San Diego, Calif., 194
Santa Barbara, Calif., 122,
     130–45, 179
Saudi Arabia, 155–56
SBCED, 144
Scallops, 172
Schaaf, John, 141
Schachter, Oscar, 175
Schaffer, Alex, 54
Science, 59, 240
"Seeding" air, 128
Selenium, 125
Senate Interior Committee, 147,
     148, 157, 158
Serwer, Daniel, 175
Sewage, 167, 168–70, 173, 179,

     186, 187, 194
Sex and the Offender, 55
Shellfish, 168–69ff.
Shell Oil, 119
Shells, unexploded, 167
Sherman Antitrust Act, 218
Ships, 167. *See also* Oil
Shrimp, 179
Sidenberg, Lois, 143
Sierra Club, 138
Silk, Leonard, 219
Silver, 112, 113, 188
Silver iodide, 128
Singh, Khushwant, 64, 76–88
Sinha, Ramesh Chandra, 80–81
Sittler, Joseph, 241
Smog. *See* Air
Snow, Lord, 68, 69
Socialism, 220
Socony-Mobil Oil, 119
Sodium fluoride, 125
Solar energy, 118
Solo, Indonesia, 91, 100
South America, 72, 112, 209. *See
     also* Latin America
Soviet Union. *See* Russia
Spartina grass, 173
Standard of living. *See*
     Economics
Standard Oil of California,
     119–20
Standard Oil of New Jersey, 120
Standard Oil of Ohio (Sohio),
     159, 160
Standley, Eugene W., 138
Stanford, 193–94
Stanolind Oil and Gas, 120
"State of the arts," 6–7

Steady state, 215
Stearns Wharf (Santa Barbara),
    140–41, 143
Steel, 117, 183, 184, 217
Sterba, James P., 64, 89–101
Sterilization, 212
Strauss, Donald R., 57
Strontium 90, 204–5
Stuart, Marvin H., 139
Styron, Rose Burgunder, 55
Suez Canal, 206
Sukarno, 95
Sulastri, 98–99
Sulfides, 125
Sulfur, 186
Sulfur dioxide, 125, 126, 185, 186
Sulfuric acid, 126, 186
Sullivan, Walter, 65, 111–20
Sumerian civilization, 207
Summerland, Calif., 136
Sunlight, 181–82; solar energy,
    18
Sun Oil Company, 131
Suradji, Edi, 100

Tanzania, 209
Taxes, 59
Teague, Charles M., 141ff.
Technology, 10–11, 65, 115–20,
    221, 229–30. See also
    specific areas
Tellurium, 125
Texaco, 144
Texas Company, 120
Third World, 230, 231. See also
    Developing countries
Thorium, 117
Tidal waves, 135

Tietze, Christopher, 48, 50
Tigris River, 207
Tin, 112, 183, 184
Tires, 186
Todd, Paul, Jr., 56
Torrey Canyon disaster, 130, 207
Trade, 230–31
Trans Alaska Pipeline System
    (TAPS), 153
Trees, 184
Triticale, 75
Tritium, 205
Trivedi, Vijay Dutt Deo Dutt, 77ff.,
    86
Tussing, Arlon R., 158–59
TVA, 41

Udall, Stewart, 135, 138, 139
Underdeveloped countries. See
    Developing countries
UNESCO, 207
Union Carbide and Carbon, 120
Union Oil, 120, 131ff., 142ff.
United Nations (UN), 9, 21, 26ff.,
    113, 167, 178, 220; Develop-
    ment Program, 74
United States of America, 20, 25,
    34, 36–61, 70ff., 130–63,
    190ff., 209–10, 214ff.,
    223–32, 236 (see also
    specific persons, places);
    and pollution (see Pollution;
    specific pollutants); use of
    resources, 112–13
United States Steel, 120
Ur, 208
Uranium, 117, 204, 216

Valdez, Alaska, 147, 152, 154, 160
Ventura County, Calif., 131, 136
Vietnam, 9, 230
Vogt, William, 56

Wagh, Bhao Jai Rao, 80
Ward, Barbara, 64, 102–10
Washington, D.C., 58
Washington, State of, 160
Waste. *See* Pollution
Water, 39–40, 103, 164–80, 187,
    201ff.; India's monsoons
    and, 77ff.
Wealth (*see also* Economics):
    pollution and, 194–96
Weapons, 167
Weather, 64, 76–88. *See also* Cli-
    mate
Weber, Max, 240
Weingand, Al, 139, 142, 144
Weir, John R., 116, 118–19

Welland Canal, 206
West Falmouth, Mass., 171–73
Westinghouse Electric, 120
Whales, 222
Wheat, 9, 64, 73–75
White, Lynn, Jr., 240
White House Conference on
    Health, 42
Wilderness Society, 163
Wild Harbor River, 171–73
Williams, Daniel Day, 241
Winds, 167–68
Wirin, A. L., 144
World Health Organization, 177
World War II, 127–28, 149

Yeasts, 210, 218
Yucatán, 209

Zinc, 126, 170
Zooplankton, 168

1957   1722